THE OPENING OF ALASKA

By
Brig. Gen. William L. Mitchell
U.S. Army Air Corps

Edited by Lyman L. Woodman
Lt. Colonel, USAF-Ret.

Pictorial Histories Publishing Company
Missoula, Montana
and
Cook Inlet Historical Society
Anchorage, Alaska

The Cook Inlet Historical Society, established in 1955, holds its business and social meetings in the Anchorage Museum of History and Art at 121 West Seventh Avenue, Anchorage. Its collection of historical materials is maintained at this location.

Library of Congress
Catalog Card Number: 82-71848

ISBN 0-933126-93-X

Published by:
Pictorial Histories Publishing Company
713 South Third West
Missoula, Montana 59801
and
Cook Inlet Historical Society
Anchorage, Alaska
1982
Second edition, 1988

The Cook Inlet Historical Society is pleased to acknowledge the generosity of Mr. and Mrs. Robert B. Atwood of Anchorage who provided funds in support of the first printing of this book, the third issuance of our publications program.

CONTENTS

ILLUSTRATIONS

Photo credits. Code letters following listings above indicate the sources of illustrations: A = U.S. Army; AHL = Alaska Historical Library; AL = Lieutenant Allen's report; CIHS = Cook Inlet Historical Society; HBC = Hudson's Bay Company's "The Beaver"; HW = Harper's Weekly; LC = Library of Congress; LLW = Lyman L. Woodman; NA = National Archives; SI = Smithsonian Institution, C.R. Goins; UA-F1 = Univ. of Alaska, Fairbanks, Farnsworth collection; UA-F2 = Univ. of Alaska, Fairbanks, Wilkensen collection; UW = Univ. of Washington, Curtis collection; Unk = Unknown; WP = Walter T. Phillips, Palmer; and YA = Yukon Archives.

FOREWORD

William Lendrum (Billy) Mitchell was born in Nice, France, December 29, 1879 while his parents were temporarily abroad. His father was John Lendrum Mitchell, veteran of the Civil War and U.S. Senator from Wisconsin. Raised in Milwaukee, Billy attended Racine College of Wisconsin, a preparatory school, then entered Columbia (now George Washington) University in Washington, D.C. At age 18, and still a student, he enlisted as a private in the First Wisconsin, a volunteer regiment, anxious to play a part in the Spanish-American War.

His father's influence soon asserted itself, for within a few weeks he was recommended for a commission by Brig. Gen. Adolphus W. Greely, Chief of the Signal Corps. As the Army's youngest second lieutenant Mitchell was assigned to the 2nd Volunteer Signal Company in the spring of 1898. He learned the signal code, taught himself the use of the typewriter, and soon was assigned in the Occupation of Cuba where he supervised the stringing of 136 miles of telegraph wire in Santiago Province.

Lieutenant Mitchell was posted to the Philippines in July 1899, and at age 20 was Acting Chief Signal Officer on the division staff of Gen. Arthur MacArthur. He was responsible for the establishment of many miles of telegraph line serving the troops in action against the rebel Aguinaldo. While in the islands he became acquainted with Col. Frederick Funston, who had prospected in Alaska, and listening to his tales of the far north raised Mitchell's interest in the territory.

After his service in the Philippines Mitchell planned to resign, but General Greely asked him if he would be interested in going to Alaska where establishment of a telegraph line connecting the Army posts there was going slowly. He accepted the assignment of making a survey of conditions affecting the construction and reporting his findings to the Chief. This resulted in his investigatory trip in the summer of 1901 and consequent report to General Greely that the line could be built more rapidly if the soldiers worked throughout the winter, packing in equipment, tools, and supplies and caching them for use in the summer months. Greely sent him back to Alaska in the fall of 1901 to carry out his plan. Construction of the telegraph line was under the charge of Col. George M. Randall, commanding the Department of Alaska. By now a first lieutenant (youngest of that rank in the Army), Mitchell was entrusted with the building of a portion of the system, primarily along the route between Fort Egbert (at Eagle City on the Upper Yukon) and Fort Liscum (at Valdez). His account of these two Alaska tours appears in this heretofore unpublished manuscript, "The Opening of Alaska." The original manuscript, one of thousands of his papers now in the Library of Congress, is not dated. It seems to have been written around 1935.

Following his Alaskan duties in 1903, in recognition of which he was promoted to captain (youngest in the Army), Mitchell commanded the 1st Field Signal Company at Fort Leavenworth, Kansas, and was an instructor in the Signal, Infantry, and Cavalry Schools.

A graduate of the Army Staff College in 1909, he served again in the Philippines during 1909-1911. While there, he carried out an undercover reconnaissance of Japanese activities in the islands between Formosa and the Philippines. He also visited battlefields of the Russo-Japanese War and studied other military activities in the area. In a subsequent report to the Army General Staff's War College Division in 1912, Mitchell indicated that war with Japan was inevitable and that the Philippines were in great danger.

During 1913-1916 he served on the Army General Staff, the youngest (at 33) ever given such a post. He spoke five languages and had some knowledge of two Philippine dialects. At age 36, when he was ineligible for military flying training (due to his age and being married) he took pilot training on weekends at his own expense, paying the Curtiss School at Newport News, Virginia, $1470 for the course. He was now a major with the Aviation Section of the Signal Corps.

In World War I, Mitchell progressed quickly in rank and assignments, becoming a member of Gen. John J. Pershing's staff, and the commander of air forces in the American Expeditionary Force as a brigadier general. He flew numerous missions and was the first American officer to fly across enemy (German) lines. Mitchell recommended that Eddie Rickenbacker, an excellent auto mechanic assigned to Pershing's staff as a chauffeur, be allowed to transfer to the Air Service. This happened, and the ex-Indianapolis track driver became America's ace of aces, with 26 victories.

After World War I, Mitchell was Assistant Chief of the Air Service, pursuing ardently his conviction that airpower deserved greater recognition. He urged that the Army's Air Service become a separate air arm with more and modern equipment. The establishment of a defense department with coordinated air, sea, and ground forces was one of his resolves.

Mitchell's exploits in the AEF and his exuberance in vocalizing on aviation's future gained him notoriety. He was a natural for publicity. His pronouncements gained increasing audience and newsmongers adopted his boyhood nickname, "Billy," in writing of "this irrepressible airman," as Maj. Alexander P. DeSeversky called him. Gen. Henry H. Arnold wrote in his *Global Mission* of Mitchell's "fine war record and leaping mind . . . this dashing, colorful doer-of-deeds who cut red tape . . . the Billy the public loved and whom the Air Corps loved."

In 1920, to call attention to aviation's capabilities, General Mitchell organized the Army air-mapping tour of Alaska in which Capt. St. Clair Streett commanded the flight of four DeHavilands from New York to Nome and return.

Following a personal visit to Hawaii and a number of Asian countries in 1923 and 1924, Mitchell submitted a 325-page report in which he reiterated his prediction about war with Japan. He warned of Japan's air strength and the likelihood that she would strike without warning. In 1925, as a result of his continued agitation concerning a budget-conscious government that seemed determined to keep air strength at a minimum, he was transferred, with the rank of colonel, to a minor post in Texas. After the destruction of the Navy dirigible *Shenandoah* in September he charged the War and Navy Departments with "incompetency, criminal negligence, and almost treasonable administration of the national defense." For these statements he was court-martialed and suspended from the service for five years, with loss of pay and allowances. He resigned in 1926.

In February 1935 when Congressional hearings were held concerning proposed military bases, including one in Alaska, he was invited to testify. Several military representatives spoke on behalf of the Alaskan base, but Mitchell's testimony on February 13 gave the session lasting significance. He spoke at length and with great forcefulness on the theme which was to give him immortality—the importance and value of air power in war. But there was also a corollary to those passionately held and unflinchingly maintained beliefs which time would completely vindicate, namely, the strategic importance of Alaska to the coming era of air power whose prophet he was.

"Japan is our dangerous enemy in the Pacific," Mitchell declared. "They won't attack Panama. They will come right here to Alaska. Alaska is the most central place in the world for aircraft, and that is true either of Europe, Asia, or North America. I believe in the future he who holds Alaska will hold the world, and I think it is the most important strategic place in the world." The legislation under consideration authorized construction of the bases, but Congress failed to provide the funds. At the outset of World War II, Alaska was virtually defenseless and the nation was ill-prepared for the conflict which engulfed her.

In January 1936 Mitchell fell ill with influenza complicated by heart trouble while at his home in Middleburg, Virginia. He was removed to a hospital in New York City where he died on February 17, 1936, the dedicated officer long considered "the father of the U.S. Air Force," and termed by some after his trial as "Prophet Without Honor."

His contributions to, concern for, and infatuation with Alaska have been recognized in the naming of Mount Billy Mitchell, a prominence a few miles north of Valdez, Alaska.

PREFACE

"The Opening of Alaska" is Billy Mitchell's title for these reminiscenses of his experiences while working on the military telegraph line in Alaska during 1901-1903.

The system of government telegraph lines and cables was developed by the Army in Alaska starting in 1900. It had its origin in the conditions growing out of the discovery of gold in the Klondike region in Canada in 1896 and gold strikes along the Yukon River in central Alaska and at Nome. The several findings drew thousands of people to the north country and gave impetus to Alaska's settlement. It led also to the assignment of a larger military force here than had been required previously. Posts and camps were established at and near the gold fields so military units could (in the absence of adequate civil government and law enforcement personnel) help keep the peace and ensure the safety of people and property. And they would give aid to the destitute—the thousands of unsuccessful individuals among the hordes of prospectors and others who entered this vast country in search of riches.

The initial thrust in communications in 1900 was to interconnect the principal Army installations. They were widely separated, at Eagle City and Tanana on the Yukon River, at Nome and St. Michael on Norton Sound, and in the southern sector at Valdez on Prince William Sound, plus a camp at Skagway. Headquarters of the Army's Department of Alaska was at Fort St. Michael, with Col. George M. Randall, 8th Infantry, commanding. The only inter-post communication before telegraph lines were built was by horse, mule, backpacking, riverboat, or steamer during "open season," and by dogsled, snowshoes, and sleigh in winter.

People and businesses in the sprouting mining camps and at busy trading posts were hampered in contacting each other and in communicating with the "Outside"—a term applied to any place that is not in Alaska. What few representatives of civil government were stationed in Alaska's interior likewise had no direct contact with one another or with Juneau, which in 1900 had become the capital of what was then called the District of Alaska.

Heroic efforts had been made to place a telegraph line through this north country in 1865-67, before Alaska's purchase. A project launched by the Western Union Telegraph Company was aimed at constructing a line in western Canada, down the Yukon River and across Alaska (then Russian America), under Bering Strait, and into Siberia. Its purpose was to connect America with Europe through Asia. Charles S. Bulkley, recently released from duty as a Union Army colonel in charge of military communications in the Southwest, was in charge of the project which was private enterprise with U.S. Government support.

Many miles of line were constructed in British Columbia and some on the Seward Peninsula before the project was cancelled after the successful completion of the Atlantic cable. Several of Bulkley's survey parties produced records of exploration which became valuable reference material later, including the period of Congressional deliberation on Alaska's purchase.

Further attempts at telegraph construction in Alaska would come with the U.S. Army's arrival in the new territory.

Colonel Randall, who had been serving in Alaska since late 1897, was in Washington, D.C. on January 27, 1900 when he wrote to the Army Adjutant General regarding the need for a military telegraph line to connect his stations. He submitted a proposed route map and suggested the matter be referred to the Army's Chief Signal Officer for a cost estimate. He recommended that if the plan were approved, the "signal bureau" (Army Signal Corps) be directed to start action on it.[1]

On February 3 the Chief Signal Officer, Brig. Gen. Adolphus W. Greely, estimated the cost of the project would be $450,550, including $10,000 for station equipment, and recommended that the proposal and estimate be endorsed immediately to the Congress for consideration. Greely indicated the need to obtain funds quickly so that operations could start in April and carry on through the short summer work season.[2]

At about this same time, Alaska's Governor John G. Brady wrote in his annual report to the Secretary of the Interior: "Wires should be put up from Valdez to Eagle City, and from Eagle down the Yukon to St. Michael and Cape Nome." Brady also favored cables connecting southeast Alaska with Dutch Harbor in the Aleutians.[3]

On May 26, 1900, Congress passed an act appropriating $450,550 "for the purpose of connecting head-

---

[1] H Doc 427, 56th Cong, 1st Sess, p.2.
[2] Ibid.
[3] An Rpt, Gov of Alaska, to Sec Interior, 1900; H Doc 5, 56th Cong, 1st Sess, Misc Rpts, Part II.

quarters . . . at St. Michael by military telegraph and cable lines with other military stations in Alaska . . ." A special provision of the act of considerable interest to civilians stated that "commercial business may be done over these military lines under such conditions as may be deemed by the Secretary of War, equitable and in the public interest . . ." Personal messages were covered under the heading "commercial business."

Thus was born what was soon to become the Washington-Alaska Military Cable and Telegraph System, popularly called "WAMCATS." Mitchell's assignment was to help get it started. Construction of the system was the responsibility of the Signal Corps under the Act of May 26, 1900. Its successful completion was in great part due to the personal interest of General Greely. His own arctic duty as a lieutenant in the 1880's inspired his enthusiastic support. Most of the line construction and some of the maintenance was carried out by "troops of the line," mainly infantrymen and artillerymen assigned to the several posts.[4] It was a project unique in the annals of telegraphic engineering in respect to its immensity and the remoteness, inaccessibility, climatic severity, and the wild and uninhabited nature of the region to be served.

Tentage, food, wire, insulators, tools, and other materials had to be moved by sleds or pack animals. Trails and unmarked terrain often were so rough that but a few miles of travel could be made in a day. In some cases, 150-pound coils of wire were carried 145 miles by packhorse through virtually virgin territory. Swift icy streams, swampy morasses, tangled underbrush, canyons and mountains, thick timber, deep snow, treacherous ice, and temperatures that froze the quicksilver in thermometer bulbs drained the strength of man and beast. Added to the discomforts of frequent falls of rain in summer were the pestiferous mosquitos, en masse, and forest fires which impeded construction or wiped out existing lines making replacement necessary. Shortages of proper food and remoteness of medical aid were common.[5]

In his annual report for 1905 (by which time all posts were inter-connected and Alaska was tied in with Seattle) General Greely recommended the system be gradually turned over to private industry. He felt that this should be done "as the future development of Alaska and the coincident extension of private enterprises may render possible. At present," he said, "no private corporation could efficiently maintain and operate the land lines. They are maintained now by men receiving from $13 to $54 a month, with rations, in a country where day laborers earn from $4.50 to $15 per day. Only loyalty to his oath of enlistment keeps the American soldier on this arduous, dangerous, and monotonous duty."[6]

Some perspective of the early land lines and cable system may be gained from the route map which appears elsewhere in this book. The laying of the submarine cable between Sitka and Seattle in 1903 was an outstanding achievement in American military history. The Army cable ship BURNSIDE placed the 1,070-mile line at an average depth of 6,000 feet, and to an extreme of 10,200 feet.

The WAMCATS route map shows the 107-mile wireless (radio) segment crossing Norton Sound to connect Fort Davis and nearby Nome with Fort St. Michael. The antennas installed on both sides of the Sound were 210-foot masts, then the highest ever erected on the Pacific coast. When that portion of the system began regular operations in August 1904 it was the first wireless put in service on the American continent used for commercial operations.

In 1936 WAMCATS was renamed the Alaska Communication System (ACS). It continued as an Army service to Alaska until 1962 when it was transferred to the Air Force. In 1971, some 66 years after General Greely recommended the functions be turned over to private enterprise, ACS facilities and its service responsibilities were sold to RCA. Except for restrictions placed on the use of circuits between Seattle and Ketchikan, and between Seattle and Juneau during part of World War II, WAMCATS and ACS service was always available for private use and commercial business.

As Billy Mitchell says in this story, "In new countries the first effort is to get means of communication. In Alaska the telegraph system was the wedge which cleft open the country to communications." He was proud to have been chosen to contribute to that effort.

This heretofore unpublished manuscript has been edited with restraint so as to retain the flavor of Mitchell's entertaining style of writing. He was not an anthropologist or historian, so there are some inaccuracies in his discussions of these topics. Also, the manuscript was written some 30 years following his Alaskan service and the passage of time may have clouded some

---

[4] The term "troops of the line" did not refer to the telegraph line. Those words differentiate between the service and support branches such as quartermaster, signal, and medical corps, and the direct combat type of organizations, the infantry, cavalry, and artillery.

[5] *The Story of the Alaska Communication System, 1900-1943,* an undated manuscript obtained by the Editor from the 1931st Communication Squadron, Elmendorf AFB, in 1967.

[6] An Rpt, Chief Signal Officer, dated Sept. 30, 1905, in An Rpts of the War Dept for FY 1905. H Doc 2, 58th Cong, 1st Sess, p. 220. In this report General Greely commented: "Even today there are more than 1,300 miles of line through a country where no wheeled conveyance can travel in summer."

details. Some missing first names of his acquaintances have been supplied, key dates have been inserted, place names have been corrected or brought up to date in spelling (the first time they appear), and footnotes have been added to clarify some statements. A more complete or detailed editing would have required many more annotations. This has been avoided so as not to detract from the original account.

Several members of the Cook Inlet Historical Society have assisted in the preparation of this publication, notably President James E. Moody, Director Gary C. Stein, and James Ducker. Cover concept by Teri Hibarger; maps and cover art by Monty Henninger, Jr., both of Anchorage.

Kenneth N. Gilpin, Jr., son-in-law of General Mitchell and husband of the late Lucy (Mitchell) Gilpin, has kindly permitted our Society to publish this story as part of its information and education program.

The cooperation of personnel in the Manuscript Division of the Library of Congress was helpful in making the Mitchell Collection available for research.

The courtesy of the American Heritage Publishing Company, in supporting the concept of publishing the full manuscript, is greatly appreciated. A portion of the original material appeared in American Heritage Magazine in 1961, copyrighted by Lucy Gilpin.

In the text, footnotes are by the editor, and brackets show editorial corrections and additions to, or clarifications of the author's material.

Appendixes include a bibliography and a WAMCATS construction progress report of 1904.

Lyman L. Woodman
Lt. Col., USAF-Ret.
Editor

Anchorage, Alaska
April 14, 1982

INTRODUCTION

By

General William Mitchell
Former Commander, Air Forces, AEF,
and Director, Military Aeronautics,
U.S. Army[1]

The following account of one who actively participated, laid out and worked on the Alaska telegraph system is told, I believe, for the first time. To a young lieutenant in the United States service, it seemed as great an undertaking as the Lewis and Clark Expedition, Fremont's trip to California, or the opening of the routes along the Mexican border to the Pacific Coast.

Three and a half decades ago, conditions in the whole world, especially in an economic and a military way, were quite as they had been for long periods before. The only difference in means of transportation was the steam engine, applied on land to railroads and on the water to steamships. In the interior of Alaska, away from the coast line and navigable streams, all movement from one place to another was either done by men or animals, with packs on their backs, or by dog team, as it had been for centuries. At that time our nation still had the pioneering spirit of expansion and we were looking for new fields to conquer. We had come to America as a nation of seamen. It took us many years to become a nation of woodsmen and pierce the great forests that curtained off the middle west from the Atlantic coast. It took years for our people to become plainsmen and reach the Pacific Coast. The thorough reconnoitering and opening up of Alaska marked the end of that period.

Today, at least temporarily, we are thrown back on ourselves. Our country has become industrialized. We are over-producing in many lines and these things have to be sold in foreign markets. The day has passed when a man who finds himself restricted in business or means of livelihood may take his rifle, go to the woods and carve out a new home for his family, or go west and develop something entirely new. Now with our congested centers of populations, our various means of transportation which have to be coordinated, the over-production of foods in one place and shortage in another, unemployment, the problem of old age without adequate means of livelihood, we are gradually being forced toward a planned existence similar to conditions in the older countries of the world.

One of the greatest changes that has come about in the last 35 years is that of transportation. When I went to Alaska in 1901, there were no automobiles, buses, airplanes, or submarines. There was no radio telegraph. Now we can fly through the air at speeds undreamed of then, we can talk by radio telegraph with the speed of light. Had the radio been in existence then, there would have been no necessity for laying cables to Alaska or building telegraph lines through its trackless depths.

Each of these changes has enhanced the value of Alaska to the United States. That country is capable of maintaining a heavy population, from the standpoints of climate, agriculture, and animal industry. At present, people do not like to live there. In recent years the population has fallen off considerably. Few of the men conscripted from that territory for the war [World War I] ever returned. As the pressure of population and the difficulties of livelihood increase in the United States, it is to be expected that more people will go north; but the present territorial limits of the United States will have to contain something over 350,000,000 people before this pressure will be great enough to cause Alaska to be heavily populated.

Alaska's strategic value increases constantly. Its position, halfway between America and Asia, is decisive. From Alaska, aircraft now can fly and return with one charge of fuel to New York or to Peking, China. These distances include all the vital centers of the United States and of Eastern Asia, including Japan. Our lines of trade have heretofore followed the parallels of latitude. In the future, our lines for military operation will follow meridians, or the shortest line between two points.

Air power is now the decisive element because it can go straight to the vital centers, cities, power plants, water supplies, and agricultural areas of hostile states, and neutralize them. Air power completely dominates sea power and navies. Either military or merchant fleets can be destroyed by air power in short order. Consequently, a position such as Alaska is of enormous strategical importance. The Panama Canal, according to the old navy theory, is an extremely important posision because it allows fleets to move from the Atlantic to the Pacific Ocean, without having to go around South America. However, it sinks into insignificance strategically when compared to Alaska, because in the first place, sea power can accomplish comparatively

[1] Mitchell was a brigadier general. His service in World War I was in the American Expeditionary Force (AEF).

little except through submarines, in an offensive way, and next, the Panama Canal can be put out of business without much trouble by air attack.

It does not take much of a look into the future to see that he who holds Alaska holds the world, because a great expanding nation, if it becomes dominant in the air, can now achieve world dominion more easily than the United States established its present confines. This is because aircraft have made the world one-sixth its former size, and we can speak from one continent to another with the speed of light.

In new countries, the first effort is to get means of communication. As a corollary to it, trails were established. The first railroad was built into the Copper River in 1911.[2] In 1913, a motor car drove from the coast to the Tanana River, at Fairbanks. In 1920, I sent a flight of airplanes from New York to Nome and back again without the loss of a ship or a man. This expedition was ably commanded by Capt. [St. Clair] Streett [U.S. Air Service]. The airway was established with the cooperation of the Canadian government. I hoped that it would be maintained permanently, but this has not been done.

At that time I was laying out plans for the flight of airplanes around the world, which we brought to a conclusion in 1923 [1924]. These airplanes flew through Alaska and again it was demonstrated to anyone with an eye to the future and conversant with world conditions that it was of the utmost importance for us to establish our airways there at the earliest possible moment. However, conservatism, ignorance and lack of foresight have prevented it up to this time.

In 1923, a railroad was built [completed] from the [Gulf of] Alaska coast to Fairbanks, thus connecting our Pacific Coast at Seward with the great Yukon inland water system.

At present, great as the economic value of Alaska may be, it is far outweighed by its strategical worth, and our people, particularly our legislators and those in the executive departments of the government, should become thoroughly familiar with these values. No longer is it possible to abandon a valuable territory to its own devices as we were accustomed to do in the past, and let it work out its own future. Today, if a country does not take care of its valuable possessions, like Alaska, they will be grabbed up and devoured by one of the predatory nations.

In the studies I have made of the application of military power on and across the Pacific, Alaska always stands out as the key point. With modern means of transportation in the air, we are no longer afraid of cold, fog, rain and snow or any other climatic condition. Our modern aircraft can not only operate under such conditions, landing and taking off successfully in fogs, defrosting their wings, and providing for their personnel in the coldest temperaures, but they can rise up into the so-called stratosphere where conditions are always the same and navigate with precision and assurance.

The tale which follows of the construction of the Alaska telegraph lines holds a great deal more in it than just the accomplishment in itself. Every officer and man of the armed services who worked in and around Alaska, the civilians whose help made a successful termination of our work possible, all learned much of its great value to us and the necessity for maintaining and keeping this territory as our bastion of defense in the Pacific.

[2] The Copper River & Northwestern Railway was completed in March 1911. Several other lines had been built earlier, including Seward Peninsula RR (1906); Yakutat & Southern (1904); Council City & Solomon (1907); White Pass & Yukon Route, partly in Alaska, (1900); and Tanana Mine (Valley) RR (1905). Howard Clifford, *Rails North,* Superior, (Seattle, 1981).

1 ALASKA AND ITS HISTORY

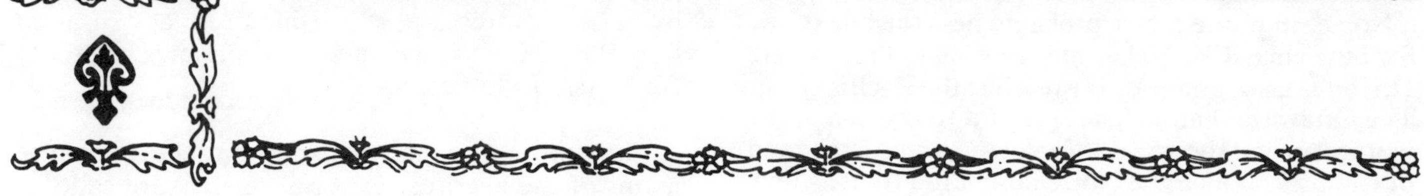

From the time of the discovery of Alaska by white people, up to the negotiations which terminated in its acquisition by the United States, the story of this north country reads more like a fantastic novel than true history.

Alaska comprises about the same area as all the United States east of the Mississippi. The distance between its westernmost island and its farthest point east is about the same as from San Francisco to Eastport, Maine. From north to south, the distance is about the same as from Duluth, Minn., to New Orleans, La. Naturally in such a vast area, there is a great difference of climate. The Japanese current washes the Aleutian Islands and all the southern coast. Its effect is to warm the air and charge it with moisture. When this warm air meets the cold air coming down from the North, a tremendous precipitation of rain and snow results. Eighty feet of snow fell on Thompson Pass, north of Valdez, the last year I was in Alaska. Throughout this area, the climate is much like that of Puget Sound. Vegetation is luxuriant. All the hardier grains, vegetables, and grasses can be grown to advantage. Livestock of all kinds can be raised with ease, as they subsist on the native grasses without extra feed. The long sunny days of June cause very rapid growth and vegetables mature quickly.

In central Alaska, the climatic story is entirely different. This is the vast Yukon watershed, one of the great drainage systems of the world. The Yukon is navigable for steamboats for 2200 miles. This area is shut off from the Pacific Coast by the mountains of the Alaska Range, the highest in North America, and by the coast range, almost as high. It is cut off from the Arctic by the mountains which are the ends of the Rockies. The rainfall is moderate and there is comparatively little snow, because where it is very cold the air cannot hold moisture. It seldom exceeds four feet in depth on the level. In winter the temperature goes as low as any place in the world. While southern Alaska is wrapped in fog, rain, and snow, this section has perfectly clear weather most of the time. When it is very cold, the winds do not blow. During the summer, when there is constant daylight, things warm up and vegetation grows quite well. This area is full of fish and game, and capable of sustaining life for a considerable population.

North of the Arctic hills, conditions are similar to those in all Arctic countries. The timber gives way to the mossy tundra and small low bushes that skirt the Arctic Ocean.

Alaska is enormously rich in minerals of almost all kinds, in oil and coal. Its fisheries, not only of salmon but of deep-sea fish, seem almost inexhaustible. Furs have been more than a gold mine in the past, but on account of injudicious handling and lack of regulation, they have greatly deteriorated.

Until about 1800, this immense territory remained practically unknown to the civilized world. Even in the United States we knew very little about anything west of the Mississippi until after 1800.

Centuries ago, Chinese and Japanese sailors ventured into Bering Sea, and at some time or another visited the North American mainland. Siberian natives and those of Alaska cross the Bering Strait frequently, in boats and on the ice. The distance is short, only 52 miles, and in the middle are the two Diomede Islands, 6 [2] miles apart, one owned by Russia and the other by the United States. Consequently, our territory touches that of Russia. The greatest distance across the water is 23 miles.[1]

The Chinese and Japanese found they could gain more in commercial trade further to the south on the Asiatic hinterland, than on the forbidding coasts and against the fierce natives of the American continent. It is strange that although the Chinese were the greatest sailors and invented and employed practically all the magnetic and celestial navigating instruments in use today, they never developed any great navigators.

[1] Evidently he refers here to the miles from Russia's Big Diomede Island to the Alaska coast.

The Norse may have visited Alaska. There is some evidence to show that these hardy people had colonies or stations all the way from Labrador to Mexico. Montezuma, in his will, made when he was about to be executed by the Spaniards, said that he was descended from a white man who had come over the seas in a ship with the wings of a bird. This must have been a Norse ship. The Norse probably held the line of the St. Lawrence River. They may have had a fort where Detroit is now, and possibly reached the Pacific coast. The Ottawa Indian language is said to contain many Norse words. The word "Canada" means "the land of cabins",[2] which the Norse taught the Indians how to build. It is thought that the mounds found in many places in America are the remains of fortifications which the Indians learned to construct from the Norsemen.

The Norse may have reached Alaska by overland trails and the McKenzie [Mackenzie] River, by way of the Arctic shores or Hudson Bay. However, the knowledge they may have gained about that country was destroyed when the Genoese and Venetians sent their cruisers along the north coasts of Europe to Greenland and America to extirpate the Norse pirates. In doing so, they raised the American Indians against them wherever they could. (The Norse called the Indians "Screelings".) These punitive expeditions, the Indian massacres, and the plague of the Black Death wiped out anything we might have known from Norse sources about the interior of America. The Norse, however, were here from about 1000 A.D. to 1490, a longer period of time than we have been here, since the discovery of America by Columbus.

The Aleutian Islands and the shores of Alaska are inhabited by the "long-eyed people". They are short, well built, intelligent and hardy. If dressed in the same costumes and mixed with a crowd of Japanese or some tribes of Filipinos, it would be hard to tell them apart. They are known as Aleuts in the Aleutian Islands, as Malemutes in Bering Sea and as Eskimos in the Arctic. They are called Innuits by the Indians, which means "meat-eaters", as they used to subsist almost entirely on seals, whales, walrus, and marine creatures.[3] Now they have herds of reindeer. They have been able to maintain themselves both in an economic and military way against the native people around them, and have held up well in their contact with the whites.

The interior of Alaska is inhabited by people who resemble the Indians of Athabascan origin in Canada and the United States. They are fine big fellows with high ridged noses, high cheek bones and copper skins. To me they look almost exactly like the Manchus and Mongols, the Asiatic tribes of Tungus origin. These people have suffered greatly at the hands of the whites, by massacres, disease, starvation, and lack of attention. Both the coast and interior people must have come from Asia in times past.

I have often thought that some day the skeletal remains of the negritos, or Aetas as they are called in the East Indies, would be found on the Aleutian Islands. These diminutive negroid people apparently inhabited all the islands from the Malay Peninsula up through Japan and the Kuriles. Their wide distribution is one of the things that cause the negroes to claim that at one time they inhabited the whole world.

The Alaska Indians' tribal relations, their customs, and their government attained about the same degree of development as those of the Indians of the United States.

Their institutions and systems were thrown into turmoil by the coming of the Russian adventurers in the middle of the 18th century. The Russian horsemen, after overrunning Siberia in an incredibly short time, reached the Sea of Okhotsk, the shores of Bering Sea, and probably the Arctic, in the early part of the 18th century. These people were about as tough as they make them. In that, they resembled the Mongols that Genghis Khan led in his great conquest. They ate anything, cooked or uncooked, and dressed in the skins of animals freshly killed. They were ruthless in their methods, killing, burning, and destroying wherever they thought it was to their advantage. They heard about the richness of the furs in Alaska, and later about its gold. At first, undoubtedly, they went over with natives in their skin boats and later made crafts of roughly hewn planks fastened together with the sinews of animals. In these they set out boldly across these forbidding stretches of Arctic sea. There have been few examples of hardihood and initiative which surpassed this.

Our definite knowledge of Alaska really begins with the expedition of Vitus Bering, a Danish captain in the

---

[2] The word Canada was originally the name of one of a number of Indian settlements. Probably from Iroquis "Kanata" meaning cabin, lodge; Adrian Room, *Place Names of the World* (Totowa, N.J., 1974).

[3] "Innuit means 'people' collectively . . . the name applied to themselves by all the Orarians except the Aleuts and perhaps the Eastern Siberian natives of the same stock. It is in use from Greenland to Bering Strait, and thence to the vicinity of Mt. St. Elias." (Orarian, a term proposed by Dall in 1869 alluding to the coastwise distribution of the tribes of Innuits, Aleuts, and Asiatic Eskimos). p. 532. "These Innuits [Mahlemut] occupy the coast of Norton Sound and Bay, north of Shaktolik and the neck of Kaviak [Seward] Peninsula to Selawik Lake." p. 407. "The neck of [Seward] Peninsula is occupied by the Mahlemut Innuit." p. 137. William H. Dall, *Alaska and its Resources* (Boston, 1870). Elliott wrote that Mahlemoot were found on King Island and St. Lawrence Island. Henry W. Elliott, *Our Arctic Province,* Scribner's Sons, (New York, 1906), pp 426, 444-457.

Russian service. He equipped a couple of vessels on the coast of Kamchatka in 1741 for an expedition to [what is now called] Alaska. After a long cruise they came in sight of land, probably around where Sitka is now. They sent a couple of boats ashore and waited for them to come back; but they failed to reappear and the watchers saw only big fires on the shore where the boats had landed. From this they judged that the landing party had been killed by the natives, so they left that vicinity. It is probable that the natives killed all foreigners who appeared, and in this way held off the Asiatics. Bering's ships became separated, and Bering himself touched the Alaska coast around Yakutat Bay, where he discovered and named Mount St. Elias, 18,000 feet high, which was thought for a long time to be the highest mountain in North America. Mount McKinley, in Alaska, is the highest, being 20,300 feet.

Bering worked his way back toward the Kamchatka coast but upon reaching the Commander Islands was wrecked on one of them, which now bears his name. Here they ran short of supplies and scurvy appeared among them. Bering himself succumbed. The men subsisted on sea creatures, and particularly on the Arctic seacow or dugong, the largest member of this peculiar family, which they exterminated. Although it is now extinct, museums have obtained complete skeletal remains from the piles of bones left by the Bering expedition.

Some of the survivors eventually returned to Kamchatka in a boat which they made of the wreckage of their vessel. Chirikof, the commander of the other vessel, returned to Kamchatka with his ship.

The tales told by the crews about the riches of Alaska urged others on. They explored the coasts and the great rivers, and made enormous profits from the fur trade. Their treatment of the natives was ruthless. Sometimes they made them drag their sleds, compelling them to work night and day without respite, while the Russians took turns sleeping. When the natives gave out, they would kill them and get more. This led to reprisals and massacres by the Indians but they had no chance against the brutally savage Russians with their superior weapons.

Pribilof, an expert fur hunter, discovered the seal islands that bear his name, in 1778 [1786]. It is here that the great seal rookeries of the present day are located. The enormous wealth derived from them has been a bone of contention between the United States, Russia, Great Britain and Japan, for a long time.

The Russians gradually pushed down the Pacific coast until they reached San Francisco harbor. The Russian River, just north of there, attests by its name how far down the coast they penetrated.

Eventually, the fur trading privileges in Alaska were given to a group of aristocrats called the Russian American Trading Company. Alaska was then known by the name of Russian America. Immediately difficulties cropped up with the Canadian Northwest and Hudson [Hudson's] Bay Trading Companies. The British were afraid that if the Russian adventurers were really backed by the Russian government, they might overrun a great part of North America. Hence they pushed them back wherever possible and ended up by making a treaty with Russia in 1830 [1825], which established the boundaries of Alaska, very much as they are today.

The Spanish, fearful that the Russians would come down as far as Mexico and interfere with their colonies on the Pacific coast, sent expeditions from Lower California to Upper California, which grew into the mission system that was there when the United States took it over. There is little doubt but that it was fear of the Russians that inspired the Spaniards in this project, because the natives who inhabited that region, the Digger Indians, were the most utterly debased tribes that inhabited the North American continent. They subsisted principally on grasshoppers, beetles, roots and the meat of dead animals. They did not know how to build fires or make weapons. They wandered about as individuals; men and women apparently did not stay together except for certain periods each year. Through an area such as this, naturally, there would be little or no opposition to the occupancy of the land by a determined people, such as the Russian adventurers were.

It remained for the British, under Captain [James] Cook, to map the shores of Alaska accurately. This great navigator was one of the first to be able to keep [to] the sea for long periods without having his crews decimated by scurvy. He used vegetables and citric acid to combat it, hence the name "lime juicer" [or "limey"] for British sailors.

American traders also began to realize the richness of the Alaska fur trade, fisheries, and gold, but all of them tried to keep it secret, not wishing to share their opportunities with others. It is difficult to say just how our government first became interested in Alaska. During the Crimean War, when England and France were fighting Russia, a certain American, Dr. [Thomas] Cottman of Louisiana, arrived at St. Petersburg and became very friendly with the Czar Nicholas.[4] Alaska was proving to be a source of increasing disturbance

[4] "Dr. Thomas Cottman, while surgeon of the Emperor of Russia's staff, initiated, with Count Nesselrode, the proceedings for the acquisition of Alaska and other Russian possessions of North America." *The National Cyclopedia of American Biography,* Vol 1, (New York, 1892), p.177.

between Russia and Great Britain. The Czar was getting comparatively little revenue out of it and was afraid the English might take it away from him completely. Also he thought that if the United States acquired Alaska, it might create additional enmity between that country and Great Britain and strengthen our position on the North American continent somewhat in the same way that Napoleon intended, when he sold us the territory of Louisiana, saying "Today I have accomplished something that will one day humble England's pride."

Dr. Cottman returned to the United States and advocated the acquisition of Alaska. Negotiations were begun but they drifted along in a leisurely way. They were practically consummated, the Czar having agreed to sell Alaska for $2,200,000, when the Civil War broke over the United States, when every cent and every resource had to be devoted to that struggle. The Russian negotiations remained in abeyance but Secretary [of State William H.] Seward never lost sight of the advantage that Alaska would bring to us. In the language of the day, it was called "Seward's Folly". During the Civil War, the Union had no friends in Europe except Russia. As the severity of the war increased and the Confederate States showed such marked military ability, it was feared by the Federal government that they might obtain recognition in Europe, which would make it possible for them to buy ammunition and equipment openly. To counteract this tendency, the Federal government asked the Czar if he would send a fleet on a friendly visit to New York and San Francisco, which would demonstrate to the other European powers that Russia might side with the United States in case of war between the latter and England or France. The United States was ready to fight these nations in addition to the Confederate States, in case the latter was recognized. The Czar replied that he would be glad to send the fleet but that his treasury was empty and he did not have the price of the trip. The United States inquired how much it would be and the Czar said it would cost $5,000,000. This was satisfactory to the United States, but they explained that it could not be paid until the end of the war, because if they put through an appropriation in Congress for that purpose, it would show that Russia was being paid for the visit and its desired effect on the other Europeans would be lost. The Russians agreed to this and sent the fleets, one to New York, the other to San Francisco, and the demonstration was adjudged worth the outlay. [This fleet payment arrangement appears to be hearsay.]

In 1867, after the close of the Civil War, it was decided that the $5,000,000 for the fleet should be included in the purchase price of Alaska, and an appropriation for $7,200,000 was made to buy the territory. The Russian fleet came to New York to get the money, and a man still living, Mr. C. C. Glover, of the Riggs National Bank of Washington, D.C., took the money to New York and handed it to the Russian commander. It is said that the [Russian] naval officers split up the $5,000,000 among themselves, and took only the $2,200,000 back to the Czar.[5]

It was one of the best business transactions the United States ever engaged in. Not only have we obtained an enormous revenue from Alaska since then, many times over the purchase price, but the strategical position that was handed over to us may some day be the keypoint in our future existence.

Immediately after the acquisition of Alaska in 1868,[6] troops were sent to Sitka, explorations were made up the Yukon River and some semblance of order inaugurated, which lasted for about ten years, when the troops were withdrawn and the place fell into a chaotic condition. There was no law and order and no control. The poor citizens who remained appealed to the English and others to help them at various times.

Little by little, the American fur trading companies extended their operations up along the shores of Alaska. The Alaska Commercial Company was given a franchise on the Pribilof seal islands [in 1870]. Little notice was taken by the general public of the fur trade and fisheries. The commercial companies operating in the north spread reports of the inhospitable character of the country and the impossibility of living there. At the turn of the century, Alaska was as little known as the center of the Antarctic continent. Men had an inkling of its vast riches, but these were hidden in the trackless, foodless, uninhabited wilderness and locked by the key of the King of the North, with his 70° below Zero.

[5] Treasury draft #9759 in the sum of $7,200,000 was issued and delivered to Baron Stoeckl (Russian Minister) on August 1, 1868. It was signed by the Treasurer of the U.S., the Register of Treasury, and Assistant Treasurer of the U.S. It was endorsed by Stoeckl to George W. Riggs and Stoeckl gave his receipt for that sum the same day. Printed copies of the draft and receipt appear in H Rpt 35, 40th Cong, 3rd Sess, pp 5-6.

[6] The Treaty of Purchase and transfer of the Russian possession to the United States occurred in 1867 and U.S. troops arrived in October 1867. Payment for the acquired property was made in 1868.

Extract, U.S. House Report 35, 40th Congress, 3rd Session, "Alaska Investigation," 1868.

The undersigned, envoy extraordinary and minister plenipotentiary of his Majesty the Emperor of all the Russias, do hereby acknowledge to have received at the Treasury Department, in Washington, *seven million two hundred thousand dollars* ($7,200,000) in coin, being the full amount due from the United States to Russia in consideration of the cession, by the latter power to the former, of certain territory described in the treaty entered into by the Emperor of all the Russias and the President of the United States, on the 30th day of March, 1867.

STOECKL.

WASHINGTON, *August* 1, 1868.

Dft. No. 9759 on Treasury Warrant No. 927.—C. F. H.

$7,200,000.] TREASURY OF THE UNITED STATES,
Washington, August 1, 1868.

At sight, pay to Edward de Stoeckl, envoy extraordinary, &c., or order, seven millions two hundred thousand dollars. Pay in coin.

F. E. SPINNER,
Treasurer of the United States.

No. 9759.—Registered August 1, 1868.

N. L. JEFFRIES,
Register of the Treasury.

ASSISTANT TREASURER UNITED STATES, *New York:*

Pay the within at the office of the Treasurer of the United States at Washington.

L. R. TUTTLE,
Assistant Treasurer United States.

[Endorsements.]

Pay Geo. W. Riggs or order.

ED. DE STOECKL.
GEO. W. RIGGS.

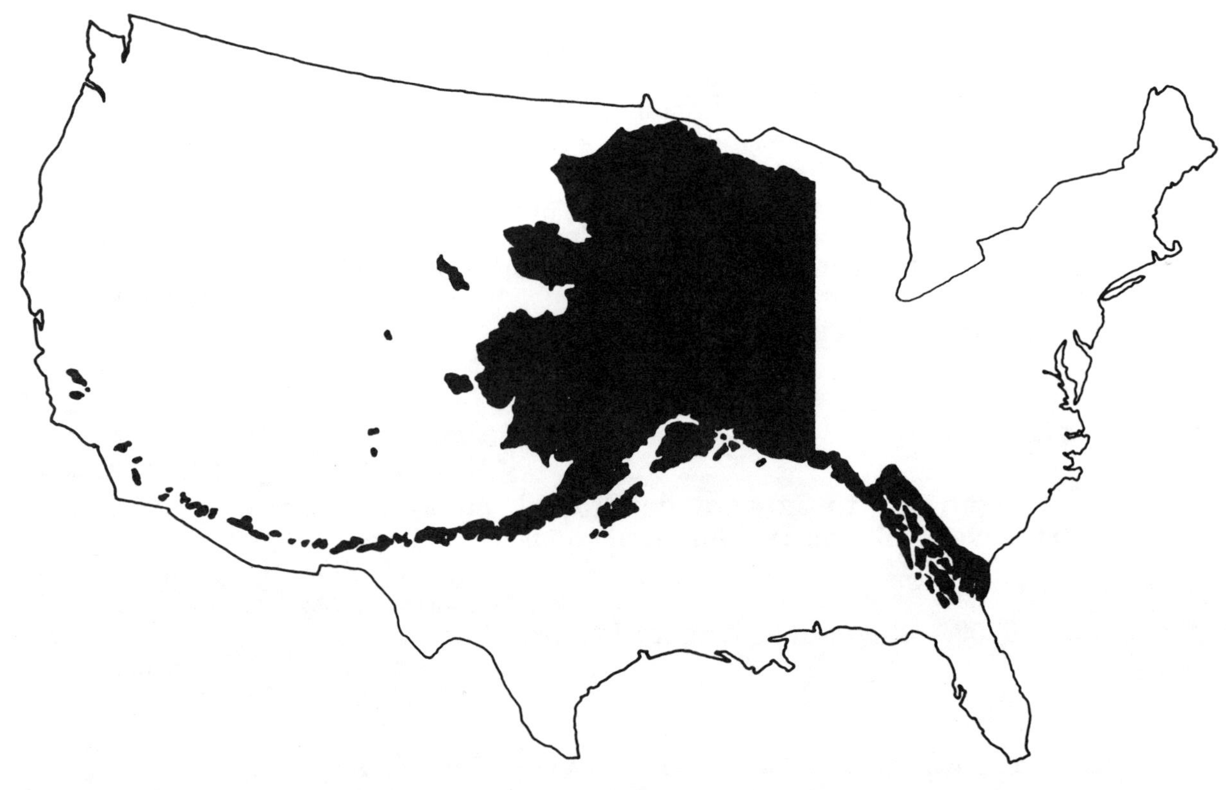

Comparing Alaska's area with that of the continental United States.

2

ORDERED TO ALASKA

In 1897, gold in fabulous amounts was discovered by "Swiftwater Bill", [Gates] on the Forty Mile (Fortymile] River, which flows into the Yukon a few miles below Dawson.[1] A horde of prospectors followed, who pierced the curtains of the Northland and found gold in great quantities all through the Yukon River basin, an area about half as large as all our country lying east of the Mississippi.

The currents from this northern Father of Waters carried the metal into the Bering Sea, where it was churned into fine dust and washed up on the beaches of Norton Sound where it could be dipped up by the saucer full.[2] This was all placer gold, the kind that could be washed out with one's hands, and did not require smelters or stamp mills. Never had such placer mines been known. Even in the palmy days of placer mining in California, Australia, and South Africa, nothing had been seen like this.

The "Great Strike" occurred about the same time of our Spanish War, and men from all continents, climes, and races trooped to the North to seek their fortunes. It was the heroic age of the United States. We had taken the West Indies from the Spaniards, their last vestige of territory in the Western hemisphere. We had crossed the Pacific and possessed ourselves of the Philippines. On the shores of Asia, American troops had assaulted Peking, the capital of China.[3] Our people were fired with the spirit of adventure such as had not seized America since the days of '49.

Those of us in the Army who had been through the Spanish War, the Philippine Insurrection, and the Boxer Rebellion were naturally more imbued with this spirit than others.[4] Three years of almost continuous duty in the field made peacetime conditions in the United States look tame to a lieutenant in the Army only twenty-one years of age in 1901.

So great had been the rush to Alaska that our government had no organization with which to maintain law and order that could cope with conditions there. Detachments of the Army were sent up hurriedly, but they were empowered to act only in case of violent disturbances, and could not administer the civil law. On the Canadian side, however, the Mounted Police, a civil body with a military organization, stepped into the mining districts and took complete charge.

The Canadians built a telegraph line, largely along the old right of way that the Western Union Telegraph Company surveyed and partially cut out in the sixties of the last century so as to connect America with Asia by way of Bering Strait. Work on it stopped when Cyrus W. Field laid the first [successful] telegraphic cable across the Atlantic in 1868 [1866], which gave communication from America to Europe. The Canadian line, finished in 1899, ended at Dawson City, Y.T., about 100 miles from the American-Canadian border. There was no means of communication from the United States to Alaska other than steamboats, canoes, and in winter, dog teams. In summer, it took six weeks for a letter to go from the Yukon country to the United States, and during the winter, in some places, it took six months. Not only was it necessary for our own domestic welfare to connect our posts in Alaska to the United States by telegraph, but friction with Canada, England, Russia, and Japan over such questions as the international boundary, and fishing and sealing rights in Bering Sea, was becoming constantly more acute.

[Brig.] Gen. Adolphus W. Greely, one of the ablest soldiers the United States ever possessed, was Chief of the Signal Corps at that time. He had had vast experience in the Arctic, having at one time attained the "farthest north" himself. The Army hung back from attempting to lay telegraph lines through this trackless

[1] Coarse gold was found by Howard Franklin on the Fortymile River on the Alaska side of the boundary on September 7, 1886. Alfred H. Brooks, *Blazing Alaska's Trails*, Univ. of Alaska and Arctic Institute of No. America, (Caldwell, Idaho, 1953), pp. 328-331.

[2] This transport of gold and its dipping up by the saucerful appear to be hypothesis and exaggeration of the times.

[3] U.S. troops were protecting American citizens there during the Boxer uprising.

[4] Mitchell was not involved in the Boxer uprising. He became acquainted with conditions in China in 1900 while en route to the states from the Philippines via Asia and Europe.

General Greely COURTESY U.S. ARMY

and forbidding territory, but Greely went right ahead and obtained an appropriation from Congress for laying a cable from Puget Sound to Alaska and connecting it up with telegraph lines down the Yukon and across Bering Sea [Norton Sound] to Nome.[5]

At that time cables were in demand and none could be bought in Europe, so Gen. Greely had one made in the United States, the first long deep-sea cable ever constructed here. It was laid down from Seattle to Juneau, Alaska, thence to Skagway, and on to Valdez, [in 1904], a distance greater than from America to Europe.

During 1900, the Army attempted to build the telegraph lines but aside from some wonderful expeditions by individuals, comparatively little was accomplished.[6] At first the Army attempted to use enlisted men of the infantry to work on the lines. Most of these were young, totally inexperienced in the north and unwilling to work for $15 a month where civilians were getting from $1 to $3 an hour, with board.[7] To take care of himself and work in the Arctic winter temperatures, a man had to be an expert. As an example: I remember visiting a camp of these young infantry soldiers along the Yukon River, where the ice freezes 6 or 7 feet thick. The Alaskan custom is to chop a hole to within a couple of feet of the water, then fire a bullet through it. The water seeps up through the small hole and makes a pool, where it can be dipped up easily.[8] Instead of this, the boys had chopped a hole two feet in diameter clear down to the water. One of them was sent down with the only pail in the outfit to get some water. As he dipped the pail in, he felt the pull of the current and thought a shark or something had hold of it, so he turned it loose and down it went. It is seldom realized how ignorant most city dwellers are about conditions in the open, especially when it is cold.

To find one's way across a trackless wilderness for hundreds of miles is a very different thing from going from one street corner to another, or along a well travelled highway. Men were back to conditions that existed west of the Alleghenies 200 years ago.

Alaska attracted and interested me not only because it was our last frontier, but also it represented a stepping stone to Asia. During my service in the Far East, when I was in contact with soldiers of foreign nations who participated in the Chinese campaign of 1900, English, French, German, Russian, Japanese, and Chinese, it was just as evident to me then as it is now that we eventually would be drawn into the political and military maelstrom of Asiatic and Pacific Ocean politics. Alaska being our closest point to Asia, it was obvious that at some future time its strategic importance to us would be very great.

On my return from the Philippines, I asked Gen. Greely to send me to the North.[9] He gave me a detachment of soldiers organized at Fort Myer, Virginia, and ordered me to Alaska, to investigate conditions connected with building telegraph lines, to distribute the men at the various stations down the Yukon, and to report my conclusions upon my return.

The month of July 1901, saw us arriving in Seattle, Washington, the great outfitting point for travellers

---

[5] On May 26, 1900, Congress authorized $450,550 for construction of communication lines connecting posts in Alaska, as a responsibility of the Chief Signal Officer. *U.S. Statutes at Large,* Vol. 31, p.206, 56th Cong, 1899-1901.
It was July 1900 before any equipment and supplies arrived at Valdez, and August at Nome and Fort St. Michael on Norton Sound and in the Yukon Valley. That summer and fall there were six working parties on the project. The team working north from Valdez continued on the job that winter. *The Story of the Alaska Communication System, 1900-1943,* op. cit.
By November 1900, infantrymen from Fort Egbert at Eagle City had constructed a telegraph line from that post 11 miles to the Canadian border, and Capt. Charles S. Farnsworth, 7th Infantry, the post commander, was able to communicate through to the States over an extension of the Canadian telegraph system. In the spring of 1901, detachments of Company E, 7th Infantry, from Fort Egbert, cleared the telegraph trail and cut and placed poles reaching a point 40 miles southward toward Valdez by mid-April. Captain Farnsworth reconnoitered 143 miles of the route. The only "hanging back" was on the section south from Fort Egbert. Captain Farnsworth did not receive expected pack mules needed for the work. Also, route instructions promised by Colonel Randall were not forthcoming. Work south from Fort Egbert resumed late in February 1901. Letters, Farnsworth to Capt. W.P. Richardson, Oct. 18, 1900; Farnsworth to Gen. Greely, Apr. 11, 1901; and Farnsworth to Maj. C.A. Booth, May 6, 1901. Farnsworth Collection, Alaska & Polar Regions Dept., E.E. Rasmuson Library, Univ. of Alaska, Fairbanks.
General Greely's part in "obtaining an appropriation" lay in his estimate of construction cost and favorable report on the proposed project to the Secretary of War. H Doc 427, 56th Cong, 1st Sess, p.2.

[6] Official records show very good progress in 1900, considering the few weeks of construction time available after tools and materials arrived from the States. See Appendix A.

[7] Unit records (National Archives) reveal that during 1900-1904, "troops of the line," men of the 3rd, 7th, 8th and 13th Infantry, plus members of the 32nd Coast Artillery, handled most of the construction in the field. In the next few years, the 10th and 22nd Infantry also worked on the lines, assisting with repairs, line replacement, and performing maintenance. Signal Corps soldiers concentrated on the technical aspects, on installation and operation of communications equipment. Annual reports by General Greely compliment the troops' work performed under very difficult and hazardous conditions.

[8] M.W. "Slim" Moore of Anchorage, who hunted and ran dogs for 50 years in Alaska and talked with many pioneers, said he had never heard of this method of getting water as "an Alaskan custom." Interview with editor in October 1981.

[9] Ruth Mitchell, in her book, *My Brother Bill,* Harcourt, (N.Y., 1953), and Emile Gauvreau, in *William Mitchell,* Dutton & Co., (N.Y., 1942), indicate that General Greely asked Mitchell to accept the Alaska duty. There were only 46 officers in the entire Signal Corps at the time.

to Alaska. The city was wide open, with saloons, gambling dens, dance halls and all the paraphernalia of the old frontier towns. All sorts and conditions of men were encountered: bankers, lumberjacks, clergymen, section hands, college professors, farmers, clerks, most of them travelling under assumed names. No one asked "What is your name?" but instead, "Pardner, what name do you go by?"

The night after I arrived in Seattle, an old-timer, George Mattock, had just come to the city to spend the second fortune he had made in the North. His first one had been consumed over twenty years before. George had never seen an electric light, a street car or a large church. He came into the Rainier Grand Hotel late one evening, at that time the "toniest" place in Seattle, dressed in his rough clothes and proceeded to the dining room. At a table near him sat two young men, very much dressed up, with female companions, ordering a large dinner. After waiting a long time, George called a waiter over and said, "I want something to eat". The waiter said, "Pardner, wait a few minutes, because two dudes over here are ordering a $25 dinner." George pulled a long poke of "dust" out of his pocket, hit the table with it, and shouted, "I'm hungry! Bring me $2000 worth of ham and eggs!"

The next morning early he hired all of the hacks in Seattle and had them come to the hotel. Getting into the leading hack, he invited anyone who wished to come with him and make a round of the town. He stopped at each saloon and bought drinks for everybody. Soon the crowd was tremendous, not only overflowing the insides of the hacks but occupying all the room on top. A few buses were pressed into service but these proved inadequate. As a last resort, about fifteen hearses were obtained and filled to capacity. This party lasted for two days when everybody was so tired out that they stopped by common consent and George went on down to Portland.

Occurrences of this kind were frequent. It was remarkable how little personal injury was done among the men. In the old frontier towns, everybody carried pistols. In the north country, nobody carried them. This was because in the days of horseback riding, Indian fighting and cattle herding, pistols were a necessity and men wore them all the time. In the north, rifles were carried to kill game and pistols were a useless incumbrance.

I expected to have difficulty in holding my men in Seattle, because many were recruits who had seldom been any distance from their homes on farms or in villages, and knew little about the world in general. They drank in the stories of the easily acquired fabulous wealth in the North, and the futility of serving in the Army for $15 a month when they might be making millions; but Sergeant Pollner, the old non-commissioned officer I had in charge, knew the game and with the exercise of rigid discipline, coming from wartime experience, got them through it in fine shape.

In a few days we embarked for Alaska on the old steamer *Cottage City,* a wooden ship scarcely 200 feet long. The route lay through the Inland [Inside] Passage, that labyrinth of islands, passages, and swift currents that stretches from Puget Sound to Southeast Alaska. This is one of the most dangerous routes in the world for shipping. Fogs, rains, and snow storms blind the eyes of the mariner, while the rapid currents push him on the rocks. Not a single ship floats today that was in service at that time. At Seymour Narrows, where we had to wait for slack water for several hours, the currents have a speed of ten to fifteen miles an hour on the half tide. Many a ship has been wrecked on this treacherous spot.

The scenery through this Inland Passage is grand and wonderful. The mountains, which rise sheer from the water, are covered with enormous cedar trees, six or seven feet in diameter. Indentations in the coast are fjords that run inland for miles, very narrow and extremely precipitous on the sides. The country abounds with game. Goats, sheep, moose, and various kinds of bears are found on the tops of the mainland ridges, while the forests contain many of the most valuable of North American fur bearing animals. The small islands are full of white tailed deer and black and brown bears.

One of our first stops was at Ketchikan, a salmon cannery nestling in the side of the mountains at the mouth of a sizable stream, whose clear waters rushed down beside it. The cannery itself was built over the water and the current quickly carried away the cleanings from the fish. Along this coast, within a few feet the depth of the water will increase from a fathom or two, to hundreds. There are salmon canneries all along the Alaska coast. Their crews, mostly Chinese and Indians, arrive before the salmon runs in June, work for a couple of months until the complete catch is canned and then return home. During the winter these establishments are deserted except for a few caretakers.

Within a few minutes after landing, two of my men came rushing up to me, very much excited, both holding a large salmon in each hand, whose tails dragged on the ground. "Lieutenant, Lieutenant, come and see the fish!" they shouted. Within a few hundred yards I came to the stream, where the fish were literally pushing each other out of the water on to the banks. I had heard stories of places where you could walk across the river on the salmon's backs, but I had never believed them until I saw this stream. I was to see the same thing many times afterward.

The captain and crew of the ship were competent, strong, hardy sailors, most of them Scandinavian, up to any emergency. The passengers were a motley aggregation, ranging from the professional prospector who had served his time in South Africa, Australia, South America, British Columbia and the Caziarc [Cassiar District,] and Black Hills of the United States, to missionaries, dance hall girls, ex-desperadoes, adventurers, and a few government agents. When a person is seized with the disease of gold hunting, it seldom leaves him, even after he has made a big stake. Usually he spends his fortune quickly. After living in the greatest wealth and affluence for a short time, he puts his pack on his back, takes shovel and rifle in hand and steps into the wilderness. In another generation, this type may have passed, one of the hardiest, most capable and attractive that America has produced.

In the evenings there was considerable drinking in the bar, with loud arguments, and blows struck now and then. It was shortly after the assassination of [President William] McKinley [September 6, 1901.] One night as I passed the barroom, a huge bearded man was declaiming that the President had gotten just what he deserved, and that the head of any State which allowed certain individuals to gain fabulous wealth and kept the ordinary man almost in a state of slavery should be gotten rid of, and that he himself would be willing at any time to kill any such President. I had never heard such opinions expressed before and my first impulse was to kill him right there, but then I considered that he was drunk and that my best course would be to go to the captain and tell him about it. After I related the incident, the captain said, "Lieutenant, some of the boys get to talking a lot in the evenings but they don't mean anything by it. But if you think too much of a rumpus is going on down there, I will stop it."

I told him the rumpus didn't worry me but that the sentiments being publicly expressed were wrong and would have a bad effect on everybody, particularly on the soldiers I had on board. He said, "All right. Come with me." He went directly to the bar, where the big fellow was still shouting. The captain was only five feet seven but he was broad. Without a word, he grabbed the orator by the neck, hit him in the jaw, threw him down, kicked him in the stomach, dragged him out of the door and threw him in the brig behind bars. "Keep your mouth shut until you sober up, or I will gag you," were his parting words. That was the last of that sort of thing on board. It turned out that the bearded man was an ex-murderer, fleeing from justice in the state of Oregon.

Next we stopped at Wrangell at the mouth of the Stikine River, an old Russian colony where considerable gold had been produced and where fur trading and fisheries were carried on.[10] An old fellow, [Capt. William] Moore, who had a patent on the townsite of Skagway, ran steamboats up this river. This was an assumed name, as he was really a Russian.[11] He was a tremendous man, about six feet four. Instead of using a pistol or rifle in combat, his ordinary weapon was a crowbar. His wife was an Indian and he had several sons, who helped him handle his steamboat. It was said that whenever he and his sons had a difference of opinion, they would anchor the steamboat, get out on the bank and fight it out. Another story told of Moore was that at one time he was arrested by the British authorities for piracy. The steamship which he had seized was taken into Victoria, B.C., anchored, and the head of the cylinder removed so that she could not leave. The guards went ashore for the night and as soon as they had gone, Moore set to work to build a wooden head for the cylinder, which he completed during the night, got steam up and made his escape.

Juneau was our next stop. This town, the capital of Alaska, occupies an imposing site at the head of a narrow waterway, with mountains rising straight up from the water thousands of feet on each side. All around it are solid rocks, containing gold. As we approached the wharf, we could see crowds of people coming and going in considerable excitement. As we tied up to the wharf, we heard that the steamer *Islander* had just struck a rock at the mouth of the Lynn Canal and had sunk with all hands on board. Thirty-two bodies from the wreck were then on the wharf. The *Islander* was a steel ship and sunk like a rock. A wooden boat, if injured, would float for a time, but a steel one, as constructed then, went down at once when its bottom was ripped up by the sharp rocks under the water. The bottom of the waterway here is of very irregular character. Soundings at one place reveal thirty fathoms and within half a mile go down to five hundred fathoms. Hundreds of thousands of dollars in gold were on the *Islander* and I do not believe that it has been recovered to this day.

Directly opposite Juneau was the Treadwell mine, said to be the greatest free milling gold mine in the world. The ore was dug out of the sides of the hills, from a big open place called the "Glory Hole," and was put into the stamps, where it was crushed and then washed out in the sluices. We were told that $2 of gold to the ton paid, and that they had found a great area back of Juneau where the ore ran $14 to the ton. All the rock along this part of the Alaskan coast was gold bearing, we were told. At the door of the great stamp

[10] Gold was found in quantity upstream, not at Wrangell.
[11] Moore was born in Germany in 1822. Pierre Berton, *The Klondike Fever,* Knopf, (N.Y., 1958).

mill, whose noise and clamor almost deafened one, was a sign bearing the playful injunction "Visitors will please observe silence in this building".

We stopped at Skagway next, which lies at the head of the Lynn Canal. The word "canal" here is a misnomer, as it is not an artificial waterway but a long narrow indentation. The upper end had been silted up a good deal by the discharge of two streams, so that the water was shallow. The tide here was about thirty feet, so that piers a mile long had to be built out from the town to accommodate the steamers.

I landed my detachment and reported to Capt. [Henry W.] Hovey of the 24th Infantry, who had a company of negroes [Company L] in garrison at Skagway, and we were assigned to quarters for a few days.

Skagway, the gateway to Alaska, presented an interesting contrast to anything I had ever seen. It was a wide open town. On the one hand were men coming out of Alaska and the Yukon, some with a great deal of wealth, and some disheartened, penniless and crippled. On the other hand, throngs were coming in daily to take their places, some never to return. As in all frontier towns, there were crooks, confidence men, and flim-flammers of all sorts, although the ordinary "bad man" had been pretty well eradicated. One particularly dangerous band, the "Soapy Smith" gang, had been cleaned up a short time before [in July 1898.]

Soapy Smith was such a picturesque character that he deserves more than passing mention. Skagway was full of stories about him when I arrived, most of the resident population having known him and his gang personally. From the many fantastic tales I heard, I have been able to piece together the following short account, which I am satisfied is substantially correct.

His real name was Jefferson Randolph Smith, and he was born in Georgia, of a good family, but he turned out to be one of the most sensational, interesting, and dangerous characters of the old West. As a boy he went to Colorado with his father. As a young man, he was described as tall, lithe, and attractive, with flashing eyes and a black beard. He started out in the flim-flam game by selling small packages of soap. It was supposed to clean perfectly, to cure baldness, and even to wash one's sins away for 25ᶜ a cake. Around some of the cakes he wrapped $20, $50 and $100 bills, in plain view of the spectators, and announced that if anybody wanted to take a chance on these prizes, it would cost them $5 a throw. Then he tossed them in the pile with the others and stirred them around. His confederates in the crowd, dressed as cowboys or miners, would come up, pay their $5 for a chance and pull out a $100 bill. That would get the crowd going and the dollars would be raked in by the hundreds. After the "trimming", as they called it, the gang would meet in a hotel room, turn in their prize money to Soapy, who would then pay them for their work.

Soapy was neither a murderer nor a ruffian but rather a sort of errant knight of the frontier, quick on the trigger, and with mental qualities far superior to most of those around him. It seemed impossible for him to try to make money by honest methods. He championed the cause of the outcast, was charitable to the down and outers and was square with his companions.[12]

He always operated with a crew, organized into "steerers" and "cappers." There were always plenty who wanted to join his well organized gang. When the soap game did not work, he turned to the shell game, of which he was a master, and his gang would seek out the strangers whose pockets were full of gold and lead them to the slaughter. When any place got too hot for him, he went on the to the next town. In some places, Soapy became the most prominent and almost the most respected citizen. He even built a church at one place, subsidized the parson, and gave to charity.

One of his most ambitious schemes was concerned with raising a military force along the lines of the French Foreign Legion for President Diaz of Mexico, to be used against the Yaqui Indians. Soapy proposed that Diaz give him 40,000 pesos to start the organization, but old Don Porfirio smelled a rat and gave him only 4000. He went back to Denver, opened an office and was getting along pretty well with his recruiting, when the old president of Mexico changed his mind and called the whole thing off. Diaz had found out about him, and sent him word that if he ever showed up in Mexico again, he would be shot by a firing squad.

In 1897, Soapy heard that gold had been discovered in the Klondike and that camps of fabulous wealth were being established in that territory. The stampede was on to Alaska and Soapy went along with it. Dyea and Skagway were the southern portals of the country, with Skagway rapidly becoming the more important of the two. Soapy and his confederates rendezvoused at Seattle and landed in Skagway [in January 1898.] The place was filling up with joints and dens of all kinds, with dance hall girls from the Barbary Coast, card sharpers, confidence men, dice experts, and shell game artists.

Soapy had everything figured out beforehand and his mind was definitely made up to be Boss of Skagway. He had been warned to be careful, but he considered

[12] This characterization of Soapy is uncommonly kind.

of course he got a rake-off on everything. Honest miners who came out of the interior with their hard-earned pokes of dust were set upon and robbed without mercy, then thrown out.

During the winter, the miners who waited to go into the interior indulged in every relaxation the town offered. There were no moving pictures, radios or things of that kind then. Men had their fun in saloons, dance halls, gambling dens, with occasional prize fights, wrestling matches, and individual exhibitions by magicians, dancers, and singers. Smith's gang ran these things also.

The spring of 1898 saw the greatest rush to the north that ever occurred. Every sort of old steamboat was pressed into service and dumped their living cargoes off at Skagway. For each successful miner who came out, ten tried to go in. The ships leaving Skagway were laden with gold.

When Soapy heard that troops were being raised for the Spanish War, he issued a call for volunteers, and when they were recruited, started drilling them. He called them the Skagway Guards, [Company A, 1st Regiment, Alaska National Guard], and offered them for service to the Secretary of War, who advised that they were not needed at that time.

Soapy planned a great patriotic celebration on the Fourth of July, 1898. He invited Gov. [John G.] Brady of Alaska to come and deliver the Independence Day address. The Governor accepted, there was a big parade, at the head of which rode Soapy Smith as grand marshal; there were fireworks, decorations, and flags, all provided by Soapy, and the affair was a tremendous success.

During all this time, forces were busy working for his downfall. The law-abiding people of Skagway were disgusted and ashamed of the way things were going. Just across the Canadian border there was nothing of this sort, because the Northwest Mounted Police maintained perfect law and order, a much less difficult task on the "inside" than in a coast town like Skagway. In Dawson, for instance, especially in the wintertime, a criminal could not escape without leaving a well defined trail, while in Skagway, all one had to do was go down to the wharf and get on a boat. The respectable citizens decided to band together and stop the continued defiance of law by Soapy and his gang.

The straw that broke the camel's back blew into Skagway from the Klondike on July 8th, in the person of a man name [J.D.] Stewart, who was on his way back to Canada with his hard-earned gold. He was spotted by one of Smith's gang. These fellows would travel the trails with packs on their backs filled with straw. They camped with the returning miners, got in with them, then told them where to go and what to do in Skagway, gradually working them into one of the places where they could be robbed. They inveigled Stewart into one of their "trimming parlors", [Soapy's saloon], gave him drinks, and when he tried to leave he was robbed and left alone. As soon as he got out, he went to the Town [U.S.] Marshal [Taylor] and told his story, but little attention was paid to it. Stewart did not give up, but told his troubles to every citizen he met, and public indignation began to mount.

The Committee of 101, a Vigilante organization, decided to take action. Meetings were held, speeches made, and all respectable persons urged to assist. Many were afraid of Soapy and would not take part, but assistance came from unexpected quarters also. The old Russian pioneer of the Stikine, Moore, came out with his crowbar to join the throng. [Frank H.] Reid, the City Engineer, was one of the most active in denouncing Soapy and his gang. All agreed that the town officials had failed to provide protection against the crooks and it was time for the people themselves to act. The Committee went to Soapy and asked that Stewart's gold be returned to him, but Smith refused, saying that the man had lost his gold in a fair and square game. Feeling grew higher and both sides began to arm. The town was rapidly reaching a state of anarchy. Word was sent to United States Judge Sehlbrede [U.S. Commissioner C.H. Sehlbrede] at Dyea, asking him to come over to Skagway. He came at once, sent for Soapy and told him to have the gold restored, but Soapy again refused. Judge Sehlbrede then told him that if the gold was not returned by 4 p.m. that day, warrants would be issued for himself and his gang, and they would be brought in, dead or alive.

In the meantime, the citizens continued to organize themselves for resistance to Smith's crowd. As the time expired which they had allowed Soapy to return the poke, a crowd began gathering outside his place. Soapy came out alone, armed with a rifle, and told them, "If you have anything to do with us, we are ready for you. I have 500 armed men who will stop you." He looked the crowd over, then turned and walked down the street, stopping at the various saloons and greeting his followers as he went. Most of his men were really cowards at heart and many of them were already quietly slipping out of town.

The Vigilantes and Committee of 101 decided to have a meeting that night and determine definitely what should be done. Just as the meeting was being called to order, it was noticed that some of Soapy's men were in the crowd. The leaders decided to move the meeting to the end of the Juneau Wharf, which was nearly a mile long. Every man coming on to the wharf could be checked, so it would be hard for anyone not wanted to attend this meeting. A committee of four was appointed, with City Engineer Reid as chairman, to see that only responsible men were admitted.

In the meantime, Soapy was going from saloon to saloon trying to recruit his followers both internally and externally for the coming fray. He announced that he was going down to the meeting himself and talk to them. His companions tried to dissuade him, saying it would be sure death, but he walked out, Winchester in hand, straight down to the pier. As he approached, Reid saw him and called to him to halt and put up his hands. Instead, he put up his rifle. At this, Reid pulled the trigger of his pistol, but the cartridge failed to explode. This instant's delay gave Soapy his chance and he fired simultaneously with Reid's next shot. Both fell, mortally wounded, Soapy shot through the heart. He was dead in a few minutes, and Reid died in the hospital twelve days later. Mrs. [Harriet] Pullen, that remarkable woman of the North, came on the scene searching for her young son, just as this happened. She has recounted it to me many times.

It did not take long for the Committee of 101 on the end of the pier to learn what had happened. They surged forward with but one thought, to clean up the remnants of the Soapy Smith gang. Bursting into saloons and dance halls, they seized whom they could but many of the criminals had already heard the news and fled out to the mountains and woods. The order was to kill anyone who resisted. Forty men were captured, beaten up and lodged in jail, while a huge crowd milled around outside, eager to lynch them. A company of United States Infantry [Company B, 14th Infantry] under Capt. [Richard T.] Yeatman, brought over from Dyea, arrived just in time to prevent the execution of the prisoners.[13]

A thorough search was made for the gold dust which had been the primary cause of the disturbance, and it was found, but some $500 worth was missing. However, Stewart was happy to get back what remained.

Soapy's body lay where it had fallen until next day, when it was removed to the morgue by a poor widow whom he had helped. It was reported that a commission as a Captain in the 36th Regiment, Volunteer Infantry, was found in one of Soapy Smith's pockets after his death. This was probably a forged document. His funeral was held in the church he had founded and he was buried in Skagway cemetery. Sometime later, a huge representation of a human skull, thirty feet high, was carved out of the rock above the town, with the inscription below it, "Soapy Smith."[14]

A great concourse of people turned out for Reid's funeral and a large monument was erected over his grave. With the departure of Soapy Smith and his gang, law and order were more firmly entrenched in the North. Although old conditions continued to some extent, they were never organized and the people terrorized by a single gang as in Soapy's time.

Company L, 24th Infantry (Negro), in the July 4, 1899 parade in Skagway.

COURTESY ALASKA HISTORICAL LIBRARY, SCINCIC COLLECTION

[13] J.M. Tanner, a Skagway resident at the time (and later a Territorial Senator) was appointed special officer by Commissioner Sehlbrede when the Smith-Reid ruckus broke out. Tanner, in charge of the Citizens Posse (not Vigilantes), knew both men and was present when they shot each other. Tanner stated in 1915 that Stewart was "relieved" of his poke of gold by Smith's gang, either in a shell game or by a crony of Smith's who grabbed the gold and ran with it, hiding it in Smith's saloon. Tanner stated that U.S. Marshal Taylor was on Smith's payroll in this case. The Posse arrested 26 members of the gang. Mitchell's account is fairly accurate, according to Tanner's first-hand report. Letter, Tanner to C.L. Andrews, November 20, 1915, in Andrews files, Sheldon Jackson College Library, Sitka, AK.

[14] The figure was painted on the face of rock in a cliff overlooking the community.

FROM WHITEHORSE TO EAGLE

3

Within a couple of days we took the train to White Horse [Whitehorse], at the head of navigation on the Yukon. The White Pass Railroad [White Pass and Yukon Route], a line 121 miles long, from Skagway to White Horse, had just been completed. [July 1900]. Before its construction, men had to pack in with loads on their backs over this terribly rough country, in the heat of summer or the prodigious cold of winter. A wagon road, built by a man named [George] Brackett, had succeeded the foot trail and was still used to some extent. Freighters with horses and mules were still operating over the passes in competition with the railroad. One of them attempted to bribe me to send all our equipment across in that way, by offering me ten percent of all payments made by the government. After that he was excluded from bidding on anything.

In the month of August the weather is fine through here, and the mosquitoes are diminishing rapidly. The scenery is grand, a succession of tremendous snow capped mountains, high inland lakes and rushing streams.

Arriving at White Horse [August 19, 1901], we received our first introduction to the Canadian [Northwest] Mounted Police. This efficient organization patrolled all of the Canadian Northwest. They exercised civil functions as well, and could try minor offenses and fix sentences up to three months. Anything over that had to be held for a higher court. No liberties were taken by the rough pioneers with the Mounted Police, because even if only one member of the force moved into a locality to exercise authority, and anything were done to him, reinforcements were immediately sent there and the culprits tracked down, no matter where they went or how long it took to find them.

There were many rumors of insurrections and expeditions across the border which the Canadian police took rather seriously. Some miners did not like the Canadian mining laws and the more turbulent elements wanted to take matters into their own hands. It was apparent however that the Canadian police had a good grip on the situation, and that law and order prevailed.

We saw the great White Horse Rapids, which mark the end of steamboat navigation from the Bering Sea, 2200 miles away. Above the rapids, the Yukon can again be navigated by steamboats for several hundred miles.

A little stern-wheel river steamer, a wood burner called the *White Horse,* was to take us to Dawson City. We embarked and proceeded down the river, stopping now and then at wood camps to replenish our fuel. One of these had a Mounted Police station, where I had my first sight of the Yukon moose. He was a young fellow, five months old, and at that tender age was about as large as a mule. He would run into the shed at the back of the Police Station and make himself quite at home. When a moose stands erect, he cannot reach the ground with his mouth, as his neck is too short. He is a browsing animal and eats leaves and bark from trees. This moose had been taught to drink condensed milk. One of the constables made up a pan of milk and took it out to the shed. The moose came pattering in, immediately went down on his knees and drank the milk.

Many attempts have been made to harness moose and make them work. Success attended some of the efforts, but moose become very obstinate and when they refuse to work, it is impossible to make them pull or even move. Their trot is said to be faster than that of any other animal. They would make the fastest animal transportation if they could be properly trained.

Very few American military men had been in Dawson, and ours was the first organization. We were received with great hospitality. Although the town was in Canada, ninety percent of the people were Americans. Over 30,000 people were in the city and the diggings nearby. This location is one of the coldest in the known world. In winter, temperatures under 60 below zero, Fahrenheit, are common, and under 70 below are frequent.

Steam sailings down the Yukon were infrequent and as I wanted to get my men distributed before the 1600

Excursion train of the White Pass & Yukon Route crossing small timber trestle at Rocky Point, May 1900. COURTESY YUKON ARCHIVES AND BARLEY COLLECTION

miles of river froze up, I had to hurry. I made arrangements for a flat boat with Ben Downing, a renowned "musher" originally from Maine, who had a contract for carrying the mail down the Yukon. The word "mush", meaning to drive dogs along a trail, comes from the French *marche* and was probably introduced into the North by the French-Canadians.

Several days were required to obtain provisions and prepare for the trip, so we improved our time by excursions to the nearby diggings. Capt. [W.H.] Scarth of the Mounted Police was detailed to look after me. We took two of their horses and rode up the Klondike to the celebrated streams of El Dorado [Eldorado] and Bonanza. Everywhere the bed of the streams and the sides of the hills were being dug into and washed out in sluice boxes. Only the most primitive machinery was employed, owing to the difficulty of transporting anything to this far off country.[1] All the trees in the vicinity had been cut down. What lumber there was had been whipsawed from their small trunks.

The amount of gold taken out of some of the small Canadian claims was prodigious. An old whaling captain named Norwood had become rich from the huge quantities taken from his claim on Bonanza. At another place, Jerry Lynch, a former State Senator from California, had bought a claim away up on a bench, that is, a long distance up from the river bottom, on the side of a hill.[2] As a matter of fact, he had bought it while in a convivial mood, and the man who had sold it to him, himself convinced that there was nothing in it, felt great satisfaction on having put it over on the Senator. Lynch drifted into the side of the hill, more as a joke than anything else, and struck enormous quantities of gold. Then everybody started working on hillsides, with more or less success.

My escort, Captain Scarth, had his red coat on, while I wore my blue uniform. News of our coming seemed to precede us, and everywhere we went we could hear, "Here come the bluecoat and the redcoat—what can we do for you?" They gave us nuggets, food and drink, and I had a pocket full of gold when I got back to town that evening.

Great activity in these far north diggings only lasted four or five months, the country being tightly frozen up during the rest of the year. I really believe, however, that if gold were discovered on the North Pole, it would only be a short time before a miner would be tying his tent ropes to the stick itself. He will go anywhere, under any conditions of privation or difficulty, to get the precious metal. I shall never forget the appearance of these diggings. Here in the Arctic wilderness men swarmed along the creek bottoms, dressed in heavy denim trousers, dark flannel shirts, soft hats or caps, and rubber boots. Everywhere they were shoveling: shoveling dirt out of holes in the ground, shoveling it into piles or into sluice boxes. Everywhere, pay dirt was run where the water could get at it and wash it out. Sluice boxes covered the bed of the stream in all directions. Each man worked as if his life depended on getting the whole job done in one day. There was no eight-hour-day in those places. They worked all the daylight hours, until they became exhausted.

The following day I was invited to be present at the hanging of a man named O'Brien. It was the final chapter of one of the most dramatic incidents that ever took place in the North. The circumstances were somewhat as follows:

The day before Christmas, 1900, three young men, named Rolfe, Olson, and Clayson, started out on bicycles from the Minto Roadhouse, about 100 miles above Dawson, along the hard packed winter trail, in order to spend Christmas in Dawson with their families and friends. They were prominent young men and it was known that one of them carried a considerable amount of gold dust with him, together with the very famous "Trap Door Nugget." Among miners, peculiar pieces of gold are passed all around and soon become well-known.

Nothing was heard of these young men on Christmas or the days following. Gradually it became evident that something had happened to them, and rewards, amounting to thousands of dollars, were offered by the banks and various individuals for information leading to the discovery of their fate. Captain Scarth was detailed to the case and worked for quite awhile without obtaining a clue. It is difficult for an evildoer in Alaska to get away in the winter, because they either have to follow the regular beaten trails or else make a trail of their own through the snow and ice, which they cannot conceal. Every trail had been run down by the Mounted Police with no result, so Scarth went on down toward Skagway, looking for clues. At that place, he met an American detective named O'Brien, and they went over the case together. While in consultation, they received a report from the Mounted Police station on the Atlin Lakes, several hundred miles away, at the head of the Yukon, stating that they held a man named O'Brien for observation, because he had a Mounted Police blanket in his sled, evidently stolen

[1] Mitchell came through Dawson about July 1901 and evidently saw the diggings on Bonanza Creek just before the first gold dredge arrived there that year from the Stewart River. A.H. Brooks, *Mineral Resources of Alaska,* USGS Bull.542, GPO, (Washington, D.C., 1913.)

[2] A bench was the site of a former river channel at a higher elevation than the present channel bottom.

from one of the Mounted Police posts. It was found that this man had been sentenced to work on the woodpile at Dawson for some minor offense. Scarth wired to seize all the man's effects and bring him back to Dawson on suspicion. O'Brien protested his innocence but a search of his clothes disclosed the "Trap Door Nugget" sewed in the hem of his parka.

O'Brien had a large "Outside" dog, resembling a Newfoundland. This dog was taken to the Minto Roadhouse and up the trail toward Dawson. After proceeding a few miles, the dog left the trail and began to dig in the snow, revealing where a campfire had been. It was at a point close to the Yukon River. The police, making a close examination of the surroundings, found a bullet mark on the bark of a tree. Gold pans were obtained and the snow in the vicinity was panned. They found bloodstains and bullets both from a pistol and a rifle. The bullets had the peculiar marks which corresponded to those produced by the pistol and rifle of O'Brien. Going down to the Yukon, they found an open hole in the river, into which they thought bodies might have been thrown, so they sawed through the ice, which was seven feet thick along the bars below this place. All three of the bodies were found and taken out, in the dead of winter. A net of circumstantial evidence closed in around O'Brien which made it absolutely certain that he had shot down these young men as they came along the trail on their Christmas journey.

It cost the Canadian government thousands of dollars to bring about this conviction. O'Brien protested his innocence to the last and was pulled out of his cell swearing and shouting, and brought up to the scaffold, on which Scarth and I and a couple of others were standing. They were giving him a nine foot drop, which I thought would certainly jerk his neck off, as I had seen similar hangings, particularly in the Philippines. They said they did not care if his neck did come off, but they wanted to be sure he was dead. He came up the scaffold still cursing, and refused the services of the priest. So the hangman slipped the noose and black cap over his head and the next instant he went to eternity. His neck was stretched but did not come off. The doctor pronounced him dead at once.

The North had its own peculiar code of laws. It was a killing offense, for instance, for a man to rob a "cache" of food left by another; but if a man came to it, starving and in dire need, he might take what he needed, but must leave a note. To steal dogs, guns, or even snowshoes or equipment was as serious as taking a man's life, because these things represented the means of life. If a man in want, however, asked for help, even though it meant the last piece of salmon or the last bit of protection against the elements, it would be shared, as readily with a stranger as with a partner.

One hears the expression "The Outside" everywhere in the interior of Alaska. It is quite an apt designation, hemmed in as this country is by lofty mountains whose walls must be scaled to effect an entrance or exit. In the winter, with everything frozen tight, the vastnesses of ice and snow are an additional barrier to be penetrated. An "Outside" dog is one of a breed other than the Alaskan huskies and malemutes.

A newcomer into the country is called a "Cheechako," a word used in the local Indian and Hudson Bay trading language, or "Chinook" as it is called. This language uses only a few hundred words but it is very expressive and with it one may make himself understood all over the north, with Indians and white men alike. There is a lot of "me savvy-you savvy" in it, and considerable sign language.

The expression for a day's trip is "one sleep," the idea for which is conveyed by putting one's head down on the hand and closing the eyes. Doing this three times means "three sleeps" or three days travel. "Hiyou" [also hi-yu] means big, and a rising inflection on the last syllable indicates that it is bigger. The same word may be used for a long distance, or very much of anything; for instance, "hiyou muckamuck" means plenty of food, and with a rising inflection on the last syllable of "hiyou," means a great deal of food.

In a few days our flat boat was ready to leave Dawson. It was about forty feet long and fourteen feet wide, with sweeps at each end and bits for attaching ropes. Two men who knew the river were to accompany the scow, also Ben Downing himself. We had a sixteen foot Peterboro canoe with oars on it, with which I could explore the shores on the way down, hoping to kill or at least catch sight of some of the game that abounded in that area.

We left Dawson [August 25, 1901] with the godspeed of a great number of our newly made friends and pushed off into the solitude of the upper Yukon. It was truly a great river. In the language of the northern Indians, "Yukon" meant "the father of waters," and it was exactly that. Deep and swift flowing, with a current of from five to eight miles an hour, it was clear as a crystal. In its upper reaches, it flowed through a succession of beautiful high mountains. Its shores abounded in game: moose, caribou, many kinds of bear, sheep, ptarmigan, and several species of grouse. The waters teemed with different kinds of salmon, including the great Yukon king salmon that attains a weight of over one hundred pounds; various species of trout, a fish called "ling" [ling cod], and other varieties. The lakes in this basin contained pike and pickerel, besides trout. Through the summer, their surfaces were covered with all sorts of ducks, geese, and swans. Thirty years ago, it was a hunter's paradise and still is to a great extent.

Mitchell's crew at Dawson preparing to float down the Yukon to Fort Egbert.
COURTESY LIBRARY OF CONGRESS, BRIGADIER GENERAL WILLIAM MITCHELL COLLECTION

As we went down the river, I noticed from my map that we were going a little faster than the current. I measured the current in several places by landing on the shore, pacing off a certain distance, throwing an object into the water and using a stop-watch to measure the time it took to float from one place to another. I asked Ben Downing if he had noticed in scowing down the river that we went faster than the water and he answered yes, that as the river dropped so many feet each mile, the scow was on an inclined plane, so to speak, and due to the force of gravity, its own weight gave it a little more speed than the current.[3] Occasionally the scow stuck on a bar, but it would be pried off with long poles and put in the current again. The men became very proficient with the sweeps and toward afternoon of the first day were able to keep the scow out in the main current.

In searching the shores I killed a few ducks, spruce grouse, and blue grouse and saw many tracks of moose and bear but not the animals themselves.

We met several Indians poling their boats against the current. Their canoes are ingenious contrivances. They are made of birch bark, about nine feet long and V-shaped, and about twenty inches wide. An Indian sits in the center, and as he goes downstream, uses a double paddle. When he goes upstream, he keeps near the shore, in water about two feet deep and with a four foot pole in each hand, pushes against the bottom of the river and thus propels himself against the current. In a swift flowing river such as this, the Indian in his canoe makes better time against the current than any other craft, except the steamboat. These canoes are very difficult for the average white man to handle, as they are very narrow and cranky. In fact, most white men are scared to death of them.

The vegetation everywhere surprised me. Some of the spruce trees were a foot and a half in diameter, while poplars and birches were in some cases larger.

We stopped at Forty Mile, where the river of that name empties into the Yukon. It is about halfway between Dawson and Eagle City, Alaska. There was a mission of the Anglican church there under a very competent pastor. Schools were maintained for Indians and white people who desired to go to them. Considerable fur was brought in there from the upper part of the river and from the Ketchemstock [Kechumstuk] Indians who lived near the head of the stream. I bought a number of Alaskan sables there for $2.50 a skin. Later I found they were worth $35 on the Outside at that time.

A short time after reaching the international boundary, we came abreast of the Indian village above Eagle City, and as we were hugging the shores, the squaws and children ran out to look us over, while the Indian dogs set up a great howling. There were some quite respectable looking log cabins, but most of the Indians lived in wickiups. A wickiup is a lodge whose framework is made of poles, on which is put birch bark. A hole is left in the middle for the smoke to come out.

All of the Indians, bucks, squaws, and papooses, looked fat and sleek. They usually come out of the winter looking thin and gaunt, but as soon as the salmon run starts, they begin putting on more weight until they reach the top of their form in August. Salmon was hanging up to dry near every lodge, and its odor reached well out into the river. Even the dogs looked fat. Dogs always swarm around Indian camps. There are no other domestic animals or birds.

Northern dogs are interesting animals. When the British Northwest Company and the Hudson Bay Company first went into the north, over two hundred years ago, the Indian dogs were very poor; small, weedy little things, descended straight from wolves. They were used principally as pack animals. The Indians pulled their own sleds to a great extent. In order to improve the dogs, these companies first imported mastiffs and Great Danes to cross with the native animals, they crossed the result of this breeding with the native wolf. But the Great Danes and mastiffs gave defective feet and a defective coat to their descendants. To counteract this, Russian wolfhounds were crossed with the Indian dogs and by careful selection and crossing with the wolves again, the McKenzie [Mackenzie] River "husky," the greatest sled dog that man has ever seen, was evolved. He weighed anywhere from ninety to one hundred and twenty or thirty pounds, was very enduring, fast on his feet and had a heavy coat. Usually their tails were cut so they could be hitched closer together in harness and also to prevent their tails from freezing when they fell in the water or got wet in the winter. A bushy wet tail adds thirty or forty pounds to their weight.

The fluffy long tailed dogs that are seen so often nowadays are what are known as "Malemute" dogs in the upper country. They come from Bering Sea and the Arctic Coast and are much lighter and in every way inferior to the "husky" for work in the upper part of the Yukon.

When I first arrived at Eagle City [August 26], there were very few real Husky dogs there, most of them being inferior Indian dogs.

---

[3] In a river, mid-stream current is faster than that along shore because of the frictiion or "drag" along the banks and in the shallower areas.

DOWN THE YUKON: EAGLE TO TANANA

4

Soon after passing the Indian village, we sighted the cluster of frame buildings that was Eagle City, the little settlement which was to be our headquarters for awhile. As we pulled up to the shore, we were met by Lt. Benjamin Tillman, a nephew of old Senator "Pitchfork" Ben Tillman of South Carolina who had been in the Senate with my father. He commanded a company [Company E] of the Seventh Infantry garrisoned at Fort Egbert back of Eagle City. Ben was the soul of hospitality and I soon met everybody in the town, about fifty people.

The diggings here were nothing like those at Dawson, although a few miners were ekeing out an existence on American, Mission, and Champion Creeks, always hoping for better luck in the future.

A fellow named Tosman, one of the most amusing men I ever met and one of the greatest talkers and story tellers, had just sold a claim to some Englishmen for around $50,000 cash. I was told confidentially that he had "salted" it, in the following manner: first, he built a dam across the creek, and made some "dump gates;" that is, the apertures in the dam were closed by wooden doors which, when the water reached a certain height, would automatically fold over and allow the rush of water to go down below. There had been originally about eight feet of gravel in the bed of the creek, on which Tosman scattered about $12,000 in gold dust which he had procured at Dawson. He then ground-sluiced this cut from eight feet of gravel to about two feet. Of course the gold sank down with the gravel, the result being that when a sample was taken from the creek bed and panned, it showed a remarkable prospect. Many claims were salted in a like manner and disposed of to people who knew nothing about such matters. Old miners can almost always tell where gold has come from by merely looking at it, and it is hard to fool them.

I told Ben Tillman I wanted to see as much of the country as possible before the next steamer sailing down the river in about ten days, so he turned his pack train over to me, with two splendid guides Frank Lee and George Webb. We set right out across the high mountains, in the direction which the projected telegraph line to Valdez would take.

The country was a succession of mountain ranges interspersed with clear running streams. Timber covered the slopes about half way up, giving way to small bushes at an altitude of three or four thousand feet. After the bushes, we ran into the deep moss that covers the whole country, in which the horses and mules sank almost to their hocks and knees. It was evident that very little would be accomplished if we attempted to transport material through this area in the summer, as a pack horse could carry only 200 pounds fifteen or twenty miles a day; but in winter these same animals could pull from one to two thousand pounds over the frozen snow, for even greater distances. Nobody had tried to freight with horses and mules in winter on account of the cold, [the forage problem, more likely], and as the dogs could pull comparatively little, almost nothing had been accomplished on the telegraph line.[1] The Infantry did not consider that it was their work, nor did they relish the idea of going out in the cold of winter and freezing to death.

I have noticed in Arctic and sub-Arctic countries how little most of the residents really know about conditions in the winter time. This is because they "hole up" for the entire winter and only go a short distance away from their houses. Although this was one of the coldest parts of the world, it seemed to me the thing to do was to work through the winter getting the material out: the wire, insulators, poles, food supplies, and forage; then to actually construct the lines in the summer, when we could dig holes in the ground and set the telegraph poles.

Lee and Webb, who accompanied me, had seen much of Alaska as anyone had, and the week's trip taught me a great deal. Each day Lee and I hunted for

[1] A lot had been accomplished away from the Fort Egbert area which Mitchell had not yet learned about. See Appendix A.

No.68.

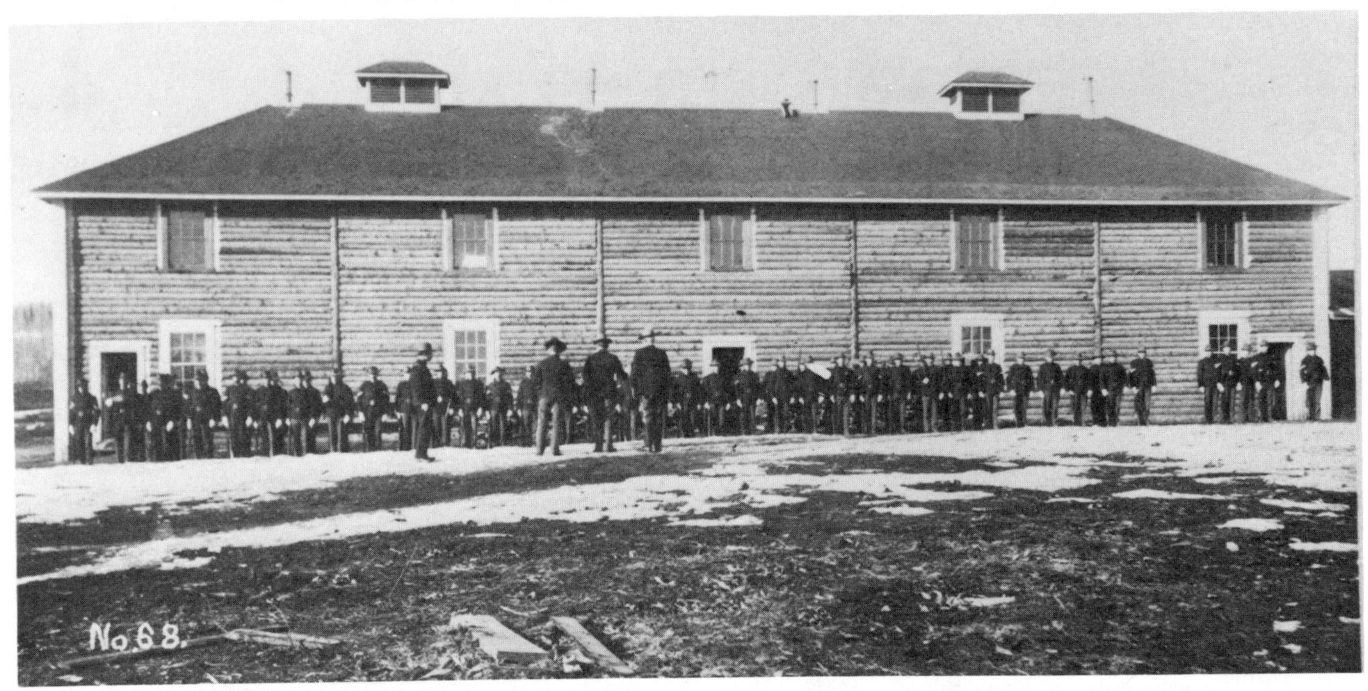

Muster of Company L, 7th Infantry, Fort Egbert, March 31, 1900. COURTESY U.S. ARMY

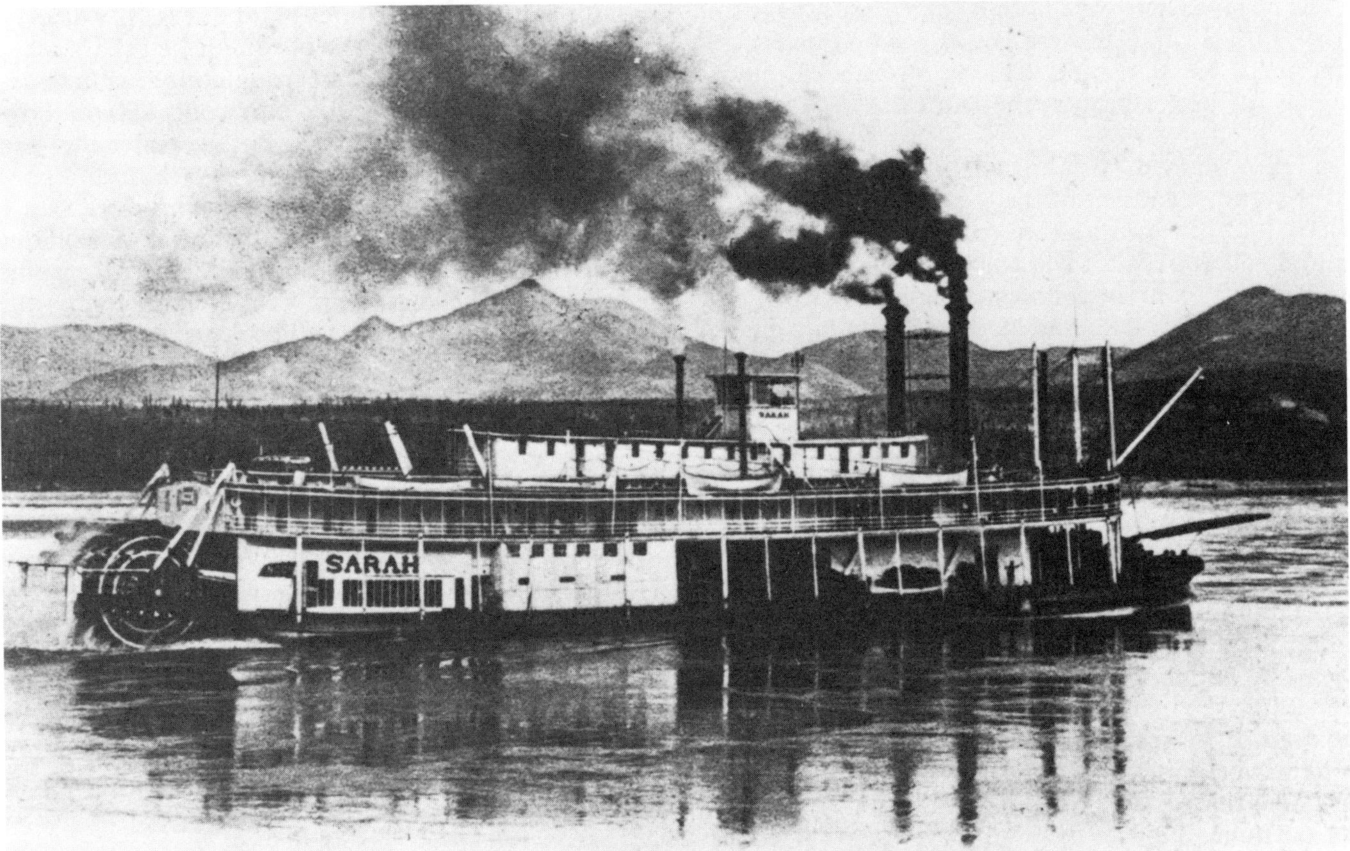
SARAH
"Sarah" at Eagle, Alaska.

The Steamer *Sarah*. COURTESY COOK INLET HISTORICAL SOCIETY

caribou and I succeeded in killing three splendid animals, although this was not the season for them in that region. They were lower down in the thick brush, grazing their calves and protecting them from the wolves. The caribou is the American reindeer, quite similar to the European, but it has never been domesticated. I believe it could be, without much difficulty. The caribou eats moss, a certain kind of white moss; the moose, a browsing animal, subsists on the foliage and bark of trees and ordinarily will not eat grass or moss; while the sheep, a grazing animal, eats grass, not moss, leaves or bark; that is why the Arctic sheep live high up among the topmost crags, where the wind blows away the snow from the herbage.

I also killed over two hundred ptarmigan, or Arctic grouse. They were in their summer plumage, and the young were about full grown.

It was toward the last of August [1901] when we encountered the first frost on the ridges.[2] Ice was beginning to form. We camped in the open as there were no mosquitoes, and in the evening ate the tenderloin of caribou, roasted the ptarmigan on spits basted with bacon, while we swapped stories of the North and tales of the wars. This was a complete wilderness at the time and except for the navigable streams, such as the Yukon, the Copper River and Kuskokwim, was an absolutely [or almost] unknown country, the Russians having scarcely penetrated beyond the coast and great rivers in their day. The trading companies spread terrible tales about the cold and impossible living conditions in the North, to keep people out while they reaped a golden harvest from the furs, minerals and fish.

We saw a couple of bears during the trip but I did not get close enough to kill them. The salmon had stopped running in the rivers and the bears were back in the timber, difficult to track. The fish seem to know when winter is coming. They leave the small streams that freeze tight and go to the deep rivers or the ocean.

Returning to Eagle City, I had come to the conclusion [in the summer of 1901] that this was the point from which the telegraph line should start from the Yukon to the Pacific Coast at Valdez, and from there [Eagle] down the Yukon or Tanana to Bering Sea and Nome.[3] It was the most difficult area in which to construct the lines, because the transportation conditions were the worst, but the distances were shortest between the places that had to be connected, and I determined that it could be done.

At last our steamer came, the *Sarah,* a big river boat much like the old passenger steamers on the Mississippi. She had all sorts of spars and lifting equipment, such as that used in the old steamboating days on the Ohio and Mississippi, to get her over shifting sand bars and mud banks with which the Alaskan rivers were infested. I learned that Abraham Lincoln was a great steamboater and had obtained several patents on machinery for lifting boats over these obstructions.

One of my fellow-passengers was "Red" McConnell, a typical prospector whom I had met in Dawson. He had been all over the world, wherever gold had been struck. He was a man of iron, broad in the shoulder and deep in the chest, with great bones and sinews. I took a great fancy to him and we had many talks, in which he gave me valuable advice on how to handle things in the North. He had a famous nugget, called the Fish Hook Nugget, which had come from Bonanza Creek on the Klondike and was almost as well known as the "Trap Door Nugget." When we stopped near an Indian camp to get wood for our steamer, he bet me that I could not ride in an Indian canoe. Few white men had ever been successful at this. I told him if he would bet me his "Fish Hook Nugget" against anything I had, I would take him up. I had a very good pair of field glasses which he liked, so he bet the nugget against the field glasses. I had been used to canoes of all sorts all my life, but this was the narrowest and crankiest one I had ever gotten into. However I managed it, and as soon as I went back on board, he handed over the Fish Hook Nugget. It was a remarkable thing, weighing about an ounce and shaped exactly like a fish hook curve, with a barb at the end of it. Unfortunately a few months later I either lost it or it was stolen from me.

At each stop for wood, I tried to get all the information possible from the wood choppers, but found they knew little or nothing outside their own immediate surroundings. Those who stayed in the winter did a little trapping. One man told me he had made $8,000 in the last two years from his traps. One of the most intelligent of the wood-choppers lived alone with his little girl and boy. He had only one arm but in spite of this he felled the trees and split them. When he had to use the whip saw, a man from a camp 60 miles away came over and helped him.

There was quite a company of returning prospectors, traders, and a few soldiers on the *Sarah*. Among others was our friend Tosman who had salted the claim and sold out to the Englishmen. Out of his ill earned

[2] Having written this story some 30 years after leaving Alaska, Mitchell's erratic chronological sequence may be excused. Earlier herein he mentioned a brawl "shortly after the assassination of President McKinley." The president was shot September 6, 1901.

[3] Except for mention of the Tanana River, this routing had already been outlined in General Greely's February 3, 1900 report to the Secretary of War.

gains, he had bought two cases of whiskey and several of champagne and was having a great time. Card games ran high in the evening, faro and poker among others. No money was used, only gold dust, weighed out on a little scale at $16 to the ounce.

Our first regular stop was at Circle City, a little mining community of log cabins built a couple of years before,[4] when quite a rich strike had been made in the back country thereabouts. There were the usual number of trading stores and three or four saloons. Tosman announced that he was going ashore and get himself a wife to complete the trip with, so he and a companion left the ship.

Circle City marks the beginning of that part of the river known as the Yukon Flats, where the mountains recede from it and the river spreads out over a great area, one hundred miles across in many places.[5] It is difficult to find one's way through this labyrinth of islands and not get into a dead-end slough and be left high and dry by the receding current. The sand bars and bottoms constantly shift and if the channels are not marked, it takes an expert to pilot a boat through safely. In some places there was scarcely four feet of water in the best channel.

The steamer blew its whistle to leave. We all went aboard and the gang plank was lifted; just one board from the after part of the ship was left touching the bank. The bow ropes were thrown off and the stern wheel started slowly. Just as the stern rope was thrown off, Tosman and his companion, with a young woman, came rushing up and leaped aboard. The ship was cast loose and full speed ahead given. In an instant we were out in the stream, gliding along with the swift current. Looking back, we could see several people on the bank, among them a man with a rifle who was shouting and waving his arms at the boat. The Captain paid no attention to him. whereat the man put off in a canoe and attempted to catch up with the steamer. He fired two or three shots, one of which hit the stern, but did no damage. It developed later that this was the man from whom Tosman had stolen the young lady with whom he came on board.

In those days in Alaska, girls worked in dance halls and saloons, or nearly anywhere, living with one person after another. Although their morals were rather lax, they were very kind to anyone ill or in need; they were hard workers, and entirely masters of themselves. This particular young woman was an amusing person. She could tell entertaining stories, dance, sing, and play on the piano. She was the only woman on board except a few Indian squaws.

We stopped at Fort Yukon, [once the site of] an old Hudson Bay [Company] trading post, where the Arctic Circle touches the river. From here the trail goes up the Poplar River to Fort McPherson, down the Porcupine to the McKenzie River and from there to Hershel [Herschel] Island at the mouth of the McKenzie on the Arctic Ocean.[6] It was from Hershel Island that the best husky dogs came. This was the place where the old Arctic whaling fleet used to winter.

One night [in 1899] as we lay before a campfire in the Philippines, Maj. Gen. [then Colonel] [Frederick] Funston told me he had spent a winter at Hershel with the whalers. They were frozen tight from October until June. They did a little fur trading and put their gear in shape for the following season, but time hung on their hands, especially when the sun did not rise above the horizon for about two months. During that time, they played indoor games of all sorts and did a lot of gambling. But as soon as it became light enough to get out on the ice, they cleared off a baseball diamond and played the great American game in temperatures down to 40 below zero. If the ball started rolling on the ice, it would not stop for a mile or so. They always used the biggest man they had as shortstop because he could lie down in front of the ball and stop it.

When Alaska was taken over [purchased] by the United States, the Hudson Bay Company had to move its Fort Yukon post back into Canada. The post office and a little trading station were the only things left at Fort Yukon.

The story was told that several years before some men representing the British Museum had gone from Fort Yukon into the barren lands east of the McKenzie River after musk ox, with the idea of bringing them out alive, as these animals were very scarce in zoological collections. They succeeded in obtaining several, which they drove and led to the McKenzie, crossed it, then went up the Porcupine[7] to within a hundred miles of

[4] Circle City's heyday had passed. In 1895, with a population of 500, it was the largest settlement on the Yukon. Brooks, op.cit., p. 332. In 1896 it was called "the Paris of Alaska," had a music hall, two theaters, 8 dance halls, 28 saloons, and 1200 citizens. The next spring it became almost a ghost town; the strike on the Klondike called the people upstream. Berton, *The Klondike Fever,* op.cit., pp.32-33.

[5] The Flats area is 180 miles long by 70 miles across. Donald J. Orth, *Dictionary of Alaska Place Names*, USGS Prof. Paper #567, GPO, (Wash., D.C., 1967.) It begins near Fort Yukon rather than Circle.

[6] The trail went up the Porcupine River (not Poplar River) and by portage to the Peel River (and Fort McPherson) and down it to the Mackenzie. James Wickersham, *Old Yukon: Tales, Trails, and Trials,* Washington Law Book Co., (Wash., D.C., 1938.) p.98.

[7] The Porcupine River flows west (downstream) from Canada to the Yukon, meeting it near Fort Yukon. Going *up* the Porcupine would take the museum men away from Fort Yukon. They may have ascended the Peel River from the Mackenzie, then cut west intending to descend the Porcupine toward the fort.

Fort Yukon. Here they awoke one morning to find all the musk oxen dead, with arrows through their bodies and their throats cut. Tracks of Indians were found all around. Some of the party attempted to follow the marauders but with no success. Later the local Indians informed the party that the musk oxen had been killed by Indians from the Barren Lands because they knew that if the oxen got out alive and were taken to a warmer zone where they could get plenty of food, that when one died its soul would return to its comrades in the Barrens and tell them of this new land, whereupon all the musk oxen would disappear, just as the buffalo had disappeared from the plains further to the south. Then the Indians would be left with no means of subsistence.

From Fort Yukon we kept on down this uninteresting stretch of the Yukon River, frequently running into shallow water, hitting the bottom and sounding our way with poles, occasionally having to use the spars to push the boat over obstructing sand bars. The next stop was Rampart City, another place with a few gold diggings behind it and a mission, in charge of Archdeacon [Hudson] Stuck, a great traveler and missionary in the North, and a man respected by all. This is not the case with some missionaries who tell marvelous tales when they come out to civilization but who do nothing but look after their own comfort in the solitudes. At [near] Rampart the shores of the Great River rose in sheer precipices.

At Tanana City, our next stop [September 18], the great river of that name meets the Yukon. The Tanana is the largest tributary of the Yukon and drains a tremendous territory. Here we saw another Indian village, with big fine looking Indians of Athabascan stock. These people have the high ridged noses, high cheek bones and hatchet faces of our own Indians on the western plains, known among old army officers as the Horse Indians. To me they have always seemed exact prototypes of the Mongols and Manchus who inhabit the other side of the Pacific. It has always been interesting to me that their tactics in war were almost identical with those of Genghis Khan, the great Asiatic conqueror.

Close by the town was the army post of Fort Gibbon, [formerly] commanded by Capt. [Charles S.] Farnsworth. We learned a great deal here about the work along the telegraph lines, how difficult it had been with inadequate equipment, inadequate pay for the men, and their inability to make the ordinary infantry soldier do this job in winter. Lt. [Hjalmar] Erickson of that garrison, a man of surpassing physical and mental energy, had made some wonderful trips alone, with a pack on his back, both in summer and winter, and found out more about the country than any other officer there.

Lt. [George S.] Gibbs of the Signal Corps, an old companion of mine in the Philippines, had just arrived to take charge of work on the line there. We arranged for mutual cooperation and laid our plans, because as soon as winter set in, we would be out of communication with one another for many months. Gibbs had a little river steamer called the *Argo.* One of the crew had just killed a great eagle, with a wing spread of about eight feet, which they had stretched in front of the pilot house. It reached almost across the front of the boat.

A few miles back of Fort Gibbon is a stream called Mastodon Creek, which derives its name from the many remains of mastodons and mammoths dug up along its bed.[8] The tusks, teeth and bones of this huge animal are found all through Alaska. This ivory is known as "fossil ivory" and is quite an article of trade in some localities. In one place in Siberia, it is said that a wooly mammoth was found in the ice, with the flesh still in such condition that it could be eaten. Its long red hair was in a perfect state of preservation.

These animals were the prey of tigers, who attacked them by biting their hind legs and hamstringing them. When the earth cooled and glaciers covered the north, these great creatures died for lack of a vegetable diet.[9] It is thought that the tigers were forced south in search of food. As they worked south in Asia, they encountered lions and drove them out. The northern tigers, found clear up into Arctic Asia, are much larger than those in the south. They have long hair and are shaggy and wooly. There are none on the North American continent.

Another prehistoric beast whose bones are found in Alaskan stream beds or in the diggings elsewhere, is the "bos primogenus," or original ox. I have been told that one miner, who was burning a hole to get out a dump, smelled the odor of scorching flesh and going there, found the meat still on the bones of this ancient animal, millions of years old. This ox is supposed to be the progenitor of the European tame cattle. The urox, now found in Poland, is said to be the direct descendant of bos primogenus [primigenial.]

While at Fort Gibbon, I saw a dog team of Great Danes hauling water. They were imposing looking animals, all of them weighing well over one hundred pounds. The five dogs could pull as much as a horse, but in the winter they were no good for trail use, because their hair was so short they could not keep warm, and their feet so big and mushy that they could

[8] Probably referring to Mastodon Creek which enters Mammoth Creek 40 miles southwest of Circle.
[9] An old theory since judged questionable.

not resist the cold. The only dog that does well in the northern winter is one with a great proportion of the wolf strain. Collies and setters are about the best of the "Outside" breeds. A dog must have real fur to resist the cold, that is, a wooly covering near the skin and long guard hair to break the wind.

Watercolor of Fort Yukon in 1867 by Frederick Whymper of the Western Union Telegraph Company's extension project.
COURTESY HUDSON'S BAY COMPANY

Rampart on the Yukon circa 1899-1900. COURTESY NATIONAL ARCHIVES, PHOTO 92-F-08-19

DOWN THE YUKON: 5

TANANA TO ST. MICHAEL

As we proceeded down the Yukon from Tanana, the character of the vegetation and scenery changed gradually. The trees became smaller and smaller and grew in clumps; the mountains were more washed down in appearance, except for the great Alaska Range to the south, where we caught occasional glimpses of Mt. McKinley, 20,400 [20,320] feet high, the tallest mountain in North America. Also the faces of the Indians we encountered showed different characteristics. Their noses seemed to be more flattened out and the corners of their eyes turned up, like the Eskimos. Their boats were made of walrus and seal skin and their parkas of fur instead of cloth, with wolverine tails sticking out from their hoods, instead of wolf and fox skins.

At Anvik we ran into a Russian mission, a dirty place kept by several Russian priests of their Orthodox church.[1] The church was typically Russian, with its many icons, and was one of the few remains of their former occupation.

While there, a "bidar" or great walrus skin boat with timbers of whale and walrus bones, loaded with furs, crossed the river. The men were Indians from the Kuskokwim River, and they had a great many fine mink and white fox skins. I bought about forty white fox for $1.50 apiece, and quite a number of mink for twenty five cents each. In the States, white fox were worth about $25 and mink $5 apiece.

I was much interested in the boat. The walrus hide was extremely tough, resisting wear and tear even from rocks against which the boat was hurled. It was lapped over and sewn three times on the seams, and all the sewing rubbed with seal or walrus oil, so that it was very dry inside. It slipped through the water with the greatest ease. It was in skin boats similar to this that many Russians crossed from Kamchatka by way of the Commander and Aleutian Islands to Alaska.

It is difficult for us in this day, with our modern boats, navigating instruments and safety appliances, to visualize how the hardy Russian pioneers, not particularly used to the sea, came straight across Bering Sea in these primitive craft, through heavy fogs, snow, rain, and blizzards, with a tremendous surf beating almost constantly on the islands where they landed. They had no navigating instruments. Their food consisted almost entirely of meat, dried or fresh; their clothing of the undressed skins of animals. Some had firearms, some merely bows, arrows, and spears. Of course a great many were lost that we never heard of, but that any of them got across was extraordinary and a great tribute to their hardihood and initiative.[2]

"Kyacks" [kayaks] are the single skin canoes in which the Indian [Eskimo] sits, with his shirt made of seal gut attached around the cockpit. There are also two and three seater skin boats built similarly. I have seen these men turn over completely in such boats without getting water into them. They have even been thrown off the decks of vessels in heavy seas without injury. They have several different kinds of paddles, and a great many spears, lances and contrivances for attacking seals, walrus, and whales. Some weapons have bladders attached as floats, and when dragged through the water they indicate the position of the prey. [Also to tire the creature for the kill, and to keep it from sinking.]

At length we arrived at the delta of the great river, where it spreads out into any number of mouths and one has to proceed very carefully, owing to the shallow waters. Out on to the bosom of Norton Sound we went,

[1] The author evidently was referring to Russian Mission, site of a church under Father Korchinski that was deemed in 1899 to be "one of the finest churches in Alaska." At Anvik, a short distance up stream, was an Episcopalian mission served by the Rev. J.W. Chapman. 1st Lt. J.C. Cantwell, RCS, *Operation of the U.S. Revenue Steamer NUNIVAK on the Yukon River Station, 1899-1901*, GPO, (Washington, D.C., 1902.)

[2] Skin boats probably were used by Siberian Eskimos crossing the Bering Sea, but the small crude craft used by Russian pioneers of the mid-1700's was the shitik, a primitive vessel whose timbers were lashed together with strips of leather. Vasili Berkh, *Chronological History of the Discovery of the Aleutian Islands,* (St. Petersburg, Russia, January 1823), included in Melvin B. Ricks' translations in *The Earliest History of Alaska,* Cook Inlet Hist. Soc., (Anchorage, AK, 1970.)

Brig. Gen. George M. Randall, Commanding Department of Alaska, (center, front row) and staff at Fort St. Michael in January 1901.

COURTESY NATIONAL ARCHIVES, PHOTO 111-SC-83596

Eskimos in their kayaks.

headed for St. Michael. Norton Sound is the great dumping ground for the waters and silt of the Yukon, and [it was thought] colors of gold could be obtained from the soil almost anywhere.

St. Michael, which commands the mouth of the river, was once a Russian post, but in 1900 [October 1897] became the headquarters for the American Army in the North, commanded by Brig. Gen. George M. Randall, a distinguished officer who had seen service in the Civil War and Indian campaigns.[3] On his staff was Major [Wilds P.] "Dick" Richardson, a great student of Alaska, who did as much as any other individual to develop her transportation systems and resources.

Reindeer had been imported into this area some years before and Laplanders brought in to handle them. The reindeer eat white moss which must be carried along for them like forage for horses, if they are taken to places where it is not obtainable. They are tremendous eaters and consume three or four times as much food as a dog, in ratio to their weight, and do not pull very much more. They are able to make very long trips, eighty or ninety miles at a time, but have to rest for several days afterward. The reindeer is not a tractable beast and when handled by an inexperienced person, becomes at times very dangerous; they not only butt with their heads, but kick with their front feet. A reindeer sled looks like a dugout canoe, and is so constructed that when the reindeer attacks the persons in it, they can turn the sled over on their heads and wait for the reindeer to go away, or for a Laplander to come and rescue them.

It was told of Major Richardson that he went out on a reconnoitering trip with some reindeer during the previous winter. At one place they ran away with him, taking the sled off the trail about three miles into deep snow. Richardson was a very big man, weighing around three hundred pounds. No snowshoes could be found in the party big enough to support his weight, so a trail had to be broken in there by the rest of the party and Richardson hauled out by hand. That was the end of the reindeer business for him.

An Indian [Eskimo] woman, "Sinrock Mary" [Mary Antisarlook], had the biggest herd of reindeer in that part of Alaska. She had the reputation of being the richest of the Malemutes. I saw her in a trading store once, dressed in fine reindeer clothes and bright red flannel trousers. She was known as a very keen business woman.

There seems to be no reason why thousands of reindeer could not be supported in this area. They would be a splendid source of meat, as well as hides. I took several short hunting trips in this tundra country, which is an endless flat plain covered with moss and low bushes. Little camps of the Indians [probably Eskimos] were encountered here and there. All of their equipment, sleds, dogs and weapons were entirely different from that of the Indians of the upper river. The dogs were much smaller and instead of being hitched one behind the other, so they could go between trees easily and around narrow places, were hitched in pairs to a long lead line which ran out from the large sleds. These sleds were two or three times the size of those of the upper river Indians, and the runners were made of bone or walrus ivory, which does not stick to the ice in cold temperatures. The winds along the coast at times are terrific but the temperature seldom gets as low as it does in the upper country.

I heard many interesting tales from the Malemutes about fish, seals, and walrus, which form a great part of their food supply. From the skins of the two latter they made clothes, footgear, and boats, but since so many white men came into the country, these animals were growing scarcer.

Among the fish peculiar to that region is one called "ice fish," which they told me could be frozen stiff and kept so for a considerable time; upon being thawed out, it would come to life again and swim all around as though nothing had happened. I did not see this fish but understand that the fact is well authenticated.[4] There is another, called the "candle fish," which is a small herring. When dried, it is a mass of oil which will burn very much like a candle if you set fire to it.

Some of the Bering Sea natives follow customs much like those of certain Asiatics. Among the King's Islanders, the women tattoo the lower lip when they are married, usually with three marks, one in the middle and one on each side; thus they can be readily identified as married women. A common ornament worn by the men is a collar-button-shaped piece of ivory which is inserted through a hole made in the lower lip. [A labret.] This ivory piece is often engraved and ornamented by carving.

Most of the walrus tusks for sale around Bering Sea have been ornamented by Malemutes with drawings of seal and walrus hunts, caribou, and moose chases,

[3]It became a U.S. post in October 1897 with Lt. Col. George M. Randall, 8th Inf., commanding. On his second Alaskan tour he came here in January 1900 as a colonel to head the new Department of Alaska. He was promoted to brigadier general, U.S. Volunteers, in February 1901.

[4] This may be the blackfish (dallia), about 4-6 inches long. Turner (Army Signal Corps) says that when the nearly frozen fish are thrown to ravenous dogs they are eagerly swallowed; "the animal heat of the dog's stomach thaws out the fish, whereupon its movements soon cause the dog to vomit it up alive. This I have seen . . ." Lucien M. Turner, *Contributions to the Natural History of Alaska,* GPO, (Washington, D.C., 1886). Also S Misc Doc 155, 49th Cong, 1st Sess, 1882.

Old Russian Church, St Michaels

From Harper's Weekly
February 1887

Eskimos from Unalakleet

An illustration from "Military Reconnaissance in Alaska," a report by Lieut. Henry T. Allen 2nd Cavalry

---

figures of fish, dogs, and wolves. Many of them have holes arranged for cribbage boards. In fact, these are so common that the story is told of a young lady who, on seeing a walrus in a zoo, expressed great surprise that its tusks had no cribbage boards on them.

Malemutes and Eskimos are said to be polyandrous, that is, the women have several husbands. Female children are said to be disposed of when too many are born. The children take the name of the mother and are looked after by her, but the fathers have to contribute to their support. A similar custom prevails among the Tibetans. It is a more or less practical way of solving the problem of over-population in a country where food is scarce and difficult to obtain.

The Eskimos live in what are called "igloos." The igloo is a hole in the ground covered by a vaulted roof of bones, driftwood and earth, hung about in the interior with skins. The entrance is ten or fifteen feet away, through an underground passage, so as to keep out the wind. Heat is obtained from small seal oil lamps. In the winter when they are on hunting expeditions, they make camps out of blocks of ice [or hard-packed snow] in a similar manner.

Ice was forming everywhere, as October approached. We had to arrange to get out at once, as only a few boats remained. Among the other steamers in the harbor was a little ship flying the British flag, called the *Manuens*. She had been ashore several times and her bottom broken in frequently. Each time this occurred her name was changed, and now her bottom was said to be mostly concrete with which the holes had been patched.

The second morning of our stay at St. Michael, Tosman told me and my companion, Lieutenant Mack, that he had bought a yacht and wanted us to take a trip out on the bay and call at various boats, the captains of which he said were his friends. Having nothing else to do, we accepted. Proceeding to the wharf, we found that his "yacht" was an open sailing dory about thirty five feet long, with a sloop rig and a primitive gasoline engine. Two men had it, Bill and Ole. Bill was from Maine and Ole was a Swede. We started out in good calm weather for the *Manuens* which lay about seven miles offshore, but on our way a breeze sprang up, which gradually increased. We spent about an hour on the *Manuens* and indulged in a great deal of good cheer provided by the captain. Tosman had with him the young lady whom he had brought down the river, a couple of his friends, the two boatmen and Mack and myself. I noticed the sea rising and suggested that we leave, and after awhile got the crowd back in the boat. By that time the waves were running high and we had to nose straight into the seas, with the wind blowing harder all the time. The old gasoline motor only gave us about four knots speed.

Bill, the skipper of the boat, had become useless and insisted on sitting up on the boom, which was balanced on a sawbuck on the stern. Bill was dressed in a leather coat, corduroy trousers and horsehide half knee boots. He had the stump of a cigar in his mouth, and was telling us in a very loud voice: "I know more about sailing than anybody living. I learned it in Maine, and I don't care whether you like it or not." Just then the boat gave a great lurch and Bill toppled overboard, immediately drifting to leeward. He was swimming like a duck, with all those heavy clothes on, his shoulders well out of the water, and the cigar still sticking out of his mouth. All the time he was swearing loudly at everybody on board for letting him fall off.

The engine could not be reversed so Ole grabbed the tiller, turned the boat around and made for Bill, but when it came time to shut off the engine, he did not know how and ran squarely over his partner. I thought Bill was gone as the propeller must hit him, but in a moment he bobbed up behind the stern as buoyant as ever, the cigar still at a jaunty angle, the swearing more voluble than ever. Thinking it was time for drastic action, I jumped to the tiller, and made a turn so as to get to the windward of Bill. I tore the wire off the spark plug and drifted down to him. He was still swimming as strongly as ever, although he had been in the water almost an hour. The whole crowd rushed over to the gunwale to pull Bill in and nearly swamped the boat. Water got into the batteries of the engine and made it impossible for us to start it, so we had to make sail under triple reefs.

After bailing the boat, we got into St. Michael harbor just as dark was enveloping the little town. Tosman took Bill to his room in the hotel, put him to bed with all his wet clothes on and gave him a bottle of whiskey, which he drank up at once. The next morning they came out arm in arm, the greatest of friends, Bill having completely dried out and sobered up, and feeling in fine shape. These men in the North are prodigies of physical endurance. What Bill had been through would have killed half a dozen ordinary men.

Next day [October 5], I boarded the steamer *St. Paul*, the largest ship that ran to the north. She had been built in ninety days at the opening of the Spanish War, and had made two or three trips to the Philippines. We started out over the hundred odd miles to Nome across Norton Sound, arriving there next morning.

Nome City looked like a metropolis. It was said to have a population of 35,000.[5] The country was more

[5] Population peaked at 30,000, in the summer of 1900. Orth, op.cit., p.694.

or less flat thereabouts and one could see the whole town from the boat. With my field glasses, I could see that we had to land on an absolutely open beach through the breakers that were still running. There was no port whatever. Ranged along the beach and still working their "rockers" were the beach miners.

The rocker is a little wooden box, about three feet long by two feet wide. It has riffles in it, to catch the gold, and apertures for the dirt to run out of. The men shoveled the beach dirt into these rockers and then with a dipper in one hand, poured water into the top of the box while they shook it with the other. Many of them were making from $10 to $20 a day at that work. The diggings were further back. Nome was second only to Dawson in richness.

We landed in small boats running through the surf. The people were a tough looking lot, much worse than at Dawson or any place up the river. This was because Nome was easy to get to; one could come there directly by boat after the ice left and not have to take the perilous and grueling trips through the passes or over the long stretches of the Yukon. For another thing, Nome had no such efficient police control as Dawson, and there was a noticeable lack of law and order. I was told that the Federal judge there was wholly corrupt, and that a gang existed which would find out where rich diggings had been located by prospectors and recorded in the government books. The gang would go out armed with rifles, drive the man off his property, come back to the government office and destroy the page on which the former record appeared, then have the claim recorded again, as theirs.[6] The same gambling dens, saloons and dance halls existed in Nome as at other places, but of a more lawless and degraded character.

A young man named Lidy, who was a representative of the White Pass and Yukon Road, [Route] had landed with me. He was a cheery, interesting fellow, breezy in the extreme, full of dash and vim. His left hand had been cut off in some way, leaving only the stump, but it was a formidable weapon in a fight, as a jab from that was much more effective than a blow from the fist. Lidy started in playing faro and soon had won a lot of money. He began setting up drinks for everybody and soon was followed by a large crowd, who aided and abetted him in everything he did. I was looking around Nome with other officers, when I saw a big fight going on down the street, in which twenty or thirty men were engaged, with scores of onlookers. Going there, I found that Lidy had seen a man hauling water with a dog team and beating his dog, whereupon he took exception to it and the man hit him. Lidy answered with a blow that nearly killed the driver, at which Lidy's adherents and the friends of the man started a general fight which ended when about ten town marshals got into the fracas and succeeded in overcoming Lidy, after he had licked three or four of them. Then they locked him up in the calaboose.

Lidy still had hundreds of dollars on his person. The boat that we were on was the last one to leave Nome that year. If Lidy was not released from jail, he would have to stay in Nome for the winter. At this juncture, a Catholic priest with a long black beard volunteered his services and went up and talked to the authorities, at last prevailing on them to turn Lidy loose for the sum of several hundred dollars. In his gratitude, Lidy gave an equal amount to the priest for his church. I thought Lidy had been released and returned to the ship, but on reaching the vessel, I found he had not appeared. I asked the Captain to wait a little while and see if he would not come. Just at that moment we saw a boat coming through the surf with a large figure in a black cassock and black beard supporting another man in the stern seat. It was the Catholic priest holding Lidy, who had not completely recovered from the effects of the Nome "hooch." He came up the ladder and was met by the quartermaster, who asked him for his ticket. Lidy answered that he did not need a ticket and would get on the ship if he felt like it, whereupon the Quartermaster tried to hold him off. Lidy knocked the Quartermaster down and started walking up the deck. They were about to put him in irons when I went down and took him to a state room. By the next day he was all right.

He had filled his pockets full of ivory curios to give to Mack and myself, but when he took them out for presentation the next day, there was nothing left but powder.[7] They had been smashed in his numerous fights.

Some days later, on landing in Seattle several of us had dinner together. One of our new-found friends, who had come out with a fortune, insisted on giving a large party. He wanted to be original and do something other people had not thought of. He had been in the North about fifteen years and did not know much about giving parties on the Outside, neither did he know many people in Seattle. He sought my advice but I told him the party would be much more original if he worked the thing out himself and then invited us.

The next morning I received word from him to come down to the wharf at four o'clock that afternoon, and

---

[6] This refers to the claim-jumping cases in which U.S. District Judge Arthur H. Noyes was found guilty of conspiracy and contempt of orders of a higher court, was fined and removed from office. The illegal "jumping" of claims and improper judicial action were the basis for Rex Beach's book, *The Spoilers,* Harper, (New York, 1906.)

[7] This is not likely to happen to real ivory.

we would have a party. Arriving there, I found that he had chartered a schooner, with a tug boat to tow it. On board, plants were arranged about the deck to make it look like a garden, and he even had an orchestra. The cabins had food and many drinks available and there were about forty guests, both men and women. I asked him how he got the idea, and he said that he had wanted to have a private party and thought a boat was the best thing. I wondered where he had found all his guests, and he told me that when he went to Alaska, he was outfitted by the Northern Commercial Company, and he thought if they could outfit him for Alaska, they could outfit him with guests for a party, which they had forthwith done! We were towed around the Sound, the orchestra played and everyone had a very good time.

Abandoned gold dredge near Kougarok, northeast of Nome, as it appeared in 1974.

COURTESY LYMAN L. WOODMAN, 1974

"Carbonano Bill" rocking $2,000 a day at a gulch near Nome, 1903.

COURTESY COOK INLET HISTORICAL SOCIETY

The beach at Nome, July 1900.

COURTESY A. CURTIS COLLECTION, UNIVERSITY OF WASHINGTON LIBRARIES

6

PREPARATIONS FOR LINE CONSTRUCTION

I submitted a report of my observations in Alaska to General Greely, Chief Signal Officer, to the effect that the people trying to build the telegraph lines stayed in the house too much in the winter, and that if they got out and worked when it was cold, the lines could be built. Whereupon [in October 1901] General Greely ordered me to return to Alaska and build them, and I was delighted at the prospect.

In order to arrange details of supply and personnel during the next two years when I expected to be in the North, I went down to Portland, Oregon, and Vancouver Barracks, Washington, on the other side of the Columbia River. This was one of the first garrisons put on the North Pacific Coast. It was picturesquely situated on a gently sloping eminence, commanding the great Columbia and Snake River systems and the trails running north and south along the Pacific Coast. Its appearance at the time was much the same as during our Civil War. The same old brass cannon, with their trails and limbers, were used for firing salutes. Many distinguished officers had been stationed there as lieutenants, among them Gen. [Ulysses S.] Grant, who went there during the first part of his service before the Mexican War. General Grant used to jump his horse over the trail of one of these old cannons for exercise. He was one of the best horsemen ever in the service.

Grant's Pass, Oregon, is said to have been named after him. They say he used to play poker there and every time it came his turn to play, he would say, "I pass."

I returned to Seattle the first of November [1901] and took the steamship *Dolphin* for the North. This was an old sound steamer from New York which had been brought around the Horn and fixed up quite comfortably for Alaskan service.

In the Inland [Inside] Passage we encountered many whales and Orcas, the latter also known as "killers," "grampus," and "tiger of the seas." Sometimes we would see desperate fights, with the whales jumping clear out of the water, the Orcas holding on to them like bulldogs. We also witnessed fights between Orcas and thrashers, with the spray flying fifty feet in the air from their terrific combats.

The people had left the salmon canneries for the winter and only caretakers remained. I had a good chance to observe the large trees along the shores of the Inland Passage, some of the biggest cedar trees I have ever seen. I saw a schooner entirely filled with the carcasses of white tailed deer, which were being taken down to Seattle for sale. There were excellent deep sea fisheries of haddock and cod all along here.

A short while before, a whale had become entangled in our submarine cable near Peril Straits, north of Sitka.[1] In its struggles to free itself, it had severed the conductors in the cable but had not broken the armor. The cable ship *Burnside* had located the position of the break by tests and had underrun the cable. Imagine their astonishment when the whale, with a half hitch of the cable around his tail, came to the surface, dead from drowning of course, and in a partially decomposed state. The stench from the creature made it almost impossible to stay on board the ship. When the natives on shore heard about it, they put out in their boats, hacked at the carcass and got it ashore, where they tried out the blubber for oil, ate the meat and used the bones for their boats. Only one other instance of this kind has ever been known to occur, when a whale was caught in the Red Sea on one of the first submarine cables ever laid.

We passed one island, Metlacatla [Metlakatla], belonging to Canada, where the natives had been organized into a model community by a missionary. They were very industrious, wove baskets, did lots of handiwork, made blankets, fished and trapped, and became very prosperous. They had good houses, schools, chur-

[1] In writing this manuscript in the 1930's, Mitchell misremembered when the whale incident occurred. It was reported by the *Seattle Post-Intelligencer* as happening in July 1905.

ches, and were said to be a model community in all respects. No white people were allowed to own property on the island.[2]

Upon arriving at Juneau, I met my old friend, Major Field, with whom I was later to have a strange adventure. He had been one of my commanding officers in the Spanish War, and now had charge of the cable operations between Juneau and Skagway. The contract had been let for this stretch of cable, a little over one hundred miles, to a civilian contractor, and the distance had been scaled off the chart in a straight line, on which basis the contract had been let. When the contractor started to lay the cable from the Skagway end, he soon found that on account of the irregularity of the bottom, which consisted of subterranean mountain peaks with valleys between, that he was running over his estimate of cable and using twenty or thirty percent more than would have been necessary in a straight line on a level bottom. He therefore put brakes on his cable drums and stretched the cable tightly so that it touched the bottom only from peak to peak. The cable was completed [in August 1901] and paid for and it worked very well at first.

In a short time, however, the powerful currents that surged through these restricted waters ground the cable back and forth on the subterranean rocks, so that it was severed in many places. They would no sooner repair one break where the ends would be a mile or so apart, than a new one would occur. Poor Major Field felt very despondent and nervous over it. He had had bad luck with our balloon at the Battle of Santiago, and had been on the cable ship *Hooker* when she ran aground and was lost on the Island of Corregidor in the Philippines. He thought that everything was turning out badly and was afraid it would be impossible to complete the Alaska telegraph lines. I told him that we were going to do it if it took twenty years, but I thought we could finish it in two. We could get started this year, get our experience and next year would see its completion. I had the greatest respect and affection for this officer and was sorry to leave him almost alone in Juneau under the conditions.

Arriving at Skagway, I stayed at the hotel kept by Mrs. [Harriet] Pullen. This splendid woman had come to Skagway with her children when her husband died, and her means of livelihood failed in the United States. She was doing very well and educating her children in the schools in Skagway. (Her oldest son, [Don, a graduate of the Univ. of Wash.], through Captain Hovey's efforts, was appointed to West Point where he became a great athlete and football player, and graduated at the top of his class. He afterward went into the Corps of Engineers and distinguished himself in the [first] World War as Colonel Pullen.)

I had to wait in Skagway until the country in the interior froze up tightly and we could get in by sleighs. The stage sleigh line was to make its initial attempt to maintain a service between White Horse and Dawson City, a distance of about four hundred miles.[3] It was in charge of an old sergeant of the Mounted Police who was to drive the first stage in himself. The company kindly consented to allow me a seat in it. Each passenger could only carry twenty five pounds of baggage. We were to be notified from White Horse, the end of the railway, when the ice was safe.

In the interval of waiting, I found a great deal to do. A lot of telegraph material had been shipped to Skagway to wait for the opening of the river in the spring, so as to be shipped by boat to me at Eagle City, and I arranged for its transportation. I scaled the nearby mountains in search of mountain goats, which greatly resemble the Asiatic ibex. Their pelts and small horns make fair trophies, but the meat is not particularly good to eat, and except for the climbing, they are not a very sporting animal to hunt.

I also went over to Dyea, where the Dyea [Chilkoot] trail of the old-timers began. Men used to carry loads of over two hundred pounds on their backs over this trail. It is almost straight up and down in some places. They received fabulous sums for packing things in. Men constituted themselves into regular beasts of burden and carried in all sorts of things; even large engines of various sorts were packed in, piece by piece. At one place on the trail, a great snow slide had occurred [April 3, 1898] while the pass was filled with toiling packers, and a great many had been killed [63 bodies found], some of the bodies never having been recovered. The exposure and hardships that people endured in getting into Dawson and the Klondike were appalling. At that time, two or three years after the first strike, parties who had tried to get through from Edmonton and down the McKenzie River to the Yukon were still coming in, worn, emaciated and haggard. They brought stories of many who had died on the way.

At last we received word that things were ready in the interior and I took the train to White Horse, and a new world for me. Everything was frozen stiff and the temperature was about 35 below zero when I arrived. The snow on the Pass was very deep, forty to fifty feet. It was hard to keep the way open for the train.

[2] The community of Metlakatla is on Alaska's Annette Island.

[3] This was the 330-mile Overland Trail built for the Yukon Territory government by the White Pass & Yukon Route. Gordon Bennett, *Yukon Transportation: A History,* Parks Canada, (Ottawa, 1978.)

The days were very short, we only saw the sun for an hour or two, when finally the stage was ready to go. It was a fine bob sleigh, with four seats and a driver's place. Two of us were in each seat, well covered with wolf robes. We had axes, chains, ropes, and equipment for helping in case we got into any trouble. The company consisted of a banker, a surveyor, two employees of the stage line and two women, one who kept a roadhouse in the Klondike and the other who had been in a dance hall but had since married. They were all oldtimers in the North, perfectly able to take care of themselves anywhere, and a jolly lot.

Relays of horses were provided every twenty-five miles. As the bells jingled through this frozen land, my companions in the sled sang and made up poems and improvised songs about our trip. Our trail lay across some of the lakes around that part of the Yukon. On Lake La Barge [Laberge] a horse broke through but we got him out. At another place, the sled turned over, and at another we had to unload it and ease it around the side of a hill. The women worked just as hard as the men and seemed just as strong.

The accommodations on the route were good for that part of the world, bunk houses where we used the sled robes to sleep in. We had plenty of baked beans and bacon, caribou and moose meat, and tea. I never knew before why people in the North generally drank tea. I thought it was from preference but as a matter of fact it is from necessity. In the intense cold, coffee has a very bad effect on the system, causing biliousness and other complications. Tea is more heating and more refreshing than coffee. [Also easier—lighter—to carry.]

At one roadhouse there was only one towel at the little basin where melted ice furnished the water for our ablutions. One of my companions said he had been in a roadhouse on the Klondike a while back, when a newcomer complained about the towel by the wash basin being dirty. The old woman who kept the roadhouse said, "Stranger, there has been three hundred men use that towel and you are the first one to make a kick." Towels and soap were great luxuries, so excessive was the cost of transportation. In fact, beer and champagne were approximately the same price, because the initial cost was entirely secondary to the charge for transportation.

As we neared Dawson, the temperature dropped further and it was 48 below zero when we pulled in. [Lieut.] Ben Tillman has come up from Eagle City to meet me, with two of his dog teams, and we had two very pleasant days with Mounted Police officers who were commanded by a Major Zachary Taylor Wood, a grandson of our own President Zachary Taylor, his family having gone to Canada at the time of the Civil War.

Dawson looked entirely different from its former appearance on my visit a few months before. The diggings were all closed for the winter. There was as much darkness now as there had been light before. A few people were burning [thawing with fire] holes in the ground and getting out "dumps" of dirt containing gold, to be washed out in the spring. Very little travel went on except the mails and a few people going out for prospecting or trade. Many were alert and anxious to hear of new gold strikes, because they could make much better time across country with their good dog teams in winter, than travelling in summer.

The Yukon was a majestic sight. In places the ice was smooth, but at others tremendous blocks of ice were piled up, making formations resembling castles and towers. Where warm springs existed, the river was open and great clouds of vapor arose from the surface.

The effect of the cold air was exhilarating in the extreme. Men and beasts ate two or three times the amount they did in the United States because so much had to be consumed to keep up the heat of the body.

I had a great deal to learn in this north country. In Northern Alaska, there are approximately three months, December, January and February, that are very dark. During six weeks of this time the sun is not seen at all.[4] The rest of the time it only shows for a few minutes during the day. It is quite dark until 9 or 9:30 in the morning, and from that time until four, the light is about the same as twilight in the temperate zone. the actinic rays of light which affect a photographic plate and make an image are very few and far between. If you want to take a picture at this time of the year, the camera must be allowed to remain open for an hour or two to make the impression which in summer could be taken instantaneously.

These dark days have a very depressing influence on some men, making them melancholy and causing them to lose hope, particularly if they are alone or with only one companion. This is more marked when they have little to do, or are of a very lazy disposition. Although no men under my direct command committed suicide, others in nearby areas did. All the suicides occurred during the dark days.

During four months of the year, two in the spring and two in the fall, there is about equal daylight and dark. These seasons in the upper Yukon are the finest I have ever seen in any country. In the fall the weather is perfectly clear, the air fine and bracing, and conditions are ideal for hunting moose and caribou.

---

[4] At Barrow, in winter, the sun does not rise above the horizon for 67 days.

White Pass Stage Line operating between Whitehorse and Dawson, 1900. COURTESY YUKON ARCHIVES AND MACBRIDE MUSEUM.

The end of the spring season is marked by the coming of the salmon up all the streams and the flight of migratory birds. One species, the Hawaiian finch, a small bird, flies all the way from the Hawaiian Islands to Alaska, over a broad stretch of water, 1800 miles,[5] where there is no possible place to alight. For many years after this was first reported, scientists refused to accept it, but it has been proved. The Hawaiian plover does the same thing. Some Alaskan birds are said to come all the way from South America. [The Arctic tern is one.]

For a couple of months in the summer, there is practically continuous daylight. People sleep, get up, have their meals and visit around almost anytime they want to. For a few days when this period begins, even though it has come gradually, it is hard to accustom oneself to it, but in a little while it is easy to sleep any time. The scourge of summer is the mosquito. The further north you go, the worse they are, right up to the Arctic Ocean.

During the summer, the rivers are the main highways and arteries of communication. Indian canoes, and the row boats and steamers of the white men move in supplies and take out gold and fur. The winter trails become impassable for dog teams and the summer trails on the ridges can be traversed only with difficulty by horses and mules.

There used to be no diseases in the north, no malaria, typhoid, or epidemic diseases such as smallpox, scarlet fever, or plague. The vigorous life that men led outdoors resulted in very few digestive disorders. I never had a case of pneumonia among my men in the north. Practically the only thing the doctors had to look after were frostbites and accidents, when the men got to fighting among themselves. I have never seen such a healthy lot anywhere.

The Indians were quite susceptible to the white man's diseases, as they had never developed an immunity to them. Chicken-pox would carry them off by the hundreds. Many contracted tuberculosis, not only by direct infection from white men, but also from adopting the white man's clothing. They bought gaudy cotton fabrics to make their clothes, which of course could not keep them as warm as their buckskin and fur garments. The white man's food, such as flour, which they did not know how to make into bread, upset their digestions. Certain tribes in the North never used to have any salt, and many ate nothing but meat for considerable periods; still under these conditions they remained healthier than after the coming of the white man.

Here in Dawson I learned a good deal about the effects of intense cold on different substances. No leather shoes could be worn in winter, and for that reason it was impossible to skate. Dawson's only skating rink was heated by large stoves. Some people wore felt shoes around town.[6]

Rubber would break in two at a temperature of 30 degrees below zero, and around 50 below, kerosene oil froze and the lamps would begin to go out. Mercury would freeze up at about 35 below. Prospectors use mercury for catching the gold in their sluice boxes, and I have seen them throw the mercury in solid bars into their sleds when starting out to their diggings.[7]

Naturally a mercury thermometer is no good in the North. For recording low temperatures, one must use alcohol or some other non-freezing liquid. After awhile I stopped all my men on the trail from having thermometers, because if they looked at them and saw it was 60 or 70 below, they would get to talking among themselves and not want to go out in the cold. As they were well fed, clothed and protected, they could stand the cold weather, and as they had orders to work every day, irrespective of temperature, a thermometer with them was merely a nuisance.

While in Dawson, I got together a little equipment in the way of moccasins, socks, mittens, and a parka, a long hunting shirt made of bed ticking impervious to the wind, with the hood lined with fur which projected in front so as to ward off the wind. I also bought a fur cap. The old-timers warned me not to put on too many clothes, because when you run with the sled you become overheated and perspire, and when you cool off, you freeze.

In a couple of days [on January 1, 1902] Tillman and I started with the two dog teams for Eagle City and Fort Egbert. I tried to make Forty Mile, about fifty miles away, the first day. Our trail lay down the Yukon River, over a great deal of rough ice. In places the wind had drifted snow over it, so it had to be broken again with snow shoes. Tillman's dog teams were not in particularly good shape, as they were not used enough. I attempted to

---

[5] Honolulu to Anchorage, 2,477 nautical miles. *Distance Between U.S. Ports,* NOAA Pamphlet, U.S. Dept. Commerce (Wash., D.C., 1978.)

[6] Leather footwear is usable with proper sox.

[7] Leroy Napoleon "Jack" McQuesten, famous Yukon trader, kept bottles of quicksilver, whiskey, kerosene, and Perry Davis Pain Killer on a shelf outside his store at Circle City. They froze in descending order, the Killer holding out till last. Berton, *The Klondike Fever,* op.cit., p. 30. Diane N. Macdougall wrote of the "Sourdough Thermometer" in *The Beaver,* (Hudson's Bay Co., summer, 1973.) The article said McQuesten's line-up included "quicksilver" (mercury) which would freeze at −40 degrees F; coal oil at −50; and Jamaica ginger (a ginger extract used for flavoring) at −60 degrees. Perry Davis' Painkiller turned white at −60, crystallized at −70, and froze solid at −75 degrees. St. Jacob's Oil (a liniment also known as Jacob's Oel) would not freeze even in the coldest weather.

mush one of the sleds in the way the others did, but soon found I had a great deal to learn. By noon we had covered 28 miles, but my shoulders and back were practically paralyzed and my legs were in the same condition, in spite of my being in excellent physical trim.

While mushing behind the ordinary sled and holding on to the handlebars, one is pulled along by the dogs and greatly assisted in covering the ground. Also there is a little step on the back of the sled where one may stand and get a ride occasionally. When heavy loads are carried on the sled, a gee pole has to be used to keep the sled on the trail. This pole, six or eight feet long, is attached to the right side of the runner in front, coming up to the right hand. The musher takes hold of the pole which throws him around when his sled hits a hard place or depression in the trail, while the lead line from the sled to the dogs, either of rope or moosehide, runs between the musher's feet to the dogs. This is extremely hard, grueling work. When a toboggan is used, mushers are usually on snowshoes and very little assistance is obtained from the dogs. This is also very strenuous and tiring work.

I had put on too many clothes and perspired freely, and when we stopped for lunch at noon, I took some of them off and tried to dry myself before the fire. My feet kept getting colder and I was afraid they would freeze, so I took my socks off and dried them.

Quite late that evening we made Forty Mile. Darkness had fallen but the brilliant moonlight and stars gave us plenty of light. The stars looked clearer than I had ever seen them and the moon was so bright that one could have had good shooting on game. After preparing the dog's food of salmon and rice, we had our dinner and went to bed. I slept the sleep of exhaustion, as I had seldom been so tired after any exertion. The trip had been a series of new sensations: handling the sled in the rough ice, with the cold beating on my face, and my breath freezing as it left my nose and mouth. The moccasins on my feet felt as light as feathers; the winter trail on the packed snow was springy.

We rose early the next day. The dogs were undisciplined and we had to chase them into the deep snow and sit on the head of one while the others were being put in harness. All had to be watched so they would not chew through their leather traces and escape.

I found that Ben Tillman was even sorer than I was but Webb, one of the packers, was not quite so bad. We made about 25 miles before lunch. The weather was around 40 below but the air was still and the going very good. The sleds were poor, as the runners were not very hard steel and stuck to the snow. At forty below, ordinary iron will stick to the ice like a roughlock. Ordinary steel does not slide smoothly. Chilled steel is quite good, wood is better and ivory or bone is the best.

While mushing the sled about an hour after dinner, I was thrown down with great force and hit my knee cap on a projecting piece of ice. It knocked me out completely. My leg became stiff in a few minutes, and I thought the fluid under the kneecap had been pierced. Tillman and Webb put me in one of the sleds, shifting the cargoes a little, and drove until we struck a cabin about 10 miles further on, near the U.S.-Canadian border, where they built a fire and left me, going on to Fort Egbert. My leg gave me intense pain but by putting hot and cold applications on it a great deal of the soreness was taken out. The next day Webb came for me with a horse, which I rode in. All that winter my leg continued to give me trouble. One's knees are always affected by the cold, and as they are not as sensitive as other parts of the body, the sinovial [synovial] fluid under the kneecap may freeze before one knows it. That is why one sees so many men in the North crippled in the knees.

Malemute Chorus COURTESY COOK INLET HISTORICAL SOCIETY

7

SURVEY BY DOG TEAM

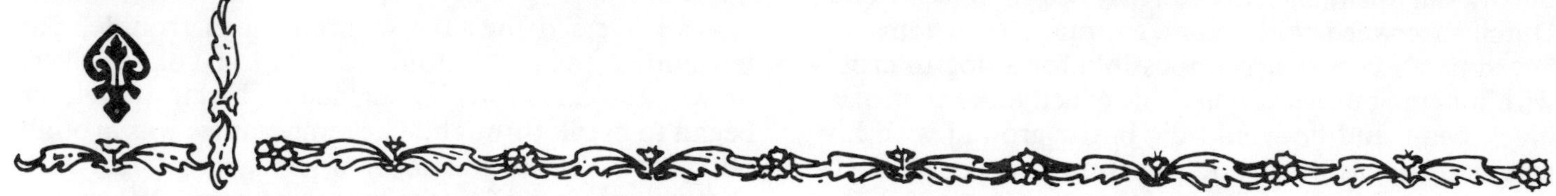

I found the garrison at Fort Egbert in rather a poor state of discipline. There were a great many recruits and few older non-commissioned officers. On account of the cold, drills were held irregularly and little target practice was carried on. The men did not like to work on the telegraph line, or anywhere in the cold for that matter. It is difficult to handle a group of men without giving them plenty of work, and in the North it is hard to find enough work for them to do while in garrison. I suggested to [Lieut.] Ben Tillman that he put them to chopping wood, but he said that was not popular in the North, as it was a punishment meted out to prisoners in the Dawson jail. This was rather a drawback, as we had to have a supply of wood to keep warm; however, the only men who chopped wood at Fort Egbert were those under sentence for some minor offense.

The darkness of the winter days brought a spirit of melancholy and unreality to persons from the Sunny South. Tillman was a splendid fellow, a man of great personal bravery and courage, but he felt very lonely and homesick. He had been engaged to a girl at home before he went to the North, and had recently received a letter from her stating that their engagement was off, that she was going to marry someone else. I asked Ben if he had written to her often. He said he used to write her a great deal but finally he had written a very long letter, in which he told her all about Alaska, describing the rivers and trees, the mountains, the fishing and game, the Indians, how very damn cold it was, and ended by saying that there was nothing else to write about so he would not write very often in the future. I told him that was probably the reason for her action and he agreed that it might be.

No trails existed over the mountains where the telegraph lines were to go, nor was their course definitely located, so the first thing we had to do was to survey their route.[1] The first line would be between Eagle City and Valdez, where the submarine cable from the United States ended, a distance of about seven hundred miles through a trackless wilderness, with no means of subsistence for men or animals except game, which could only be found at certain seasons of the year.[2]

My orders specified that all transportation in the post should be turned over for my use, and I made preparations to get my outfits out on the trail as soon as possible. I began to buy dogs to use for light sledding and reconnaissance work, selecting each one myself. Out of some two hundred dogs that I bought, I was only fooled on one. The first dog I obtained was a McKenzie husky leader called "Pointer", owned by a squaw man named Jack Lawrence, a mail carrier. My attention had first been drawn to Jack when he neglected his squaw for a week or so, to remain in Eagle City celebrating. She came up with a long knife, found where he was, grabbed him by the nape of the neck and marched him home.

Pointer was the greatest dog I have ever seen. He weighed about one hundred and twenty pounds and was perfectly sure on the trail. He could feel through the snow with his feet for an old trail and unerringly find it. We could depend on him to protect the sled and the team under all conditions. He would face the worst of storms and pull me out of places where I had broken through the ice, when it looked all but impossible. If he could get his front feet on anything, he would pull out the swing dog next to him, and between them they would pull out the next dog and gradually the whole team. He was so fierce that we had to cut his fangs off to keep him from chewing up the other dogs. He became tremendously attached to me, and from that time on during every trip, including the longest one ever made in Alaska, Pointer was my constant companion and friend.

[1] Not so; see Chapter II, footnote 5.

[2] The Army's submarine cable between Seattle and Sitka was laid in August 1904, and completed from Sitka to Valdez on October 3, 1904. The wilderness trail probably seemed like 700 miles long, but the line strung from Eagle to Valdez was 420 miles long. *The Story of the Alaska Communication System, 1900-1943,* op. cit.

The next lot of dogs I bought were from the Indians [Eskimos] who live on the Kobuck [Kobuk] River that runs into the Arctic Ocean.[3] They often came into Eagle City to trade. They were powerfully built men and their dogs were remarkable. One dog that I got from them, named "Moose," looked like a bear and weighed 140 pounds. The Indians told [Arnold] "Dutch" DeHeus, one of our men, the Moose really was half bear, and Dutch afterward told people so, many of whom believed it. Of course it is impossible for a dog to cross with a bear; but Moose had fur exactly like that of a black bear, and he would dig in the ground with his forefeet, just as bears do. Sometimes he would reach up to a limb of a tree with his forelegs and stretch himself, another habit of bears.

When we first bought these dogs from the Indians, they [the dogs] hated us. Even when we fed them, they were as fierce as wolves and would jump at us. We would have to knock them down with the stocks of our loaded whips, or grab them by the necks and choke them. But after they became used to us, they hated the Indians just as fiercely in return.

Gradually we got together wonderful teams. I selected the best ones, mated in size, gaits and in weight, and organized them into two teams. Taking a man named Emmet with me, I made a reconnaissance into the country of about one hundred and fifty miles, to see for myself where the lines should go and how we could stand the weather. When doing this advance reconnoitering, we always travelled light, often not carrying a tent but digging a hole out with a snowshoe and banking up a fire of logs opposite it, sleeping in the reflected heat of the embers. Sometimes we slept in a hole in the snow with the dogs lying on top of us.

It was necessary to push through to the south and find where the men working under Capt. [George C.] Burnell were located, who were coming north from Valdez. He was supposed to work north over Thompson Pass, in the Alaska Range of mountains, and meet me somewhere on the Tanana River, three hundred miles from each of us.

Emmet and I sought and found the Mentasta Pass, south of the Tanana River, which leads into the Copper River. Just south of the pass lies Mentasta Lake, the headwaters of a small river called the Tokyo, [Tokio] which is fed by warm springs that make glaciers.[4] A glacier is the result of warm water that flows out of the ground, which is gradually built up in the form of ice until it topples over and begins to move.[5]

We traversed the lake without much trouble, but once down the precipitous sides of the Tokyo River, on whose treacherous icy surface we had to travel, we began to break through. The temperature was around 60° below. There was layer upon layer of ice, with about three feet of water between them.. When our moccasins and trousers were wet, they would freeze instantly and become hard as boards the minute we got out of the water. In one place I broke through with my sled, clear to my shoulders, and if my leader Pointer had not gotten a foot hold on the ice beyond and pulled out Hunter, the second dog, and the rest of the team, I would probably have been there yet. Emmet avoided that hole, but broke through in another up to his waist. We were both thoroughly wet and the dogs were incased in ice, biting at their feet to get it out. If we did not act quickly, we would be frozen to death in a few minutes. Our sled mantles, containing the supplies, although made of canvas and moosehide, were frozen stiff. Each of us had two axes lying on the top of our sleds, but the handles were incased in ice and slippery. We had silk gloves inside our mittens, but even these had gotten wet.

Fortunately for us, I spied a dry tree leaning over the river, as if it had been put there by Providence. Shouting to Emmet to start chopping the tree, as he was the least wet, I drove the team ahead to its foot, breaking through as I went, and began turning the dogs loose from their harness, jumping in the water meanwhile to keep from freezing stiff. I got two candles from the sled and lighted them with matches we carried in a shotgun cartridge case to keep them dry.

Emmet grabbed a double-bitted axe and went for the tree, but on raising it for the first stroke, the axe halve [handle] broke in two from brittleness caused by the intense cold. Emmet was now beginning to freeze.

---

[3] The Kobuk empties in Hotham Inlet, which in turn enters Kotzebue Sound and the Chukchi Sea.

[4] From modern maps it appears Mitchell went on the "Eagle Trail" from Tanana Crossing (now Tanacross) to the Tok River, and on it to the Little Tok River. He apparently turned west from it to go up Station Creek (once called Tokio River), thence to Mentasta Pass. From there he headed south on the Slana River or the Chistochina, tributaries of the Copper River. He followed that stream to Copper Center, then continued south across country to Thompson Pass.
On this journey the lieutenant covered the route of the present Glenn Highway almost from today's community of Tok to about the present Gakona and Gulkana, then along what is now the Richardson Highway past Copper Center and Tonsina to Thompson Pass. Evidently he turned back north from the Pass toward Eagle, not venturing on down to Valdez.

[5] Glacier ice develops where accumulated annual snowfall exceeds the amount annually dissipated, and a residual snow mass persists from one year to the next. Over a period of years the mass compacts and, in time through several stages, is transformed into ice. *Encyclopedia Americana,* Americana Corp. (New York, 1966.)
Mitchell was referring to stream overflow or spring water which freezes when exposed above ground. Thus "glaciation" on a roadway can occur.

I told him to jump in the water while I tackled the tree. After having chopped it about half through, my axe handle broke. Things looked bad. I had a little tin of kerosene but that had frozen. We had placed the lighted candles in a sheltered place and warmed our hands over them, because if our hands became stiff we would be unable to light the matches. I jumped back in the water, as Emmet came with his second axe, with which he got the tree down, stripping off the branches in a second, and getting them in a blaze.

In the meantime, three of his dogs had chewed through the traces and gotten loose before I had been able to let them out. But in a moment we had a roaring fire and everything was changed. In a few minutes more, I had a fine meal ready, from food I had prepared before we left. I had taken large kidney beans and mixed them with tomato sauce and syrup and ground up caribou meat, seasoned with pepper and salt. We cooked these just the way we wanted them, and put them out in the cold in pails, stirring them while they were freezing. Then we put the mixture in canvas sacks, as they were just like rocks. When we put them into a skillet and got them warm, they were ready to eat. No more concentrated and balanced food could be found. We got our water without any trouble because the ice was so thin. It is necessary to get water either from a spring or to melt ice. To eat snow or make water from snow is bad for either men or dogs, as it makes one all the more thirsty.

Within a few hours we had dried everything, repaired the harnesses where the dogs had chewed through, and prepared the dog food of equal parts of bacon, rice and king salmon. I always carried the best food obtainable for the dogs, and fed them in individual dishes so as not to lose any of the substance in the snow and ice. Each dog was trained to come to his own dish, while I stood over them with a twenty foot whip, ready to pounce on any animal that tried to steal his neighbor's food or make trouble.

We whittled out a couple of new axe handles from spruce wood, and started out again next morning. The intense cold had frozen the surface of the river much better than the day before. We put muckalucks [mukluks], the Eskimo water boot, on our feet. These are of walrus hide, with sealskin tops, and extend to the knee. They are the only boot that will stand the extreme cold of Arctic winter. We greased them with seal oil which smelled to heaven but was very effective.

There was a mail station somewhere in the vicinity, and we expected to meet the mail carrier coming north from Valdez at any time. We should have met him the day before, but I figured he had been delayed. Soon I could see by the action of my lead dog that he smelled a habitation. It is remarkable how these animals show by their actions what lies ahead of them. We were running along at the base of a steep bank when I noticed ahead of us a place where a sled had evidently broken into the ice, which had frozen over, and then made a trail up the river bank. Peering over the top of the bank, I could see the top of a tent. It was about lunch time. Yelling "gee" to the leader, I jumped up the bank with the team in front of me. There in front of the tent was a sled, on which a man was sitting, with his head leaning over on his hands. In front of him, sitting immovable, was a large black dog, at least half Newfoundland or some other outside breed. I called to the man but received no response, and going closer found that he was frozen to death. The mail was in the sled under him. Between his teeth was a match and between his knees was a box where he had tried to scratch the match when his hands had frozen.

Pieces of harness showed where four of his dogs had bitten out and left, while the only remaining companion was this half-bred Outside dog with all four feet frozen. We put the body of the mail carrier in his tent, laced it up and shot his dog, then proceeded on down the river to the mouth of the Chestochina [probably Slana River] on the Copper River, where we left word about the mail carrier's fate. Things like this happen every once in a while, and both Emmet and I had narrowly missed a catastrophe the day before.

Our camp that night was on the banks of the Copper River where it makes the great bend to the west. Within the bend are some of the highest peaks in America, culminating in Mount St. Elias, over 18,000 feet high. Mount Drum, Mount Tillman, and Mount Wrangell are great buttes rising from an almost level floor up to their full height, around 16,000 feet.[6] They are the most imposing physical features of this earth that I have ever seen, including the Himalayas, Alps, and Rockies. The following day I counted thirteen craters smoking at the same time on Mount Wrangell, which is an extremely active volcano.

Our marvelous dogs were holding up in great shape. These half wolves from the very Arctic itself knew how to take care of their feet and themselves under the worst conditions. They got along on less food than any animal I ever saw. They were getting more from us than they ever had from the Indians, and were thriving on it. All of them were about three years old, except Pointer, who was four, in the full vigor of their lives. When the trail was drifted over and hard to find, I could make Pointer "loose lead." He would run ahead

[6] Mount Drum is 12,100 feet high, and Mount Wrangell is 14,163. Orth (op.cit.) indicates that Lieut. H.T. Allen may have called Wrangell, Mount Tillman. Mount Sanford, 16,237 feet, is in the same general area and may have been the third mountain Mitchell saw. Mitchell may have mistaken areas of blowing snow for smoke. There were not thirteen smoking craters.

of the team and I could regulate the distances I wanted him to go by telling him "Mush" and "Come back." I could "gee" and "haw" him, that is, direct him to the right or left by word of mouth, and he would instantly respond. He was a one-man dog. Nobody else could handle him except me.

In a couple of days we arrived at Copper Center, at the mouth of the Tonsina [Klutina] River, where there was a settlement of Indians. I noticed one especially handsome large Indian with reddish hair and blue eyes. I asked him his name and he answered, "Me named Cross River Joe." "Who your papa," I asked. "Long time ago big soldier chief, he come here. He my papa," Joe replied, "Now me chief of tribe." "Where your mama?" I went on, inspired by some curiosity. "She live in cabin up river," he answered. I told him I would like to see his mama tomorrow, so the following day she appeared, decked out in very handsome beaded caribou skin clothes, with a large aneroid barometer hanging around her neck, like a jewel. It was of brass, polished till it shone. The conversation developed the fact that the barometer had been given her as a magic talisman by the soldier chief who was Joe's father.

Copper Center was just north of the Coast Range and here I encountered a sergeant from Valdez who had some telegraph supplies in his charge. Proceeding south from there, I came to the Thompson Pass in the Coast Range, where I met Captain Burnell. This range has one of the greatest snow falls of any place in the world. That winter it was around eighty-five feet. In the spring, when the soft snow melted away, the hard winter trail, stamped down by men and animals, was left standing twenty or thirty feet above the level. Great difficulty was being experienced in holding a telegraph line through this area, and Burnell figured on putting in the shore end of a submarine cable through here. [This was done in 1903.]

All this country is full of copper. The real name of the so-called Copper River is "Etna," an Indian word sigifying "big" or "principal" river, whereas what is called the Chitna [Chitina] is the real Copper River, "chitna" meaning copper in the Indian tongue.[7] All sorts of copper implements, knives, arrows and cooking utensils, are made and used by these Indians.

I had now traversed the whole route on which the telegraph line was to run from Eagle City to the coast.[8] We made all arrangements possible between ourselves for its completion. I returned over the trail we had broken and fortunately got through the Tokio River without breaking through again.

On this trip I fell in with the Middlefork [Middle Fork] Indians on the Forty Mile River, whose chief, Joseph, became one of my great friends and companions later on. He had thirteen families under him. Their country began about 100 miles south of the Yukon and extended over to the Tanana divide. They were great hunters, trappers, and fishermen.

Every Indian tribe had its own clearly defined hunting grounds and boundaries and each hated every other tribe.[9] The only time they got together was in their general hate for the white man. All of them, however, respected the soldiers, especially the "soldier chiefs." I was the first officer to come into Chief Joseph's camp. As he heard my men calling me Lieutenant, he always afterward addressed me as "Chief Klutina," that being his rendition of the word "lieutenant." I was later known by that name to all the Indians in that part of the country.[10]

Upon arriving at Eagle City and Fort Egbert, I found that our sled trains were working better, although the equipment was poor and inefficient, and the horses and mules not what they should be. I took careful note of all these things so as to remedy them the following summer.

---

[7] The old Athabascan name for today's Copper River was "Atna." The Chitina River is a 112-mile tributary to the Copper River. The word "chitina" is said to mean copper river in Athabascan.

[8] "The whole route" would have taken Mitchell to Valdez on the coast, 25 miles beyond Thompson Pass where he met Burnell.

[9] This comment on inter-tribal hatred seems to be a generality of dubious validity.

[10] "Klutina" came from the Ahtena (or Atna) Indian word "Khlu-ti-tna" meaning glacier river. The Klutina River joins the Copper River at Copper Center.

DISCIPLINE AND TRAIL PROBLEMS 8

The day after I returned to Fort Egbert, one of our dogs went mad, jumped out of the corral and started across the parade ground straight for some men who were chopping wood. The sentinel on duty shouted to them to get out of the way, and shot at the dog but failed to hit him. Seeing what was happening from my cabin, I rushed out for my rifle. We always kept them outside because to bring them in would made them sweat and rust. I took aim and fortunately killed the dog with the first shot. This madness in the North is not hydrophobia, but seems to result from extreme exposure. On dissection, the animal's brain is found to be congested. It is like apoplexy or spinal meningitis in a human being. It seems to be communicable from one dog to another, by biting.

Tillman had told me of some trouble that day between our soldiers and some men in Eagle City, in a saloon, and said that some of his men had been put in jail. Just after dinner, Sergeant Pollner of the Signal Corps, my First Sergeant, came to me and said that the whole infantry company had gotten the keys to the arm racks in the barracks, that the non-commissioned officer in charge of quarters had issued ammunition, and they were about to march to town to take the jail and free their comrades. The Assistant United States Marshal, Robinson, had deputized all the citizens, who had posted themselves on the roofs of the cabins, ready to shoot any soldiers who attempted a jail delivery. These citizens were trappers, hunters and frontiersmen, expert shots and cool as cucumbers. The poor recruits in the infantry company would have been killed to a man had any such trouble started. I ran over to Tillman's cabin and told him what I had heard.

In the twilight, we could see a group of men with their rifles disappearing on the other side of the hill behind the barracks. Without a word, Tillman threw on his cap and parka, took two revolvers and rushed toward the place where the men could be intercepted before they reached the town. I ran after him, and just as we reached the road, the men, armed with rifles and cartridge belts, came marching along in columns of fours under their non-commissioned officers, headed for the town.

Tillman jumped squarely in front of them, a great big fine looking fellow, with his long black hair pushed back from his forehead. He gave the command "Halt" in a loud, firm voice, and said, "Men, you are going back to the barracks. You may kill me, but I will kill four or five of you before you go any further. Column right, march!"

Not a word came from the men. They came to a "right shoulder arms," and he marched them to their barracks, fell them in, had the roll called, their names taken, and all the guns put back in the racks. Then in a calm, straightforward manner he told them what they had done: that they were all liable to be shot for such an attempt; and he particularly reprimanded the non-commissioned officers. He finished by telling them that no punishment would be given now, but that if anything like that happened again, he personally would see that the non-commissioned officers got what was coming to them. The all knew what that meant and there was no further trouble from that source.

I found that Sergeant Pollner had prepared the transportation and supplies for my forthcoming trip up the Yukon into Canada, and up the Forty Mile River to the point where we intended to cross it. We had obtained permission from the Canadian authorities to go through their territory. I decided to go that way because there was no trail broken over the mountains for horse sleighs, and the equipment we had was not suitable for that kind of work. Sledding along the rivers made the distance further but did not require anything like the exertion incident to scaling the mountains and ridges.

There are two ways to organize a transportation system across country where all food and forage supplies must be carried along. One is to establish a chain of stations a day's march apart, and have the sleds go loaded one way and back empty, the number of animals and men constantly diminishing as the supplies are eaten up, until the base cargo taken out is delivered at the trail head.

The other way is what is called the "cache" system. A point is selected about a day's march off and everything hauled there and deposited. Then a second point is selected and everything taken there and so on, until the objective is finally reached.

The horses ate forty pounds of hay and oats each day, twice as much as they do in temperate regions, and as the average horse could only pull about a thousand pounds and do an average of ten miles a day, this meant that in twenty days they would have eaten [almost] that weight in food [800 pounds], gone only two hundred miles, and landed nothing there.

The sleds, harness, horses, and equipment were very poor. Nobody had ever operated big organizations up there in the winter. I was told it would be impossible, that the horses and men would freeze to death.

I determined to use the cache system until I had gotten out enough supplies to enable us to lay a telegraph line to the Tanana River during the winter, a distance of about 300 miles. Then in the spring we would erect it.

The mule skinners had organized among themselves to prevent our going on the trail at this time of year, and to stop my getting other men to take their places. They received fair wages and led lives of absolute idleness, doing nothing except gambling and drinking. In spite of their opposition, Pollner had had the sleds loaded and each had its 4-mule outfit with it. The days were very short at that time. No sun shone at all, and we had only the twilight to work in. On the day we were to start, the men were late getting up, and I could see that they meant trouble. I instructed Pollner to put a soldier on each sled, in addition to the civilian driver.

At last all the mules were harnessed and we pulled out in column on the trail. I thought for a moment that they would really get started; but just as they got into the village of Eagle City and were about to go down the bank on to the ice of the Yukon River, the packmaster, a man with a lame hip, jumped off the leading sled and stated that neither he nor his men would go any further. I told him to get his men together, and go back to my office at Fort Egbert, get their pay and get off the military reservation in half an hour; then I ordered the soldiers to proceed on up the Yukon toward Forty Mile. I had found out from three or four of the men beforehand that they would stay with the game, [Frank] Lee, [George] Webb, Emmet and "Dutch" De Heus. I immediately doubled the wages of all packers, created new positions of packmasters, assistants and scouts, and got some very good men in place of the worthless ones discharged.

When I was convinced that the wages had to be raised and more money was required to meet current expenses, I wired General Greely, by way of the Canadian lines through Dawson, that we needed additional funds. He telegraphed back that he was sending me all the money available under the current appropriation, which, the telegram stated, was $50,000. This was very encouraging and I immediately obligated it on equipment, salaries and services.

A disbursing officer of the government is not supposed to spend public money until he gets a warrant from the United States Treasury, showing that the funds have been set aside to his credit. Had I waited for this, the whole winter would have passed with nothing accomplished and we would have been retarded a year. An officer who always follows the letter of the Book of Regulations instead of the spirit seldom gets anywhere. Three months after I received the telegram, a warrant came through the Treasury. But it was for $5,000 instead of $50,000! The telegraph company, in transmitting the message had made a mistake in the figure; instead of sending the word for "five", they had sent the word for "fifty". Of course I was responsible for the other $45,000. That did not worry me very much, because I did not have it. Had it been $450 or something like that, they probably would have taken it out of my pay. If you get a large enough amount up against you and it has been properly spent, you need not be alarmed. I wired back to [General] Greely, telling him what had occurred and he made a personal appeal to Congress, with the result that a supplementary appropriation was passed at once covering the amount in question.[1]

Slowly and laboriously my train made its way toward Forty Mile on the Yukon. We marked out where each station should be on the direct line and put a couple of men with a dog team in each one. These places were from twelve to twenty miles apart, depending on the roughness of the ice and the location of good shelter and water.

Some of the mules broke through the ice on the river, at places where glaciers or warm springs kept it thawed, and their feet immediately froze. We tried to shelter the animals in tents at night, but made the mistake of taking off their collars, and their shoulders froze.

---

[1] It is unlikely that a young lieutenant in an organization commanded by a brigadier general with a staff of senior officers would be able, independently, to acquire and use funds in the manner described.
At the time there was no telegraphic communication between Fort Egbert and General Randall's headquarters at Fort St. Michael, so essential messages from Egbert to Washington, D.C., and back via the Canadian link made sense. However, Egbert was commanded by Captain Farnsworth, so although Mitchell may have initiated the matter and handled the problems on the trail, it is more likely Farnsworth was responsible for the messages and the actions resulting therefrom, as Mitchell's superior on the scene. (Editor)

Horses' lips froze where the bits touched them. We had a good deal of barley and corn in the feed, thinking that was heating, but it froze so hard the animals could not chew it, and when we got it in shape for them to eat, it made them perspire so that when they stopped to rest, they froze. Although we had to shoot many frozen animals that winter, the work went on without cessation.

The trip up the Yukon to the Middle Fork of the Forty Mile, a distance of some 200 miles, gave us a cache of supplies about halfway between the Yukon River and the Tanana. From this point I sent out parties with dog teams and one-horse sleds on the direct route that the telegraph line was to follow. They cut out the right of way in the winter and established their camps. The [#9 galvanized] telegraph wire was strung out on the ground and we worked over it with buzzer instruments. Great cold insulates the ground, otherwise the electric current would escape into it.

Gradually it began to dawn on people that we were going to build the telegraph lines and that it was possible to do so in the dreaded winter. Those who had failed accused us of wasting equipment and endangering the lives of men and animals, but I never lost a man or even had one seriously frozen. We were beginning to get our experience and our losses of animals were diminishing.

One of the conditions which facilitated our work was that I personally conducted all the reconnaissance across country and led the organizations on their first trips. I kept constantly on the trail inspecting them and attending to whatever situations arose. I had learned to do this in the Spanish War and Philippine campaign, principally from the old Civil War trained officers who, under difficult conditions, always took the lead themselves and blazed the way.

In February [1902] it became necessary for me to go down [up] the south fork of the Forty Mile River to what was known as the Mosquito Flats, where the Ketchemstock [Kechumstuk] Indians lived.[2] My trail along the line, over hill and dale, was now getting pretty good for the dog teams, but the heavy sleds with horses and mules still had to stick to the roundabout road by way of the Yukon and Forty Mile. The little streams up which our trails led were infested with snowshoe rabbits. These great white hares would jump up ahead of the dogs and the whole team would go wild trying to catch up to them. Occasionally the dogs would smell caribou or moose and the same performance would occur.

The spring migration of the caribou was on and we often saw them over the tops of the hills, in the distance. Thousands and thousands of these animals made a great herd that lived between the Yukon and Tanana. I have watched them go by my camp in endless procession for four days and then the stragglers kept on for a longer time, while the wolves picked up the weaker ones and quickly dispatched them.

While crossing the top of one divide, I looked down about 2000 feet below and saw two caribou being chased by six wolves. Just as they reached the vicinity of our trail, the leading wolf struck down one of the caribou. Instantly the other wolves jumped on both of them. They were not over two and a half miles away when this occurred. We came down the divide running as fast as the dogs could go, as they were wild to get there, but when we arrived, nothing was left of the caribou except a few pieces of hair and red bones. These great doglike animals make short work of any creature they are able to overpower. I got one and tried to drive it on the sled but it was sulky and morose and would not work properly. After it was fed it wanted to lie down for an hour or two and rest. It is the custom of the wolves to gorge themselves and then do nothing for a few days until the pangs of hunger drive them out again.

At the edge of the Ketchemstock country I was met by Chief Charley [Charlie] of these Indians. We had tea and a good talk together. He had a beautiful silver tip fox skin which in those days was very rare. We had a great trade over it, which ended by my giving him an order on the store in Forty Mile for certain amounts of powder, lead, caps (as they still used muzzle loading rifles), flour, bacon, beads, bright colored wool and large buttons.

The Indians all like flour but few of them knew how to bake bread. I have seen an Indian make up a batter of flour and water, then take a can of baking powder, make holes in the top and sprinkle the contents of the can over the batter like sugar. After attempting to cook this mess before an open fire, he then ate it with apparent relish. It would have killed an ordinary person.

The constant use of baking powder had such a bad effect on my men that I took it away from them and had them bake "sour-dough" yeast bread. Soon they learned to make just as good bread as could be had from any bakery.

I accompanied Chief Charley to his village, which was quite a respectable cabin community. On a hill nearby were the graves of his departed warriors. Each

[2] "Mosquito Flats, a 13-mile wide swamp at the junction of Wolf Creek and Mosquito Fork. Flats named by Lt. William Mitchell, U.S. Army Signal Corps, in 1902." Orth, *Dictionary of Alaska Place Names,* op.cit., p. 659.

was inclosed in a sort of fence, with the body in a cache supported on long poles. Strung round about it were the pots and pans that had belonged to the dead man, intermingled with streamers of various kinds to keep away the evil spirits.

These Indians had a clever scheme for killing caribou. For miles along the low range of hills bordering the Mosquito Flats they had constructed a series of fences about eight or nine feet high. These led into pens something like a fish trap. When the caribou began to come into the vicinity of these stockades, Indians posted on eminences would signal to other waiting on each flank where the caribou herd was located. They signalled by means of smoke from a fire built in a hole, alternately holding a blanket over the pit and pulling it away, thus allowing puffs of smoke to escape. The Indians would then run out on their snowshoes and surround the caribou, driving them along the fences and into the pens. Once they were secured, the squaws and children attacked them with bows and arrows and spears, and butchered them. Every bit of the caribou is saved, his hide, his feet, horns, entrails and even his skeleton. From the hides they make clothing. What meat they cannot eat immediately, they dry, and the bones are used to make all sorts of implements.

Aborigines never exhaust a country of game, as white men do with their superior weapons and wasteful methods. The average Indian in the North was a poor shot with firearms. This was because he did not have much chance to practice, as ammunition was expensive, and he never took a long shot. They were remarkable hunters, however, and would stalk the game until they were within a few yards of it, when every round they fired took effect. A good white hunter would usually kill more game than an Indian, but at the same time he would use up more ammunition. Indians were wonderfully adept at killing all sorts of game with bows and arrows, such as caribou, moose, birds of all kinds, even fish. The larger animals were now becoming harder to approach and more difficult to kill with arrows, consequently the Indians were forced to use guns. In the winter, while snowshoeing, they still used their old weapons, the arrow and spear.

The days were now becoming longer, with the attendant menace of snow blindness. I had dark glasses issued to each man, with instructions that if they lost them they should blacken their faces with charcoal, especially the nose and under the eyes. Snow blindness is an extremely painful thing. One good remedy is to apply wet tea leaves to the eyes and remain in the dark until the pain and inflammations subside. While returning from my trip to Chief Charley's country, I met a Negro and a white man going out to some diggings on the Forty Mile River. The Negro had on snow glasses and the white man had his faced blacked.

I felt we were now making real headway. Our men had a good organization and good discipline. They were well clothed and fairly well equipped, and we were spreading the lines along at a rapid rate. It was a sure thing now that unless something unforeseen occurred, we could finish the system in two years.

I established a wheelwright's shop at Fort Egbert where we made all our own sleds, harness and horse shoes. We built stables at each camp so the horses could be sheltered each night. We had discarded all bits, and drove the horses by means of halter. On each collar we hung a hammer to knock off balls of snow and ice whenever they formed on the horses' feet, to prevent them from freezing. We used single-horse sleds instead of double ones, with runners of concave chilled steel that did not stick to the ice in low temperatures. Our trains consisted of eight or ten horses and mules, which followed the lead animal and kept on the trail handled by two men. We had regular gangs running up and down the trail to keep it open and trestle over the places where warm springs existed.

We sent pack saddles and "aparejos" for the mules out along the trail, where we would organize pack trains in the summer. As the weather became warmer, the teams could pull two or three times the load they did in the cold of winter. We had a schedule made out which showed just what load each sled should carry in accordance with the temperature.

SPRING INTERLUDE: HUNTING AND FISHING 9

Gradually the streams showed signs of breaking and we came back from the trail to Fort Egbert, putting our dogs in the corral for the summer. The snow melted from the hills and ran down, forming pools of water. From the south, ducks began to arrive, first by tens, then by hundreds and thousands. In May, the Yukon River was still frozen.

One night we heard a tremendous cracking like cannon shots. It was the ice in the river. People began yelling and discharging firearms. Next morning when I looked out, I saw that it had broken and the river had begun moving. This is the great annual event in the North. All winter long private bets had been laid, specifying the day, hour and minute when the break-up would come and the ice begin moving at a certain point. A stake was erected on one bank and a tree or rock selected on the opposite side, from which a sight could be taken by two or three people, to decide when the river would break up, at its particular locality, in which people took chances, just as in a ship's pool.[1]

Everyone who is able to gives a party, and they visit between cabins at all hours of the day and night, drinking to each other's health for the coming season.

The grandeur of the break-up at Eagle City is impossible to convey by words. A great bend in the river here has as its background an enormous mass of rock called Eagle Cliff [Eagle Bluff, 2,000 feet high] against which the ice piles up for more than a hundred feet. Great cakes from five to ten feet thick grind and crash together with a noise like an artillery preparation for attack, for two or three days. Every day the river moved more and more and finally was clear.

For about two weeks during this period, it was impossible to go anywhere. The snow drifts had not melted through, the winter trails along the streams had been swept away by the waters, and the summer trails along the tops of the ridges were still impassable for horses and mules. We utilized the time to put away the winter equipment and prepare for the summer. I selected two good horses for my own use on the trail and for hunting, a big black named "Nigger" and a bay named "Frank," the sole survivors of the Castner Expedition of two years before, which had become lost in the wilderness. They had to kill most of their animals and barely found their way to help on the Yukon.[2]

One day while shooting ptarmigan on a hill near Eagle City, I suddenly came upon the body of an Indian, with the whole side of his head torn off. He had a bow in one hand and a quiver of arrows on his back. Near him was a hole between some rocks on a hillside, and the snow all around was covered with blood and bear tracks. Putting buckshot into both barrels of my shotgun, I followed the bear's trail into a little open stretch of spruce timber. Within a hundred yards I came upon him, stone dead, with an arrow piercing his heart.

This is probably what had happened: the Indian saw the breath of the bear rising from his den, as he prepared to come out from his winter hibernation. Going to the mouth of the cave, the Indian shot him through the heart as he emerged, then ran. But the bear, enraged at the pain, saw him and being more active than the Indian calculated, jumped out and happened to catch him right in the head with the first blow.

Not far behind the breaking up of the ice came the salmon running upstream. Lieutenant Fitzpatrick and I were walking along the bank of the Yukon near the Indian village above Eagle. Several emaciated Indian dogs, looking like living skeletons, were also patrolling the banks, looking into the water. These poor creatures, when sledding stopped, had been thrown on their own resources and were fed nothing by their owners. They had to eke out an existence catching rabbits, mice, ground squirrels and such. Suddenly one of the wretched looking creatures jumped into the water and disappeared beneath its surface. I said to Fitz, "That dog

[1] The largest such pool conducted now is the Nenana Ice Pool held on the Tanana River at Nenana.

[2] Lieut. Joseph C. Castner, 4th Infantry, led a small exploration party of Capt. Edwin F. Glenn's expedition into interior Alaska during 1898-99. *Compilation of Narratives of Exploration,* GPO, (Washington, D.C., 1900.)

has certainly committed suicide as he is despondent from being in such a condition." But just then he emerged from the water with a fish about three feet long between his jaws, and his companions rushed to help him devour the dainty morsel. In a moment it was gone. Within a week, every dog in that vicinity was as sleek and fat as a seal.

It was now the latter part of May [1902] and instead of darkness, the days were all light. Before the snow had half gone, the mosquitoes made their appearance. Wild flowers began to cover every available inch of ground. The soil is tremendously fertile and almost anything can be grown that will mature in the short summer. We raised excellent vegetables and even matured some wheat, although it went to stalk a great deal on account of the great amount of light.

Soon we were able to get out on the trail with saddle horses and pack mules, and get the men started digging post holes. The earth was still frozen and we tried many methods for getting the holes down. Blasting did no good, the ground was so springy that it just bounded away and closed up again. Using steam points from a boiler was too cumbersome, as it took too much equipment to carry a boiler along and too much work to get fuel. So we used very sharp digging tools which were sharpened and tempered every few days by blacksmiths who went from place to place with their pack mules.

The ground in the North practically never thaws out completely, unless the moss is stripped off and the earth exposed to the direct rays of the sun in May, June, and July. In places the ground may thaw for a foot or two down, but below that you strike the frozen earth. The top of the moss thaws and becomes almost like a bog, as the frost holds moisture in it. We often dug holes into the sides of hills where we put our game to keep, and it would never thaw, even through the summer. In some places where there are warm springs, or heat comes from volcanic activities, the snow is melted and there is even green grass all through the year.

The herds of caribou were now separated into two parts, the bulls by themselves and the cows and calves together. All had dropped their horns and the new ones were beginning to spring out in the velvet. The moose with their calves were in the heavy brush and exposed themselves as little as possible, waiting for their calves to grow big enough to fight the wolves on their own account. An angry moose is a very formidable animal. One blow from its front feet will kill the largest wolf, which hesitates to attack one alone unless it is badly crippled.

One day I sat on the banks of the North Fork of the Forty Mile fishing for grayling. My wheel dog, "King," had escaped from the summer dog corral and followed me out. He was a big husky with a short tail and weighed about 120 pounds. I was catching one grayling after another, with a little brown hackle fly, when I heard a yowling behind me and King dashed out of the brush with his head full of porcupine quills. He was trying to brush them out with his feet, without much success. He ran down to the river and put his poor head in, trying to cool his mouth from the agony caused by the quills. I tried to pull them out with my hands but it hurt him so he began to bite at me. Being a very big dog, he was hard to handle. I got a rope and snubbed his head up against a tree and put a stick in his mouth so he could not bite, then pulled out the quills with a pair of pliers. I expected that he would have a lot of trouble from the little particles remaining in his flesh, but he never seemed to. It cured him from the porcupine habit, however.

A short distance below me, almost in front of the men's log cabin, a Hospital Corps man was also fishing, and so engrossed that he paid little attention to anything else. Out of the corner of my eye, I saw a large bull moose swimming across the river straight toward him. As the moose was much nearer the cabin than I was, I had no opportunity to run there and get my rifle in time to get a shot at him, so I waited to see what would happen. The man didn't see the moose until he was within 25 feet of him. Then he leaped up and ran for the nearest tree, a spruce from which the limbs had been cut for 8 or 9 feet from the ground. With one jump he grabbed a branch and swung himself into the tree in an instant. I have never seen anything so quick. The moose, which had very large antlers, passed directly under the tree. I don't think he had even seen the man, or anything around there, as he was intent on following the trail of a doe [cow moose], that being the rutting season.

Seeing me, the man came down from the tree and told the most lurid tale of having been charged by a moose, which had nearly gotten him. Of course he had every reason to believe that what he was telling was the whole truth.

Next morning I started back to Eagle City, a distance of about 40 miles, intending to ride it alone in one day. One of my pack trains was going back at the same time, empty. I left my dog King with them, instructing them to keep him, but then about ten miles out, I heard a yap behind me and saw that King had found me out.

A good many moose were all through this region, and King would run up and down their tracks every little while. About midday, when I had covered a little less than half the distance, I heard a lot of yowling and baying in a clump of alders, and looking up at a little eminence, I saw what I thought was one of our dun-colored mules, but soon recognized it as a large moose, making over the hill. It was sneaking along so rapidly and stealthily, taking advantage of all the cover, that it disappeared in a moment. It is remarkable how a huge animal like a moose can almost fade into invisibility in a perfectly open place.

I galloped around to the bottom of the hill and almost ran into her. Drawing my rifle, a 30-30 Winchester carbine, I fired as she ran away, and she fell dead. This is one of the few times I ever killed an animal from horseback. It was largely a chance shot. I hit her in the hindquarters, a little below and to the right of her tail. The bullet ranged forward into the heart cavity and killed her instantly. There were no game laws in those days and we killed meat whenever we needed it.

King kept up his baying, and to my surprise a large moose calf came trotting up to the dead mother, with King after it. It would trot up and then away, looking around as it went. I had a lariat on my saddle and tried to rope it, but the trees were in the way and I missed repeatedly. The speed of a moose at a trot is incredibly fast, and in the trees and moss it went faster than I could on my good horse. I could not make King stop his pursuit while the calf circled around the body of its mother, so at last I shot it.

Dressing the carcasses as best I could, I waited for the pack train, which came by late in the afternoon and made camp near the kill. The cow was a very large one, fat and in good condition. We had not eaten any moose meat for quite a while, so everybody pitched in and ate the hearts and livers right away.

Next day at Fort Egbert I found that a company [Company C] of the 8th Infantry had arrived to relieve the 7th [Lieutenant Tillman's Company E] which had just left [on June 13, 1902]. This new company was commanded by Capt. [Frederick] Perkins, with Lieutenants Janda and Kelly. Mrs. Perkins had accompanied her husband. Our first dinner together had as the principal dish the young moose I had killed the day before. I have never seen people eat more heartily. Each person must have eaten four pounds of it. It was the best meat I ever tasted.

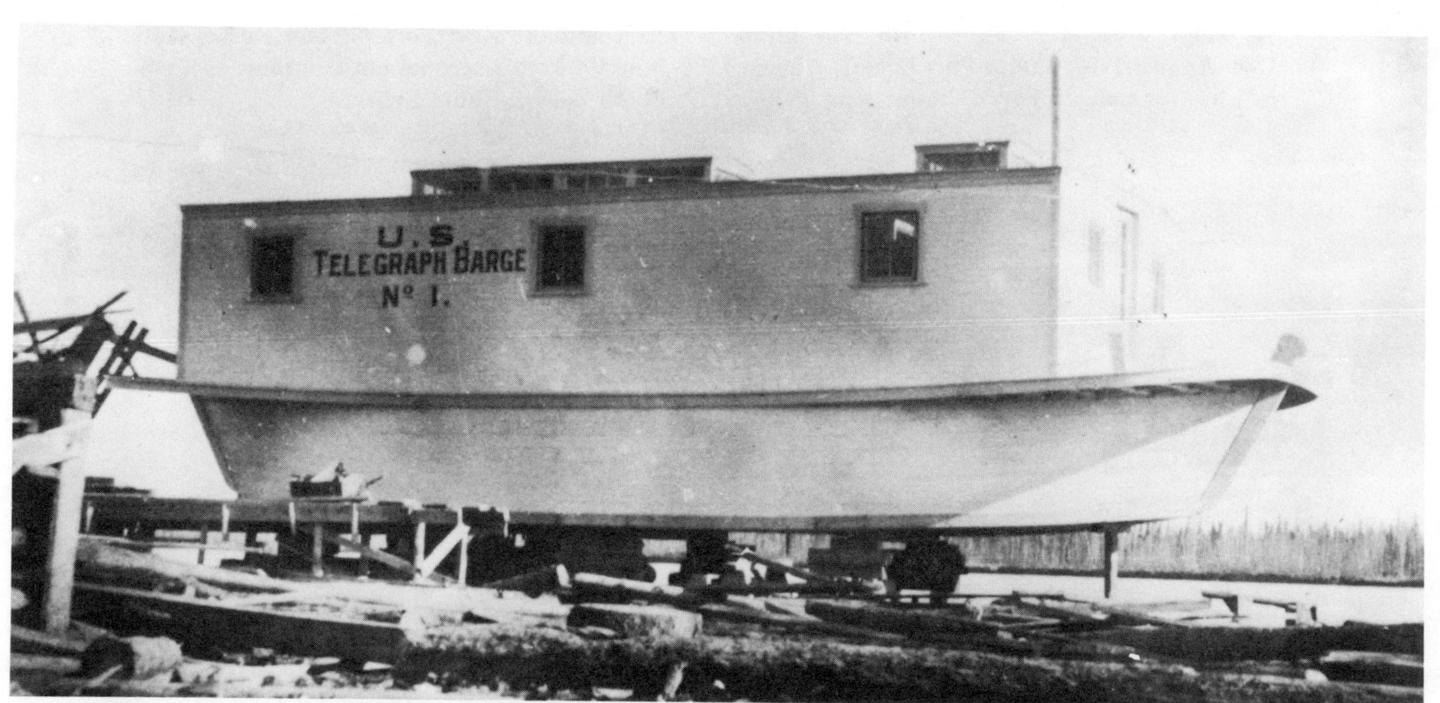

Signal Corps barge at Fort Gibbon, 1901. COURTESY U.S. ARMY, NATIONAL ARCHIVES, 111-RB-2673

Capt. Charles S. Farnsworth, 7th Infantry, was commander at Fort Gibbon during July 1899-August 1900, and of Fort Egbert, August 1900-June 1901. In a second Alaskan tour, as a major, he commanded Fort Gibbon again 1910-1911. (Photo taken at Fort Egbert.)
COURTESY C.S. FARNSWORTH COLLECTION, ARCHIVES, UNIVERSITY OF ALASKA, FAIRBANKS

Company street, Fort Egbert, 1899-1900. COURTESY U.S. ARMY

THE MAJOR'S PECULIAR MENTAL CONDITION

10

Our next project was a thousand mile trip from Eagle on the Yukon, to the Tanana River, then down the Tanana, in order to locate the mouths of its north and south tributaries and determine the best place for crossing it with the telegraph lines. I had worked first along the southern tributaries of the Yukon River to their sources in the dividing range of mountains between the Yukon and Tanana, and located these points carefully with instruments. I now planned to locate the mouths of these streams on the Tanana in a similar manner so as to estimate the approximate distances from source to mouth. We were to travel by pack mule 300 miles to the Tanana River, then build a whipsawed boat to take us down the river to Fort Gibbon. None of my acquaintances in Alaska had gone down the Tanana. Some white men had made the trip, (notably Lieut. Henry T. Allen [2nd Calvary,] in the early eighties [1885]) but they were not in Alaska at the time. It was just as mysterious a country to us then as the center of Greenland or the Antarctic continent is today.

While making my arrangements, I received a telegram from the commander of the Mounted Police in Dawson, to the effect that Major Field, my old friend, who was on the way in to make an inspection of the lines, was acting strangely, and that he had detailed two plain clothes Mounted Police to accompany him. This seemed very odd to me, and I could not imagine what was the matter.

I went down to the wharf to meet him as he came off the steamer. He greeted me with his accustomed cordiality. I noticed, however, that he was very nervous and kept looking all around suspiciously. Going out to my cabin at the military post, he was immediately called upon by the Commander and other officers. As soon as they left, I spoke to him of the trip I was about to make, of the arrangements I had made for it, and suggested that it would be a good thing for him to accompany me, as he would get an excellent idea of the country.

Major Field said he would like to go to my office and look over all phases of our work. Arriving there, I asked Sergeant Pollner to have all the maps, progress sheets and reports ready, so as to give him a comprehensive idea of what we were accomplishing. Major Field gave a hasty glance at everything and then asked the Sergeant if he would withdraw, as he wished to speak to me personally. As soon as we were alone, he said, "I want to tell you what has happened to me recently, and then I want your candid opinion about it."

His story was as follows:

"About a month ago, I was in my room in the hotel at Juneau, when I heard two men talking in the next room. I could hear one of them saying, over and over: 'Now we have him. We will kill him tonight.' After awhile, I heard my own name mentioned. I listened further and when I was sure that they were after me, I took my pistol, broke the door and jumped into the room, intending to arrest the men and take them to the town marshal. There was nobody in the room whatever. I went out and walked around the streets. Everybody stared at me. As I passed different groups of men, they eyed me peculiarly and absolutely stopped talking.

"I went back to my room and thought it over. I thought I had better consult a doctor. I went to one, and he gave me some medicine to take, but it made my brain so inactive that I stopped it."

Here the Major paused a moment and I asked him how he knew it made his brain inactive.

He went on: "Because I took a simple problem in integral calculus and it was perfectly impossible for me to work it out. I was sure then that the stuff was affecting my brain. Again I heard the men talking in the next room during the night. The door of the room was open and I rushed in, but again they avoided me. There was no one there. So I determined to come up here to you. I kept my departure a secret. Just before the steamer was to leave Juneau for Skagway, I ran down and jumped on board. As the steamer pulled out, I could see people running down to the wharf with the evident intention of getting me, because I had eluded them.

"When I arrived at Skagway, I went to the cable office and looked over the messages received that day, to see if anyone had wired ahead that I was coming, and to look out for me. I found only one suspicious message which was in code. It was addressed to the Canadian Bank of Commerce. I went to the bank and asked them to let me see their cipher, so I could decode the message, which they did. It said that a shipment was being made to the bank and to look out for it. It did not say what the shipment was or anything else about it, and I drew from that it might mean me. I seem to be followed everywhere, through the streets, mostly by the rougher element, who always keep their eyes on me.

"I went to White Horse on the White Pass Railway, and at that place I asked the Canadian Mounted Police authorities for an escort. Two men were detailed to accompany me, in plain clothes, and they took the river steamer with me. A few cows were being shipped down the river and as I looked in at them through a window, I heard the two men who were taking care of them say, 'We'll get him before long, he is going down the river now.'

"When I arrived at Dawson, the Commander of the Mounted Police met me at the wharf, and as there was another boat ready to leave, coming down here, I did not go into the town but came to you right away. I saw how everybody looked at me when I got off the boat. I am sure that I am being watched and followed, and that the first opportunity will be taken to make away with me."

He stopped speaking and I could see that my old friend was in a terribly excited state of mind. He had always been one of the bravest of men, and to see him in abject fear was a strange thing to me.

"Now," he said, "what do you think of the whole proposition?"

Without hesitating, I stated it was perfectly impossible that a plot with such wide ramifications should have been made to kill him, and that if anybody wanted to kill another in this country, they would do it at once.

"No," he objected, "They want to keep me in a state of suspense, so as to torture me. Everything I have done in the last three years has ended in failure, and I am sure that what I tell you is true."

I was confronted with a difficult problem. Unquestionably Major Field had lost his mind. If we confined him or restrained him physically, he would certainly go all to pieces and be incurably insane for the rest of his life. But if I got him out in the wilderness where he would get plenty of fresh air and exercise, hunting and fishing, and be in an entirely different scene, I thought I might get him over it. So I suggested that we start on the trip for the Tanana River the next morning.

He wanted to know if there were many Indians and if I thought they knew about the plot. I replied that there were a few, but I knew them all. They were my friends and would do more for me than for any other white man. He then asked what outfit I was going to take, and I told him one packer, four pack mules and our saddle horses. He asked to see the packer and I had the man, Hall by name, come in. He was a great big fellow, about six feet three in height, with blue eyes and a blond beard, as fine and straightforward in appearance as any man I have ever seen. Major Field was satisfied with him.

He then asked me what arms we took with us, and I told him we never carried pistols there, that I took a 30/30 rifle along, with 60 rounds of ammunition in my belt. He insisted, however, on taking two pistols and a service rifle, a Krag 30/40.

Next morning we got away. Major Field would look behind every tree, thinking he might find an Indian waiting to shoot him. At our first camp that night, the mosquitoes were terrible. I built smudges, around which the horses and mules stood, and put up our silk tent, which had a floor to it, and a hole with a puckering string to close it up. In the middle of the night a bear or wolf came near the camp and the horses made a lot of noise. Major Field thought the camp was attacked and made a bolt for the hole in the tent, knocking the whole thing down on top of us. It took some time to disentangle ourselves, then Major Field took a pistol in each hand and began running all around. I thought he would certainly shoot Hall and myself before I could persuade him there was nothing to be feared. He suspected everyone except myself, and his mental anguish was so pitiable, it wrung my heart. Of course it was a dangerous thing to be with a man in his condition and armed to the teeth, but I hoped to be able to effect a cure.

The next day we ran into a small herd of caribou. We made a careful round-about stalk and I brought him within range of a nice bull, which he killed. This pleased him greatly, not only because he was glad to make the kill but also because he was satisfied he could hit whatever he aimed at.

For several days we journeyed on and saw nobody, but one afternoon, just as we were making camp, an Indian from the Middlefork tribe came up. Indian like, he approached me, gave one grunt and then sat down on his haunches to watch what was going on. After having made our camp and started the fire, I gave him a little tobacco and papers for cigarettes, poured him a cup of tea with some sugar and we began our conversation, as follows:

"Long time me no see you, Klutina. What for you bring stranger here?"

I replied, "He is very big soldier chief, much bigger than me. He is chief of all the soldier chiefs in the North. All the Indians who see must remember he is a very big soldier chief and do everything for him they can, as he likes all Indians."

I asked him how he had done with his fur during the winter, where he had sold it, how many fish they were catching, what he intended to do the rest of the summer, and told him to tell his Chief Joseph to come in to see me in two months. After this the Indian curled up under a tree and went to sleep.

Major Field had heard him say "What for you bring stranger here" and immediately he was all off again, thinking the Indians were in league against him. For several days again after this we saw nobody, and again he was becoming quiet, although he would frequently get up at night with his weapons and look around.

Arriving at our little station [Tanacross] on the Tanana River, I ordered the two men there to whipsaw some lumber and make a boat for us to descend the Tanana River. We then proceeded south through the Mentasta Pass to meet Captain Burnell's party who were packing supplies up from Copper Center to the southern end of the pass. About halfway through the pass, we met a mail carrier running up the trail, very much excited. I asked him what was the trouble, and he said he had wounded an old brown she-bear that had two cubs. She was in a patch of alders on the trail, and three times when he had gone near it, she had run after him, so he was afraid to go back there. He showed me the alders, near the base of a hill which had some large spruce trees on it. I rode up near the thicket, and could hear her growling and the cubs squeaking, quite plainly. Going back about two hundred yards, I dismounted from my horse, went up the hill and climbed a tree overlooking the thicket. I saw her at once, with the two cubs nearby, looking up the trail in the direction where she had heard me. One shot from my 30/30 through her heart sent her tumbling over.

I thought she was dead so I shouted to the mail carrier, and he advanced into the thicket cautiously, throwing rocks ahead of him as he went. There was no sound and from my perch I could see no movement from the bear. In three or four minutes he found her, poked her with a stick then called back to me that she was stone dead and did not need to be shot again. The cubs, which were quite large, had run away and we could neither catch nor kill them.

That night the Major and I camped on a small lake which was alive with large trout jumping out of it, steelheads I believe, weighing on an average of four to five pounds each. I had left what little fishing tackle I had back at the Tanana River, so had to improvise some. Some pieces of caribou sinew, out of an old snow shoe, made a fairly good line, and I twisted a piece of Number Fourteen telegraph wire into a hook. Then I shot a ground squirrel and fastened a piece of his tail to the hook for a fly. Cutting a piece of birch about eight feet long for a rod, I fastened it to the hook and line, about fifteen feet long. I didn't know whether I would be able to hold them with this equipment or not, but wading into the icy water up to my waist, I got one at the first cast, and succeeded in landing three before a big fellow took all the equipment away with him. Major Field enjoyed this performance very much. He had also enjoyed the bear episode, and had not suspected the mail carrier.

On the following day we met a large and well-appointed pack train with the supplies from Valdez. Captain Burnell had accompanied them and we conferred again about our plans for joint action. After their hard journey, the men were certainly a tough looking lot, in their buckskin clothes, leather chaps and long beards, their faces covered with running sores caused by mosquito bites. The mules and horses looked more like skeletons than the sleek animals one sees in the United States. I could see that Major Field was becoming very nervous again. He took me aside and said he thought we had better get away from that rough crowd as he feared he might be grabbed up by them at any moment, and away off here in the wilderness nobody would every know what had happened!

His was a peculiar mental condition. Normally he was an extremely brave and happy man, not at all afraid of dying or being killed, or of any sort of personal combat with another. I had heard and read of this sort of disease, but never before realized how terrible it could be.

We returned to the Tanana River station, where we found our boat completed, so we started down the river. For twelve days we travelled on, catching fish, both salmon and trout, and seeing many animals on the banks: bears, wolves, beaver, caribou, otter, and moose. We passed through Cathedral Rapids and on down the torrents through Bates Hundred-Mile-Long Rapids. These are really not rapids in the true sense of the word; they are so called merely from the extreme swiftness of the water. The Tanana River there spreads out over a great area. It is about 60 miles wide in places, and has an unusual drop, but the bottom is smooth everywhere, with no rocks, consequently rapids in the ordinary sense do not exist.

There are great piles of driftwood on the heads of the islands, under which the torrents roar. A slip of the oar or paddle might cause the boat to go under them and be lost for good. I purposely avoided seeing any Indians on this trip, because at the mouth of the Tanana we would run into another military garrison, and I thought it best to keep the Major from seeing anyone as long as possible. He had said not a word about his hallucinations during this stage of the trip, and I thought he might be over it.

When we arrived at Fort Gibbon[1] on the Tanana River, we looked pretty tough. Our clothes were in rags. I had lost my hat in the river and my head was shaggy. Our bearded faces were full of sores from mosquito bites, but we were as hard as rocks and tough as sinews, in fine physical condition. The exercise and fresh air had done Major Field a great deal of good.

Upon our arrival at Fort Gibbon, one of the officers began to jolly us about our appearance, and immediately Major Field was all off again. He took this as an indication that the officer was linked up with the gang who were after him. His fears redoubled, and they had to send him out of Alaska under guard. He was put in St. Elizabeth's Hospital in Washington D.C. Never have I been through a more harrowing experience; the fact that he was such a great friend of mine intensified everything. Fortunately, with a year of quiet and good care, he recovered his health, and was sent back to full duty with his organization. In due course he retired from the Army, and afterward became a professor in a large university.

Part of Fort Gibbon in July 1908. Large structure was the Signal Corps telegraph office and barracks building. Signalmen tended their garden in the foreground. The telegraph line had reached this post by November 1901.

COURTESY U.S. ARMY

---

[1] Near the site of the present community of Tanana.

11

MOOSE AND CARIBOU HUNTING

In a few days I took a steamer up the Yukon to Eagle City [505 miles] and found the telegraph line actually working through to the Tanana River. It was a great event, as it proved we could overcome the worst obstacles and succeed. On my trip down the Tanana I had located the mouth of the Good Pasture [Goodpaster] River. I was sure that it was better to go over that route from Eagle City to Fort Gibbon, than down the Yukon with all its bends, as it would save several hundred miles. Accordingly, I laid out the project for the following winter.

After everything was checked up, I took to the trail again and went into the Forty Mile country. On this trip, I camped overnight with three Irishmen, who were prospecting on one of the branches of the Middle Fork. They were hard workers, always at it from morning until night, and their prospects looked good. I went out and panned with them and got 25¢ to 30¢ worth of gold to the pan. They had cut sluices out of the frozen ground for quite a distance, through which the water flowed into a gravelly area where they had erected dump gates for ground sluicing.

In placer mining parlance, ground sluicing means throwing such a volume of water over a gravelly or sandy area that the great proportion of the gravel will be washed away down the stream. As gold is very heavy, it sinks and very little except the lightest of flake gold is carried away; so that if there is eight feet of gravel and you ground sluice it, you wash away all except two feet, and that two feet will have four times as much gold per cubic foot as the eight feet had. Consequently only one fourth as much gravel and dirt will have to be shoveled into the sluice boxes to get the same amount of gold. If the Irishmen sluiced their claim, they would get $1 or more to the pan.

Quite a little grass grew up the beautiful deep valley above their cabin. We hobbled our saddle horses and turned the mules loose to graze in it. I was riding Frank, the big bay. Next morning, we found our mules and my packer's horse, but Frank was nowhere to be found. After searching awhile, I struck his trail and followed it to the sluice ditch where the water was led to the dump gates. There it disappeared.

With a stick I poked into the opening and found that the warm water coming down had thawed out a great area underneath. Although the width of the opening was only two or three feet at the top, it widened out through the action of the water underneath to about eight feet, and was ten feet deep. Into this cavern the horse had fallen, and had hobbled down fifteen or twenty yards under the ground in his attempt to escape. The water at the bottom of this artificial cave was only two feet deep, hardly up to his knees.

Holding a candle through this hole, we could see Frank quite plainly. The question then was how to get him out. The propectors had some rope and a pulley. Getting picks and shovels, we made an aperture over the horse, constructed a sling out of moose hides, rigged up a jenny with the trunks of a few spruce trees, and the five of us lifted him to the surface and hauled him out, absolutely unhurt and ready to go ahead. This horse, one of the few survivors of the Castner Expedition mentioned before, seemed to bear a charmed life, never being hurt or frozen, although he was in some tight places in the North.

The next station at which I stopped was near the Mosquito Flats in the Ketchemstock country, where a Sergeant Record was in charge, with another man. He was a great talker, always telling some fanciful tale. The wolves in that vicinity, he told me, were large and terrible, most of them being black and white. As a matter of fact, there were a lot of wolves around there on account of the caribou herds, but some were grey and some black, and I did not believe he had encountered them. He was housed in a tent, around the bottom of which he had heaped up moss and dirt, but had neglected to build a wall of logs three or four feet high completely around it.

I camped a short distance up the stream from him and got a fine mess of grayling and trout beside my little camp. I asked the sergeant to come up and have breakfast with me, so that I could give him instructions about the work while my men put the aparejos on the mules and saddled the horses preparatory to starting. The sergeant showed up with a rifle in his hands, followed by another Signal Corps man. I gave them the necessary instructions and the sergeant, saying he had forgotten paper on which to write down the orders, started back to his tent. In a moment he came running back, terribly excited, saying he had found a large bear in his tent, so large that instead of going through the door it had just walked through the side of the tent.

Taking my rifle, I went to the tent which I saw had a large rip in one side. I could hear an animal in there, chewing something. Peering in, I saw a small cub eating a side of bacon. I opened the tent door and said "Boo" at him, whereupon he ran out the hole he had made in the tent and disappeared. He was so small I did not shoot him. By that time my packer, Sergeant Record and his companion had come to watch the proceedings, and the men gave him a hearty laugh over the large bear which had scared him so that he dropped his gun and ran away.

There was a great deal of game all through this area, and many fur bearing animals. On the Mosquito Flats there were ptarmigan, Canada blue grouse, spruce grouse, pinnated grouse, and what I took to be ruffed grouse. The grass was luxuriant. I believe that cattle could have wintered on it, as there were no blizzards, the winds were not very strong and they could get plenty of protection in the timber. It was a favorite locality for moose to make their yards in.

Moose "yard up" in the winter, a number of them getting together for mutual protection and warmth. I have seen as many as fourteen in one bunch. They choose a location with plenty of trees on which they can browse, then stamp down the snow, usually four or five feet deep, for a radius of one or two hundred yards, so they can walk around without sinking in snow. This makes the "yard." They stay here until spring when the snow thaws. Moose have sharp feet like deer and break through the crust on snow, when all they can do is flounder about helplessly. Caribou have big blunt feet which spread out when they begin to sink into snow, giving them a larger supporting surface. Thus they can get through practically any kind of snow without going belly deep in it.

The summer was drawing to a close and frost began to take hold of the vegetation and kill it. I had received many new mules and horses that summer from the bunch grass country in the state of Washington. These animals knew how to paw in the snow for their food and were very hardy, but the younger ones and those new to the North, the "cheechako" mules, had not yet learned how to browse on the boughs of trees or eat the bark the way that moose did.

Frost came earlier than usual that year and I was caught on the Tanana River with a full pack train of sixty-four head of mules and twelve horses, with the country pretty well frozen up and not enough oats to get back with. The men had fed [them] more than they were supposed to. If a horse or mule is hungry enough, he will eat anything, even raw meat. It is said that the Yaks in northern Asia feed their horses meat. I therefore took all the hardtack I could find and all the spare bacon and made up bannocks, or open fire bread, with whatever flour could be spared. With this bacon, bread and hardtack I hoped to get my mules back.

The mules and horses ate these things with relish and seemed to thrive on them, as much as any food. We found they would eat anything that had salt, grease or any kind of food rubbed into it. For instance, the rags we used for cleaning the dishes would be gobbled up at once by the mules, as well as leather shoes or gloves, even parts of clothing that had been soaked with perspiration.

For several days we got along pretty well, but as this food began to give out, the younger mules grew constantly weaker, as they would not eat the boughs and bark of the alders and willows. Each day two or three fell down exhausted, unable to move. We cached their aparejos, usually in trees, to protect them from the wolverines, then shot the mules. The wolves soon got on to this and followed close behind, waiting for the stragglers which they consumed in short order.

Our packmaster was a lean old frontiersman named Bradley, who had killed many buffaloes on the plains in the old days. One day, riding with him at the head of the pack train, we talked about arms and how each epoch required a new and more deadly weapon to kill the game.

"I remember when the Indians had to have a certain kind of long bow to kill the buffalo," he said, "and then a 50 calibre Sharps rifle. Then we had 45/90 Winchester repeaters. But nowadays we have to have 30/30 or 30/40 high powered rifles to kill anything." This was true, because the game constantly became more wary and a longer range gun was necessary.

We were traveling along a ridge about 2000 feet above the bed of Champion Creek. Suddenly we heard a peculiar bleat. Bradley said to me, "That is a moose in trouble." At the same instant, a large silver tip or grizzly bear ran out of some bushes across the ridge. I told Bradley to gallop down one side of the draw and I would go down the other, the pack train keeping straight on down the ridge. I did not see the bear again.

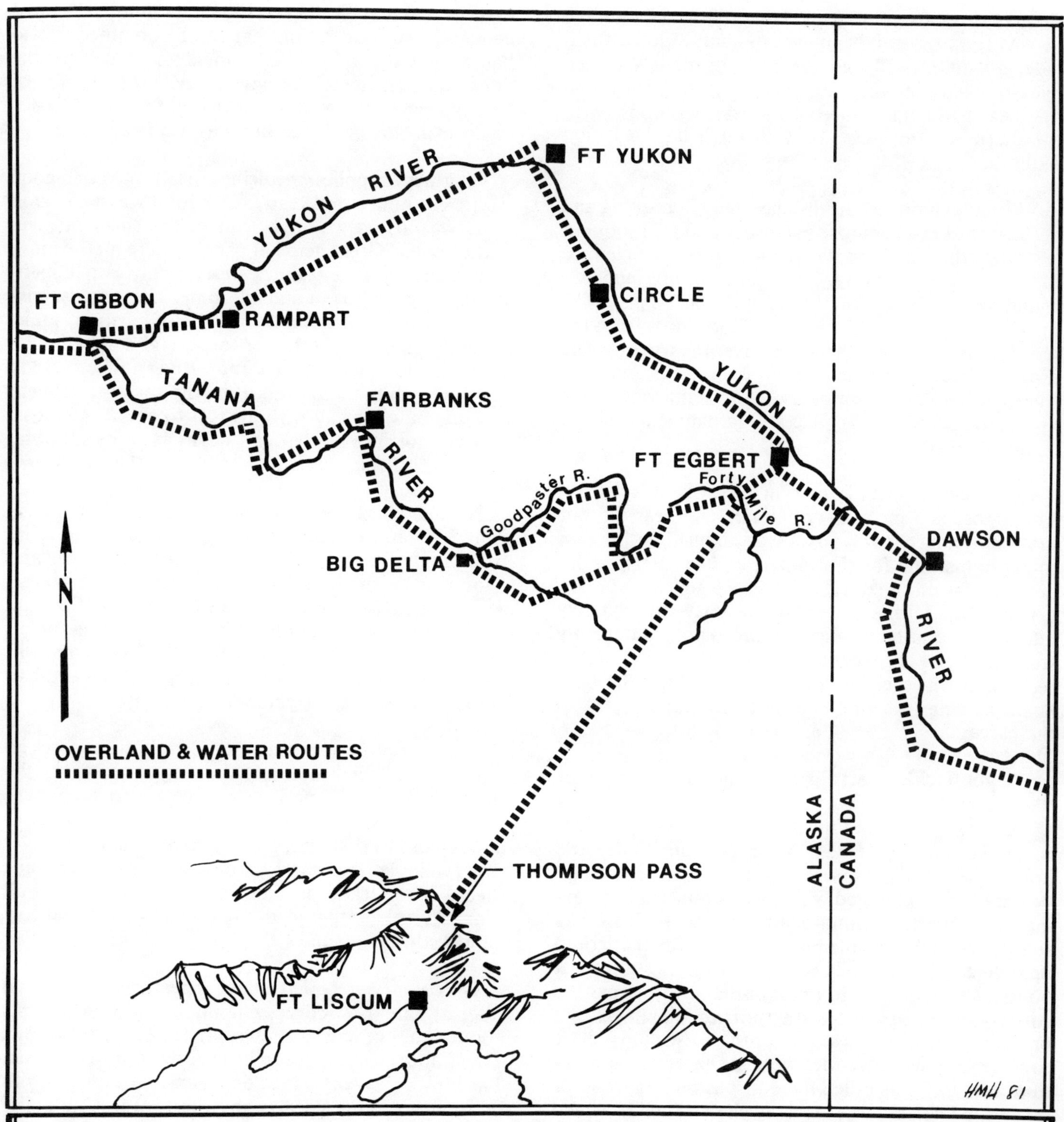

In addition to travelling the length of the Yukon River between Whitehorse, Yukon Territory, and the sea, Mitchell went on these routes cross-country and on river ice by dog team in winter, and by packtrain, raft, and boat in summer on the military telegraph project. He travelled the Goodpaster River and Fortymile River several times, and back-tracked on some exploratory routes.

Bradley caught sight of him about 200 yards off when he was coming straight toward me and began a fusillade, but he missed and the bear escaped. We then back-tracked him and came to the alders from which the bleat had come. There lay a yearling moose with the marks of the bear's bite through his back and kidneys.

We made camp a short distance away at a spring and decided to skin the moose and use his meat. I thought it strange that the bites we saw would be sufficient to kill the moose instantly, but upon skinning him, we found the imprint of four blows of the bear's paw. The underside of the skin showed the blood clots from the terrific punches given the moose over the withers. The dorsal processes that extend up from the spine were smashed flat and the spine itself and spinal cord were broken through in three places. Death must have been instantaneous.

I had never heard of an occurrence like this before. The moose is a most wary animal. The bear did not look particularly lively, as it was about time for him to get in his hole for the winter, and he certainly did not want the moose to eat, as there were plenty of cranberries around. I figured that he must have run squarely into him, and when the moose jumped up, undoubtedly startled, the bear gave him the trip hammer blows that set him down, then bit him. I do not think the bear heard us when we first saw him running away from the carcass.

We got back to Fort Egbert in the first snowfall of the season, the latter part of October [1902]. Another winter was upon us but this time we were well prepared for it. We had made new harness for our mules and horses, new sleds, horse shoes with corks that could be removed or changed with a wrench instead of having to reshoe the animal entirely to make his corks sharp. We had portable blacksmith outfits that could be pulled over the trails on sleds. We had stations at intervals of from ten to twenty miles clear across the country, each with its telegraph office, a built-up tent or cabin for the men, a stable for the horses and a place to store supplies. Two men were in charge of each station. Material was billed there just as on a railroad or steamship line, and was regularly checked and receipted for by the station keeper and passed on to the next.

The arrival and departure of each sled train was reported by telegraph to headquarters. Our great problem was still transportation. I still had to work five hundred miles away from my base.

During the summer, we had put up our own salmon for the dogs. Three of our men had fished for salmon all during the run, with nets they made themselves, then had dried and smoked it. For my own dog teams, I had them save the bellies of the king salmon, the most concentrated food ration that can be obtained. I also had procured good rice, corn meal and bacon for the dogs, and some excellent hay and oats for the horses, having learned the winter before that the use of barley or corn in this cold weather was a mistake.

Veterinary supplies, medicines for the men and good Arctic clothing stood ready. Our food was very good but I was afraid we might run a little short of meat in the winter. Great herds of caribou were on the move and when they were at the nearest point to Fort Egbert, I determined to go out and kill some. These herds, containing thousands upon thousands of caribou, make a regular migration each year for several hundred miles between the Tanana and Yukon Rivers. The caribou eats only white moss, and after the snow has fallen, he must paw it away with his feet to get at the moss. He does not shovel it with his horns as many suppose. Consequently he goes wherever there is the least snow.

The main herd always crossed on a ridge connecting American and Champion Creeks, about forty miles from Eagle City, to which we now made our way and established a small camp. I had a couple of packers, a cook and two splendid hunters, Frank Lee and George Webb. Captain Perkins, commanding the infantry garrison, had come with me at my invitation. He was an excellent shot on the target range and had killed a good deal of game in the West.

Our method of hunting the caribou was to go mounted to a high point of the ridge and survey the surrounding country until we spotted a herd, then make a circle to get down wind from them, gradually working as close to them as possible, using whatever cover was available. A herd of caribou act a great deal like sheep. If the leader is shot down, they begin to mill around until another leader takes charge. An old cow almost always assumes the lead in a crisis.

The country presented a bold appearance, ridge upon ridge of bare snow-covered mountains with their crests about two thousand feet above the stream lines below. The timber came up just a little above the stream line. The hills were well washed down and we could go with our horses or mules nearly anywhere, at fast gaits. We filled their feet with grease to keep the snow from balling in them.

On the first day at camp, I took a good look from the ridges and found no tracks of caribou, although I was sure they must be in the vicinity. On the second day, I went over the ridge as soon as I could see in the morning, and up at the head of the gulch I saw a herd of about twenty animals in repose, some lying down, some standing and pawing snow to get at the moss. At that time of the year, all the caribou, bulls, cows and calves, carry horns, and the herd presents an interesting appearance when running. Looking for them over a snowy ridge, the first thing one sees is just a lot of horns moving along, all intermingled, jumping up and crossing one another, looking like snakes winding and unwinding. I came back to camp, told Capt. Perkins, Lee and Webb, and we all returned to the ridge.

I showed them where the caribou were and then I tested for wind, first by wetting my finger and holding it up, then by throwing the dry snow up in the air. It fell back exactly where I had thrown it, which showed there was no wind where we were. I stationed Captain Perkins with Webb at a point where several ridges came together, where the caribou, if startled, would almost certainly pass. It was Captain Perkins' first trip into the interior and I didn't like to leave him alone, as it is very easy to get lost in that country.

I sent Lee, mounted on a wonderful roan saddle mule named "Beauty" toward the caribou behind one ridge, while I, mounted on "Nigger," went up behind the ridge opposite. Lee had a 30/40 Winchester rifle I had given him, from which the back sights had been knocked off, while I carried a 30/30 carbine. Each of us carried about 150 rounds of ammunition. Lee wore a mackinaw, a fur hat and mittens. As I worked up the ridge, I found that the wind was blowing from the caribou to me but that soon they would get Lee's wind and begin to move.

After a couple of miles, I looked from the top of a ridge and saw a herd of caribou running straight toward me. Jumping off my horse and throwing the reins to the ground, I knelt down and waited for them to come. The leader, a young bull with beautiful horns, was only thirty feet away before he saw me. I killed him at the first shot and the herd began to mill. I fired as rapidly as possible and loaded the carbine three times. When the melee was over, eight caribou lay dead on the snow within an area of a hundred and fifty yards, and blood trails showed that I had crippled two others, which I would follow up in a little while.

I looked across the valley to the other ridge upon which Lee was supposed to be but nowhere could I find him. The atmosphere was absolutely clear, and the distance across about 1000 or 1200 yards. As I was going up the ridge, I suddenly saw a column of caribou descending the other side, toward the creek, in my direction. If they kept on they would surely see me and avoid me, because I was on an open sidehill with a snow background. I could not gallop fast enough through the snow to turn them, and if they got in the valley line instead of staying on the ridge, they would miss Captain Perkins who was posted down below. One caribou came on, two, three, four, six, ten, until I had counted over seventy, led by an old cow. Just then, Lee appeared on the crest of the ridge about half a mile from them. I could see every detail of his clothing, equipment, and the mule "Beauty" whose ears seemed half as long as her body.

I waved frantically but got no response. I fired at the caribou to try and turn them back toward Lee, but still they came on. Then I galloped my horse back and forth against the white background to attract Lee's attention, but with no success. Keeping up the firing, running and yelling, I at last got the caribou turned. They came down to the turning point and rounded the bend, all following the cow in a very leisurely manner.

To signal Lee, I took off my parka and dark blue flannel shirt, and getting into a position with the snow as a background, I waved them vigorously in the direction of the caribou. Lee instantly got this signal and galloped down the ridge. Beauty's stomach almost seemed to touch the ground, so fast did she run. The undulations on top of the ridge kept Lee from seeing the caribou or the caribou from seeing him. Gradually each approached the other and I saw they would meet. As Lee came over the crest, there were two hundred caribou directly in front of him, only ten or fifteen yards away. The mule stopped in her tracks, squatted back on her haunches and her ears shot up. Lee leaped from the saddle and it seemed to me started shooting before he hit the ground. The old cow in the lead went down in a heap and then one after another were shot down as they attempted to take the lead. I never saw such marksmanship in my life. If only a moving picture could have been taken, it would have been wonderful. Beauty, her reins on the ground stood motionless, ears erect, watching everything.

Enthralled by the spectacle, I had almost forgotten about Captain Perkins, but I knew the balance of the herd would run down near his position. I galloped in his direction, and reached there with my horse blown, expecting any moment to see the caribou. He had not heard a single shot and had been walking up and down at his station, thinking himself entirely forgotten. He was using a Krag 30/40 army rifle, which he had used on targets at the rifle range to keep his hand in. While I was telling him about the caribou, we heard a clatter to our left. It was the unmistakable sound of the herd as their feet hit the rocks and their hoofs knocked together. In a moment we could see the tops of their horns. Perkins was completely unnerved. It was his turn to shoot and Webb and myself held our rifles across our arms. On they came, like a moving forest of horns, hardly a body yet in sight. They began passing in front of us at a range of about thirty yards, and Perkins began firing. Bang! Bang! Bang! went his rifle, but not a caribou fell. He loaded again and emptied the magazine, and still not one was touched. When they were about four hundred yards away, Perkins killed with a single shot one of the biggest bulls I have ever seen, a tremendous animal, with which he was very much pleased.

We then mounted our horses and went up the ridge to where I had left Lee. he was busy cutting the throats of some of the caribou he had killed. Twenty-nine lay dead on the ground and a few cripples had gone in various directions. I sent for the two packers to come up and pile the caribou in a heap, as I feared the wolves would get at them. The rest of the day was occupied in killing a few more, so that night we had about fifty caribou for our day's work.

The next day we killed about twenty more, which was plenty, and then I gave a day to the ptarmigan, killing about 400. I brought a pack train out from Eagle City and got all the caribou safely cached at a point where we could distribute them along the trail to our stations. They were now frozen hard and would remain frozen and perfectly fresh until the following May. The men liked the caribou meat much better than moose, beef or wild sheep, and could never get too much of it.

Captain Perkins had fixed up a sort of cold storage house for game near his quarters, and it really looked like a museum. There were various kinds of fish, salmon, and trout. There were ducks, swans and geese. There were caribou, moose, and sheep, all in prime condition and sufficient to last him all winter.

Clearing the telegraph line right-of-way along the Yukon, 1901.

COURTESY U.S. ARMY, NATIONAL ARCHIVES, 111-RB-2726

DOGSLED RECONNAISSANCE IN THE FORTYMILE DISTRICT 12

Toward the middle of November [1902] we had a hard freeze, the temperature falling below thirty [below zero]. If it is much warmer than 30 below, the warm springs keep breaking through the snow and ice, making travel difficult and dangerous. I decided to make a reconnoitering trip, to see if the country was sufficiently frozen to begin our sledding operations. I took along Arnold De Heus, a Dutchman who had been in South Africa in the Boer Republic. He had come from a family of bakers in the old country and was a fine cook and an expert at making bread. No truer, finer man ever lived than old Dutch. He was always with me on every trip after that, whether it was on horseback, with dogs or in boats.

We were going up American Creek, with the dogs almost wild, being fresh from their summer's rest. They kept sighting numerous snowshoe rabbits all along the creek. The trail here had already been broken by some miners who lived further up, and the snow was about three feet thick. As we rounded a bend about fifteen miles from Eagle, my leader, Pointer, suddenly stopped in the trail and the team piled on top of him. I yelled at him to go ahead. He answered by putting his tail between his legs and looking off the trail to the right. I glanced over there, but could see nothing except a high cut bank and some spruce trees. Again I commanded him to go ahead, and again the same action. I knew that something must be wrong but could not guess what it was. I went up to him, snapped off his traces and looped them over his back, then told him to go ahead.

He jumped on his belly in the snow and tried to waddle up toward the top of the bank. Then I knew there was something over there. Calling to Dutch to get his snowshoes and follow me to the top of the bank, then watch the dog teams from there, I put on my own snowshoes and followed Pointer. At the top of the bank I looked over and saw a miner's cabin, about seventy yards off. A little distance from it was a small dump of dirt, beside a hole with a winch over it, from which smoke was rising. It was the custom for miners to get out a dump in the winter, to be washed out in the spring, and nothing looked unusual. The dog, however, kept making frantic leaps through the deep snow in that direction. The trail from the cabin led out in another way. I would have turned around and gone back to my sleds if it had not been for the insistence of Pointer in propelling me toward the cabin, which I now recognized as belonging to Jack Cavanaugh, a miner.

I made haste over there and rapped at the door but got no answer. Opening the door, I found the cabin empty. I turned and went along his trail to the hole, and looking down it about nine feet, I saw Jack Cavanaugh's body lying across the logs with a fire burning beneath! The fire was beginning to eat up toward him, although it had not yet made much headway. Shouting to Dutch to come quickly, I jumped down into the hole, unhooked the bucket from its rope which I tied around Jack's body, under his arms. I pushed and Dutch worked the winch until we got him out.

He came to almost immediately, apparently not hurt except for a bad welt over the left temple. The dump had been dug out the day before, he told us, then he had laid his logs for the fire in the bottom of the hole. Lighting it, he came up the ladder, and near the top he must have slipped and fallen back on his head, on top of the fire, because in no other way could he account for the welt on his head, and his being where we found him.

It is incomprehensible to me how the dog sensed that something was wrong. It was entirely due to his animal instinct that we saved Cavanaugh's life. Time and again Pointer did things almost as remarkable as this.

Returning to the sleds, we continued on our way and made camp at the top of the ridge, about thirty-five miles away. From there we had to break the trail on the other side of the ridge down Champion Creek. We made slow progress and only about twenty miles were covered that day, because we had to hitch both teams together while I broke trail ahead, with Pointer loose leading behind me, and Dutch handling the sleighs.

I had noticed a good many moose tracks in that vicinity, so I went out to find one. Working up the timber line in the head of a draw, I ran into a very large bull and killed him on my third shot, each bullet having taken effect. It was more of a job to get him out than we thought, and I was anxious to keep his head and horns. We debated for some time about what to do, because the wolverines would get them unless we built a strong cache of spruce timber, which we did not have time to do. It was Dutch's suggestion that we take one of our sled ropes, tie it around the head and horns and throw the end of it over the projecting limb of a spruce tree that overhung a high bank, letting the horns hang down about six feet from the limb, which would put them about twenty feet above the ground. There it would be impossible for wolverines to reach them, either from the limb or by jumping up from the ground. This looked good to me, so we did it. We then cut out the ham, loin and forequarters, tied them up in the hide and pulled this back to our sleds.

A month later when I came back to look for these horns, I found that the rascally wolverines had bitten the rope off the limb and let the head and horns drop. They had eaten all the skin and flesh from the head and gnawed a good deal of the bone, but fortunately had not hurt the horns, which I still have.

In a few days we had a spell of weather fifty below and the country froze absolutely tight. Returning quickly to Fort Egbert, I set our organization in motion. A sled train for each station went out loaded, and by the middle of December (1902) our transportation system had been extended to the head of the Good Pasture River, a distance of one hundred and fifty miles from Fort Egbert, and a great cache of supplies made at that place.

No white man had ever been down the Good Pasture River[1] and few Indians in our vicinity knew anything about it, because the Middlefork Indians' domain stopped at the divide on the head of the river and the Good Pasture Indians, who live on the Tanana, did not come over on the north side of the divide. I had consulted several times with Chief Joseph of the Middlefork tribe about the trip I proposed to make down this river. I wanted him to accompany Dutch and myself, to help break the trail down there. He always said it was a terrible trip, and it was a tradition among his people that anybody who went down it in wintertime never came back, if they met the Good Pasture Indians.

These Indians were very bad, he explained. If they looked at you intently, they made you sick. They stole everything they could from graves, thereby being just about as bad Indians as could exist. I assured him that I could protect him against these things, that he need not worry because I had fine dogs, good toboggans which we would use in the snowshoe trails, good rifles and snowshoes, and the best of food in the north. Although I always rewarded this Indian liberally, I never agreed beforehand to pay him a thing for any of the trips on which he came. We had become great friends, having hunted and fished a great deal together, and for that reason he agreed to go with me.

Just before Christmas [1902] I made a trip with Dutch to my various stations to see how things were going, and to make sure the men were well taken care of and would have whatever we could give them for Christmas. My dog teams were in marvelous condition. The harnesses were beautifully made, each collar fitting the dogs perfectly. On the back bands, each dog carried four bells, and each dog's bell was in a different key, so as to make a harmonious jingle. Each animal had a pompom over his collar, of orange, red and green wool. Eight dogs constituted my team, with Pointer in the lead, then two brothers, big white McKenzie huskies; then another, named Hunter; then two tremendous animals, reddish in color, called Fox and Prince; then a light gray dog called Rover, while next to the sled was King, a splendid wheel dog who knew how to pull a sled back when it left the trail.

Dutch's team consisted of seven dogs, with "Whiskey" as the leader, then three brothers, followed by two other brothers that we called the "Two Savages," so wild they were when we first got them from the Kobuck [Kobuk] Indians, while on the wheel he had "Moose," the "half-bear." We had had to cut his fangs also to prevent his tearing up the other dogs. The back band of Dutch's dogs had bells all an octave lower than mine, while his pompoms were red and green wool.

We had a wonderful horse trail made across the country and with our sleds light, we went along at a great rate, often at a dead gallop. I was crossing the Forty Mile River on the way back, when I looked down the trail and saw a lone figure running with a springy step toward me and waving his hand. I brought the dogs to a halt, and he handed me a letter from the commander of the Mounted Police in Dawson, asking me to come there and spend Christmas with them. This man had run a hundred and twenty miles in two days and did not seem to be particularly tired. He was half Indian and half French-Canadian. I told him to go a couple of miles to our next station and take a rest, and gave him a note to the station keeper to look after him.

[1] However, according to the *Fairbanks Daily Times* of July 1 and August 28, 1906, at least two men, C.H. Hamilton and the Reverend Prevost, had gone up the Goodpaster in 1892.

We had to travel hard to get to Dawson in two days. Turning my teams in the trail, I made for the metropolis of the north. The dogs seemed to know that they were on the way to holiday and a rest. We jingled down the Forty Mile with our bells echoing from the hills on either side. That night we reached the little town of Forty Mile and stayed at the roadhouse, setting off early next morning for Dawson, after getting the telegraph operator to wire that we were on our way and should arrive about 4 p.m. Christmas Eve.

The Yukon River trail was rough in spots but we made good time. The winter trail along a large river follows the smooth ice as far as possible. On each side, broken fragments and high ridges of ice were heaped up where the water had pressed them aside before they froze solid. Behind them, the high and precipitous river banks thrust upward, heightening the boldness and grandeur of the scene. In some places, the ice had no snow on it and the wind whistled over the frozen surface with biting fierceness. That is where we appreciated our parkas of striped bed ticking (this breaks the wind) with hoods lined with wolverine tails, which had hair about eight inches long sticking out in front to protect the face. Inside that was an inner lining of marten skin, soft against our faces, and beneath our chins was a patch of wolf skin, because the ice from the breath did not stick to this as easily as to other furs.

Our caps were of marten skins with two or three tails pendant from the top. These caps extended over the cheeks, under the chin and well down on the back of the neck. They could be folded and tied back when desired. Over the forehead was a patch of marten skin but the back part was of woolen cloth with a silk lining. Fur is so impermeable to moisture that if the head becomes unduly heated and perspires in a fur cap while one is mushing, it is liable to freeze quickly afterward.

We wore great moosehide mittens, encrusted with beads and fringe and lined with soft wool, with white rabbit around the top. Our moccasins, made by Chief Joseph's squaw, were beautifully beaded and reached halfway to the knee. We wore fleece-lined underwear, shirts and trousers of pure wool and outer trousers of blue denim to break the wind. This outfit was warm and light, and ideal for rapid work along the trails. The minute we stopped, heavier clothing had to be put on.

About three o'clock in the afternoon, the dogs showed that they smelled the town lying around the bend of the river ahead of us. As we rounded the point about five miles from Dawson, we could see the city and the dogs redoubled their efforts to get there. We went straight down the main street at a hard gallop, our bells jingling merrily.

The Christmases at Dawson were renowned all over the Northland, and we had nothing but our trail clothes for this great occasion. I put up with Captain Cosby of the Mounted Police, one of the finest fellows I ever knew, while Dutch went with the non-commissioned officers, and our dogs were carefully housed in a section of the Mounted Police dog corral where they could not fight the other dogs or be hurt themselves. Our teams were the envy of all the dog mushers in Dawson who gathered to inspect them.

The parties given by the various prosperous citizens were endless and all very well done. The ladies had as fine Paris gowns as could be found anywhere, and wore wonderful jewels. At one dinner, we ate raw oysters on the half shell, that cost $1.00 apiece to get in. I learned afterward that the shells had been brought in separately and the oysters put on them, but they were very good indeed.

Most of the music consisted of fiddles, played by musicians who knew all the old time dances. There were some accordions, guitars, and mandolins, and a few upright pianos.

On Christmas Eve, the Mounted Police gave a great ball. All turned out in their full dress uniforms. As I had none with me, I wore one of Cosby's, who was a Mounted Police Captain, red coat and everything else, and had just as much fun as if it had been my own.

We stayed with them seven days, which was plenty long enough. Had we remained longer and accepted the lavish hospitality extended to us, both the dogs and ourselves would have lost our "trail condition."

The temperature had been falling constantly, and when we left Dawson on January 2nd [1903], the thermometer registered 62° below zero. In weather as cold as that, when one exhales the breath, the moisture congeals instantly and a distinct pop can be heard. It is practically impossible for wind to blow at this temperature. If it did, wherever it struck you, it would freeze you just the way a hot iron burns you.

Having a long nose which protruded whenever it had a chance and was constantly being frozen on the end, I hit upon the scheme of putting a little piece of snowshoe rabbit fur on it, the hairs of which stick out about an inch and a half. The moisture from my face held it there.

Ice formed all over our parka hoods from the moisture of our breath and had to be knocked off every little while. Long beards and mustaches become instantly caked with ice, and are not only an inconvenience but a menace as they might freeze one's face. That is why men in the North shave clean in winter, after having let their beards grow long in the summer to keep the mosquitoes off.

Smoking pipes froze up even when they were in one's pocket and would have to be thawed out by a fire. If a person smoking a cigar or cigarette removed it from his mouth an instant, it became a cake of ice where it had touched his lips. If the hands and feet were at all constricted by tight mittens or moccasins, they would freeze immediately. When a person gets into a condition to freeze, life will leave him and he will become as hard as a cake of ice in a couple of minutes.

One often hears inexperienced men say that after it gets below 40° below zero, a further drop does not make much difference. This is not so. 40° below is not particularly cold, or even 45°, but for every degree below 50°, the intensity of the cold seems to double.

In spite of the intense cold, we made excellent time, going by way of Forty Mile, and in three days I reached the head of the Middlefork River and scaled the high divide where I had ordered a cache of supplies to be made. Here I was met by Chief Joseph of the Middlefork Indians. He had brought an excellent outfit with him, good snowshoes, caribou skin clothing, and a 30/30 carbine. He seemed quite melancholy, however, and told me that he might never see his own people again as he was going with me into the country of the bad Indians. Although I did not expect to encounter any very unusual conditions, I knew that a long snowshoe trip with the temperature below 60° was a serious thing, particularly if we ran into any warm springs and broke through the ice. The temperature had been falling steadily. It was now under 70° below zero.

In two days we had prepared everything for the trip down the Good Pasture River. We had to change from our sleds to toboggans, which had been made for us by Chief Joseph's tribe. These toboggans were constructed of willow wood and sewn together with moosehide thongs. The baskets on them were of moosehide, sewn over three times along the seams and made waterproof. Into these we put our sled mantles of canvas and warped them down inside the baskets with moose hide thongs. These toboggans are quite limber and fit themselves to the inequalities of the ground. In this way they do not fetch up as hard a bump when they hit an obstruction as would a stiff vehicle, and are much easier to pull down the trail. Toboggans are used on a snowshoe trail, too, because they fit right into the boxlike path that has been stamped down by the snoeshoes, and do not require the handling that a sled does.

On top of our toboggans were two double-bitted axes and two extra ax halves, together with our rifles in buckskin cases, several candles, oil rags, a bottle of kerosene, both ordinary matches and wind matches, and flint and steel, so that in case our things became wet, we had several chances of making a fire. The oily rags and candles, when lighted, gave enough heat to keep a man's hands warm. If the hands did freeze, it was pretty nearly all off, especially if one were alone.

Each of us had two pairs of snowshoes, one large pair to use for going ahead, and a small pair to stamp the trail down immediately behind the big ones, or for running on a trail already broken but still soft. We used the large ones when we hunted, or went anywhere off the trail. They were made by the Cook's [Cook] Inlet Indians, who made the best snowshoes in the North. The small ones were made by our local Indians. They had been very carefully selected and the apertures and thongs exactly fitted our feet.

In addition to our dog whips, which were about 20 feet long, we carried staffs, eight feet long, that were shod with iron, with which to feel our way on bad trails, or to steady and assist ourselves while snowshoeing. Our method of progress was this: I took the lead in the morning, followed by the Indian, with Dutch bringing up in the rear behind the two dog teams. In the afternoon, the Indian took the lead and Dutch went behind him in trail snowshoes, while I watched the dog teams. We did it this way because the Indian could not handle the dogs, and although he had never been down the Good Pasture River before, he had heard about it and was quite conversant with its general characteristics.

Mitchell's Model 1894 Winchester carbine.

COURTESY SMITHSONIAN INSTITUTION MUSEUM OF HISTORY AND TECHNOLOGY, C.R. GOINS

DEADLY COLD AND STARVATION 13
ON THE GOODPASTER

We found the Good Pasture to be a beautiful stream, gradually broadening out between washed down hills, with excellent timber. We threaded our way through groves of spruce trees, birches and alders, and as we descended the river course, we began to get more and more into the bed of the stream.

The terrible cold continued, constantly around [minus] seventy. The wise husky dogs would stop every little while and bite the snow out of their feet to keep them from freezing. A snowshoe trail in cold weather is extremely hard on dogs, because even after it has been broken, in about four feet of snow, the dogs go in almost up to the bellies. As their feet go down through the snow, their toes spread out, with the web and hairs projecting so as to offer the greatest surface possible. The snow sticks to the hair between the toes and in a little while it is a good deal the same as marbles between them. An outside dog, not familiar with these conditions, will have his feet frozen in no time.

We made about fifteen miles a day, which we considered good as the snow was quite deep compared to the Yukon. Apparently the Good Pasture River country was warmer in the fall than the Yukon country, consequently had more snow. As soon as the trail had been broken, it froze right up the first night and was hard the following day. If it were not drifted by snow, it could be travelled without snowshoes, and dogs and men could run along it without sinking.

I had cut down the weight of my supplies to the lowest possible point. We figured on using the same diet as the dogs most of the time, that is, king salmon, rice and bacon. I also had a good store of my specially prepared beans, some tea and flour, with a little "sourdough"[1] for leaven. Old Dutch was wonderful at baking fine bread before an open fire. I have never tasted better. In the evening he mixed up the batter, leavening it with sourdough, put a little wind break behind his pan, which rested on balsam boughs and arranged the embers so it would give just enough heat to cause it to rise during the night. In the morning early he began baking by placing the dough in a frying pan and holding it up toward the embers until it became hard enough on one side to be turned over. He then turned it and got it hard on the other side. Then removing it from the frying pan, he propped it up with a little stick, so that it stood up in front of the fire. He usually made from four to six loaves, and for an hour or so would keep turning them around so as to bake them through. Each of us had a frying pan to eat out of, a tin cup, a spoon and fork, and our hunting knives.

I carried a little silk tent, 9' × 9', that weighed about nine pounds. There was a rope sewn in the top which we could tie between two trees, or if they could not be found, we cut two saplings, crossed them and swung the tent across the top of these. Our beds were balsam boughs about a foot deep, and on these we laid our wolfskin robes, lined with canvas. Each of us had a caribou hide suit, consisting of trousers and coat with beaver collar, which we put on at night. Sleeping bags would have done us no good at these temperatures, because these bags retain the moisture exuded from the body during sleep, freeze up and become almost useless.

As we exhaled our breaths, they would rise until they hit the top of the tent, and freeze. In the morning when we woke, before we stirred much, the tent would be ornamented with festoons of our frozen breath, hanging down like beautiful lace curtains.

I had a small light Yukon stove, especially made for this trip, that took wood about twelve inches long. We did not use it on the trail, however, but instead employed a long fire with good big back logs to reflect the heat in our direction.

[1] Sourdough is a fermented leavening of flour, water, sugar, and yeast. A small amount is carried on a journey (or a jar or crock of it is kept in reserve in one's cabin) to mix with a batter when making bread or hot cakes. A "Sourdough" is a long-time Alaskan or Canadian, particularly one living much in the open such as a trapper or prospector.

Our procedure was the same every morning. I roused the men, the Indian built the fire and Dutch cooked breakfast. I laid out the harness ahead of the toboggans, which had been placed under the sled mantles at night for protection from frost, and inspected all the dogs, examining their feet and shoulders, looking into their eyes, because dogs sometimes go snow blind. If it was necessary to put a moccasin on a dog, I adjusted it and made it to fit the particular animal. We only fed the dogs once a day, which was in the evening. After we had breakfast, Dutch put all the food away in the grub bags in his sled and tied down the mantle, while the Indian packed up the tent and folded up the bedding, which he put in my sled.

Dutch and I, standing in front of our respective sleds, called the dogs, who ran up and stood opposite their harnesses. We slipped the collars over their heads and adjusted the back bands. Some of the dogs almost harnessed themselves, but it took a lot of training, patience and severity with these fierce northern dogs to bring them to this stage.

In the evening, I gave the word when it came time to camp. The Indian, who was in the lead then, would look for a suitable place. After locating a dead spruce, which could usually be found within a short distance, we established camp at a convenient spot nearby, the Indian chopping down the tree and making the fire. Then felling a green spruce tree, he stripped off the limbs and made a bed for the tent, comparatively close to the fire.

Dutch got out the grub bags and cooked dinner, while I unharnessed the dogs, cut up their food and cooked it in the two large dog kettles, while they stood around and watched. I then spread out the pans in a double row, two feet apart and four feet between the rows. We made the dogs range themselves in the same way that they pulled in the harness. I stood at the head of the two rows, whip in hand, while Dutch distributed the food to each pan. No dog was allowed to touch his food until all was ready. They made a wild and savage picture in the semi-darkness of the evening, amid the snow and ice, against a background of dark spruces. Poised and tense by their dishes, they licked their chops eagerly as the savory odors arose. When I gave the signal "Eat!" they jumped to the pans and gobbled down the food as fast as possible. If one finished ahead of the others, he might feel tempted to take another dog's food. This would have resulted in bad fights which might have crippled them. Our dogs knew they would get a terrible cut from my long whip if they tried this, so as soon as they finished eating, they chose suitable places to sleep, under a bush, bank, rock or anything that afforded protection. They would turn around in small circles, gradually getting lower and lower, until they made a real nest for themselves, and curled up to sleep with their noses resting on their haunches. In the morning they might be entirely covered with snow, but they would be warm as toast.

By this system, we made and broke camp with great swiftness, only a few minutes being required for the whole thing.

On our fifth day out we ran across a trail which Joe at once pronounced to be an Indian trail, made by one of his tribe, he thought, who had left his own country and gone into the forbidden territory because it was so rich in furs. The trail went ahead on down the river. Soon we saw the smoke of a fire rising through the spruce trees, and getting closer, saw an Indian wickiup, a lodge built something in the form of a beehive, covered with bark and spruce boughs.

"Him David house. I guess he die," said Joe, meaning that the lodge belonged to a man of his tribe named David who was probably starving to death.

Leaving Dutch with the dogs, Joe and I went to the wickiup and looked in. There sat David with his head in his hands, emaciated and pale. Three children, practically unable to move, were on the other side of him, while his squaw was just able to put wood on the fire. Three dogs were in the lodge, two of them hardly able to move, but one came toward the door to try to attack us. He was so weak he fell into the fire on the way and had to be pulled out.

Joe talked to David and elicited the information that David had come across with his family at the first snow. It had grown cold so quickly that he was unable to get sufficient caribou meat to last him through the winter. The snow was so light that the game ran right through it, but it offered the maximum impediment to snowshoes. He had only killed a couple of caribou since the middle of November, and for over a month they had subsisted on the moosehide contained in their moccasins and the sinews out of their snowshoes, had eaten one dog and were about to eat the others. All these Indians seemed perfectly numb, mentally and physically, so exhausted were they. A white man under the same conditions would have frozen and died long before.

Indians are peculiarly constituted. Beyond a certain point they have tremendous powers of vitality and resistance, if they do not have to exert themselves physically to a great extent. At any great physical exertion they are very good for a few days but then they begin to get tired, and do not come back as quickly as a white man. I think this is due to the superior foods and better nutrition of the whites.

We had been hitting a terrific gait along the trail. Dutch was getting tired but the Indian Joe was becoming much more so, although neither of them said anything about it. When a person gets tired in this terrible cold, he feels it more intensely and consequently freezes more quickly. I therefore decided to give them a day's rest and at the same time try to help out this Indian family and save them if possible. If I split my own meager store of provisions with them at that time, they would eat everything up in a few days; so I gave them only meals that we cooked ourselves during the day we were there, and left them only sufficient food to last for ten days by which time I expected to return.

Naturally this was cutting down our own supply pretty low, but I knew I could get to the mouth of the Good Pasture River in four or five days more, and I expected the Indians there to have some dried salmon left, and possibly some game. We chopped an additional store of wood for David's family and fixed up his lodge. The effect of a little food on the dogs was even more marked than on the Indians.

The day's rest had stiffened up both Joe and Dutch, who showed increasing signs of fatigue. Dutch kept lagging behind when I was snowshoeing in front, so that I went back before my turn and sent him forward where I could watch him. When cold begins to seize people, they become very pleasant, and everything seems rosy to them. They want to lie down and take it easy, and when they do, of course they freeze to death in a couple of minutes.

The second day out from the starving Indians, we started in as usual, but after an hour's mushing down the difficult snowshoe trail, Dutch began to lag behind worse than ever. As we rounded a turn in the river, I looked back and did not see him. I could tell by the action of the Indian that he was worried. A little way down the stream we saw a dry spruce tree, sticking over the bank above the ice. I told Joe to go down there and make a fire instantly while I ran back on my snowshoes to look for Dutch. I found him about 150 yards back, lying on his back in the snow. I spoke to him, asking him why he had not kept up. Dutch was one of the best natured fellows in the world anyway, and he answered that he was so tired, he had to lie down and take a rest, and he didn't believe it was possible for him to move, that he was perfectly comfortable there in the snow.

It was a typical example of the stage where circulation begins to slow up, preparatory to freezing. I jumped squarely on his face with both my snowshoes and wiggled them around, then jumped on his chest and kicked him in the stomach, all the time abusing him verbally, trying to make him get up and fight me. At last I got him on his feet and slapped him in the face as hard as I could with my open hands, to make him so mad that he would exert himself. Dutch was a good man physically and ordinarily would take no foolishness from anybody, but I had a terrible time trying to rouse his ire and get him started down the trail. At last I succeeded and walked along with him, hitting him every few moments and dragging him along. As we rounded the turn, I saw that Joe had gotten the fire started in a jiffy. Flame and smoke was rising from the dried spruce boughs.

The sight seemed to work a transformation in Dutch. His eyes stuck out and he made straight for the fire. When he got there, he jumped squarely into it. We had to drag him out to keep him from burning himself. As it was, he burned a part of one snowshoe and one moccasin and it took us an hour to repair them. He now began to tingle all over and appreciate how cold he was.

I had two bottles of Perry Davis Pain Killer in each sled. This is the greatest medicine ever invented for use in the North. I do not know the ingredients, other than that it is about half alcohol and contains some laudunum, but I would hazard a guess at opium, red pepper, turpentine and tabasco juice. You can take it internally or rub it on as a liniment. It is one of the best remedies I know of for frost bite, for man or dog. I never allowed any liquor to be taken on the trail at any time. The worst offense in our outfit was to be caught with it. If a man got drunk, it not only lowered his resistance to the cold but robbed him of his judgement, and he was sure to freeze. I didn't care how much they drank or fought and carried on when they were in town, providing they did not kill each other or commit any crime; but the minute they went on the trail, it was different. The only thing I allowed them to take was this Perry Davis Pain Killer.

I gave Dutch a good swig of it and rubbed some on his neck and chest. In a little while he was well heated up. We ate a good hearty lunch there and I filled him full of hot tea. Then I put him ahead of the sleds and kept him there all the time afterward.

Five days out from David's house, or ten days out from the head of the Good Pasture River, we reached its mouth, a distance of one hundred and seventy miles. Rounding a point, we came all at once on the Indian village, a very good one consisting of ten or twelve log cabins, with caches outside of them. Birch bark canoes were piled up for the winter outside the houses, and sleds and dogs were in front of the doors. As the dogs heard our bells, they put up a great hue and cry. An Alaskan dog cannot bark, it can only howl. If one does hear a bark in the north, it is an unmistakable indication that the dog is of an outside breed.

As we came up the bank to the village, these Indian dogs ran up to my leader Pointer, apparently with the idea of biting him. Pointer grabbed one of them by the

A racial mixture in a gathering at Nuklukayet (Tanana) in summer. (From Lieutenant Allen's reconnaissance report.)

Chief Nicolai, a Midnoosky (Copper River) Indian and his two wives at left; Indian guide Mahnie and his mother at right. (Allen report.)

throat and threw him five or six feet, never looking at him at all, but keeping right on the trail. The dog beat a hasty retreat and none came near us again.

The Indians began to emerge from their houses, and I went to what I supposed was the chief's cabin, the largest one in the village. About twenty Indians had assembled there. They were quite large men and appeared huge, because they all wore white rabbit skin coats when walking around their village. Rabbit skin is the warmest and lightest fur there is, but it is very perishable, sheds very easily and goes all to pieces if wet. The Good Pasture Indians used it for the lining of clothing, bedding and for these coats.

The Indian name for the Good Pasture River was "Cheesen." This word means "the camp robber" or butcher bird. We had noticed a great number of these birds as we came down the river. The camp robber, or northern jay, is a pest around camp, where they steal any article of food they can get hold of. Old-timers say they will pick up a piece of bacon out of the frying pan if you turn your back. The word for village, in this Indian language, was "deeg," so the name of this place was "Cheesendeeg" or "the village of the camp robbers." This name was in keeping with what Joe had told me about the habits of these Indians.

Indian names for places are always much more expressive than those given by the white man, and they should not be changed. White men usually name new places after themselves, their wives, sweethearts or friends, which conveys no idea of what they are like. Why this river was called the Good Pasture, I do not know. Possibly the great herds of caribou and moose found along its banks might have suggested the name, because it is a good pasture for them.[2]

The Indians seemed tremendously astonished to see us, and examined our equipment, eyeing my Indian, Joe, curiously. He spoke an entirely different language from their own, but he made himself understood by signs and a few words common to all Indians. Several of the Good Pasture Indians spoke quite a few words of English, having been down to the mouth of the Tanana River with their furs to trade. They could also speak Chinook quite well.

I explained to them that I was a soldier chief, engaged in putting up a "talk string" as they called the telegraph wire, which I said would be a great assistance to them when installed. One asked me if it would bring more white men into the country, and I told him it probably would not, because the "talk string" would do the work of many mail carriers who otherwise would have to go through that country. One Indian said he had heard that game would not cross the "talk string," and that therefore the migration of the caribou would be changed, much to their disadvantage. This was really so. The caribou at first were very much afraid of the right of way that we chopped through the country and of the wire that was laid on the ground, because when they came into contact with it, it cut their legs. We found that caribou had become entangled in our wire in several places and pushed it a hundred feet away from its original location, but afterward let it severely alone. Gradually they became used to it and after awhile crossed the right of way without hesitation. I explained this to the Indians and told them it would make no difference with the caribou migration. In addition, the telegraph line went straight from point to point and would always afford them a fine winter trail.

They asked me why I had brought an Indian of another tribe with me, because he might find out things there which they did not wish him to know. I replied that I was a soldier chief and he was an Indian chief, that we were great friends and companions, hunted and fished together, and I had made him come with me against his will, to assist me on this trip.

The Indians seemed satisfied with these explanations and told me they were glad to see me, that I was the first white man who had ever come down the river, and they were greatly surprised that I came through in this terribly cold weather. They themselves had stopped trapping, they told me.

Pointing to the back of their village, they said that the Tanana River there always remained open, on account of the warm springs. Sure enough, there was the water flowing along, almost the same as in the summer, and the temperature was now around seventy degrees below. Fish were still in the river, which the Indians caught in traps. I saw five mallard ducks, both flying and swimming, that stayed in the river all winter!

In other places, especially in some lakes, ducks remain about the open holes up until Christmas or later. The holes become smaller and smaller as the cold increases. Muskrats and otters use them for feeding places, bringing green vegetation up from the bottom to the rim of the hole. The ducks and divers that remain fight to get some of this green stuff; sometimes one can see them grab it out of the mouths of the rats as they come up. Eventually, the ducks froze or were

[2] The stream now known as the Volkmar River originally was named the Goodpaster by Lt. Henry T. Allen in 1885 "in honor of the Goodpaster family in Kentucky." The stream now known as the Goodpaster he named for Col. William Volkmar, USA. Later, the names were transposed by explorers and the Volkmar was reported by USGS in 1903 at its present location. Orth, op.cit., p.1023. The Goodpasters were cousins of Lieutenant Allen. Heath Twichell, Jr. *Allen, the Biography of an Army Officer, 1859-1930,* (Rutger Univ. Press, NJ, 1974.)

eaten by owls or hawks; one could read the story in the wing marks on the snow and the feathers and skin scattered about.

Undoubtedly a great many birds remain behind, being sick or lame at the time of migration. Most of these perish except those along big river courses such as the Tanana. The mallards I saw near the Indian village lived there until spring. We killed one and its flesh tasted as fishy as that of a merganser, one of the few times I have ever found mallard ducks with that taste.

We took up our quarters in the chief's house, who vacated the cabin for us and went with his squaw and children to another. We did not tell him anything about David, the starving Indian we had found in his territory. These Indians did not go out more than forty or fifty miles from their village in the winter, so would not be likely to find him.

Our dogs had the greatest contempt for the Indian dogs. When any of them approached our sleds, he was warned by a growl from Pointer. Both teams would have jumped on them and killed them in short order if they had approached more closely. It was my custom to chain each wheel dog to the toboggan, who guarded it under all conditions and slept on top of the sled mantle. Each team gathered around its own toboggan, while ordinarily the leaders slept at the door of our tent. Sometimes we would call them in to sleep on top of our robes to keep us warm.

After having provided for our dogs and eaten a good meal ourselves, we settled down to smoke, and I gleaned all the information I could from the Indians about the country. I asked when they thought the breakup would come in the spring, and where they thought was a good place for us to build boats, that is, that location of the biggest spruce trees from which to saw the planks, as I intended to build boats to use on the Good Pasture River to the Tanana. The conversation shifted to when the salmon would come, whether there were many of them, how much game there was in the country and where it was located; then we began to talk about fur and where most of the different animals were caught. The Good Pasture, they told me, was the best place for marten, or Alaska sable, but the Delta River, the mouth of which was about ten miles below, was the best place for foxes, particularly black and silver tips, several of which they had obtained during the last month.

Finally, an Indian who was telling me about the Delta River, said, "Me come back yesterday from line of traps, Delta River, me catchum two white men. He heap sick, too much eat."

This was astonishing information, two white men in the country at that time of the year, and sick from eating too much! I could get no more out of him except that he had left two Indians with them, that he had given them frozen salmon to eat and they had been on the trail for a long time, coming from the Copper River. Joe elicited the information that these men were nearly frozen to death and in a very bad condition.

I determined to push down there at once and see what the trouble was. Telling one of the Good Pasture Indians to start down ahead of me, I borrowed a sled from the Indians to use instead of my toboggan, hitched my team to it, took a little rice and bacon with me, and left Dutch to look after things at the Good Pasture village.

In a couple of hours I reached the Indian camp, a little above the mouth of the Delta. Sure enough, there were two white men, one an Irishman and the other a Swede. The Indians had built a nice wickiup for them, with a comfortable fire which made it quite warm. The Irishman's face and hands were entirely black from freezing, and his ears were all shriveled up and sloughing off. The front teeth of both men were broken off from having tried to bite into the frozen fresh salmon which the Indians had given them, and both were very sick at their stomachs from having eaten so much of it. The Swede was in much better condition than the Irishman. His toes and fingers were a little frozen but his face, except for the nose and ears, was pretty clear of frost, as were his legs, arms and back. I looked over the Irishman. The Indians had taken off his trousers and were rubbing him with snow to try and save him, but I saw at once that his legs were gone and probably his arms. He had worn suspenders to hold up his trousers and these had frozen from the moisture. There was a black streak on each side of his chest and down his back where they had extended. I did not see how the man could have lived.

I gave him a little Perry Davis Pain Killer, and cooked some rice, bacon and salmon for them. It would have been impossible to get these men back to my working parties or to Eagle City, but there was a trading station at a little place called Chena, about a hundred miles below, where a gold strike had just been made. (This was the Fairbanks strike, that name being given to it at a later time.) I therefore told the Indians that they must mush these men on down there and they would be paid liberally for it by the Government or by private individuals. Both the frozen men said they had plenty of money and produced an order from the Northern Commercial Company, to give them practically anything they wanted.

In the meantime, the Swede, whose vitality seemed enormous, began telling me what had happened to them. To begin with, he and his partner had determined to go into the upper Tanana River country, as they thought it offered the best chance for making a strike. During the summer they hired some packers to take them up the Chestachina [Chistochina] River, and carried a good outfit across the divide, which is without timber for about thirty miles. They made a good strong cache for it, which would resist wolverines or any other animals, then crossed the divide and waited for the freeze-up in a cabin on the Chestachina about fifty miles from their cache.

When the freeze came, they crossed the divide under great difficulty, then found that their cache had been robbed by the Delta Indians of everything except a little corn meal. They debated whether they should go back or go ahead, and decided that the trip back was almost as bad as the trip ahead. As they were both good shots, they thought they could kill game sufficient for their subsistence, but little did they know about hunting at that time of the year in northern Alaska. They saw sheep several times but could get nowhere near them, and in a week's hunting only killed two rabbits.

Still they decided to push ahead. Soon their scanty supply of cornmeal was exhausted. They went several days without eating, and their dogs became so exhausted that they could go no further. A dog can work from four to seven days without anything to eat. After that he dies if he is not fed. So they killed one dog, ate some of it and fed the rest to the other dogs. This carried them on a little further. Two dogs ran away, which left them only two others. These they killed both at once because they were afraid one of them might run away, and they would have to feed the remaining one anyway. They were still pulling their own sled and making from six to eight miles a day.

The terrible cold weather that we went through overwhelmed them. Their clothing and outfit was not sufficient to stand it. The Irishman began to freeze more and more every day and could not thaw out properly. When all their dog meat was gone, they chewed the dog hides, then ate all the webbing out of their snowshoes. They ate their moccasins and attemptd to make sandals for their feet out of birch bark, with spruce twigs next to the feet, to keep the snow off and raise them above the ice. Finally they ate their moosehide mittens, leaving only the woolen lining to wear, which of course soon became wet and froze their hands. By that time they were nearing exhaustion and really had expected to die in their last camp where the Indians found them.

I urged the Indians to make all haste to take them down the river. They did it and did it well, sending two sleds with two Indians each. I afterward found they got the men down there in about four days, in as good condition as could be expected. The Swede only lost two or three fingers and the ends of a few toes. The Irishman lost both legs and both arms. I saw him several months afterward and he remarked in a jocular way that he did not know whether it was better to be dead or alive in that condition. His face was a mass of scars and his ears practically eaten away.

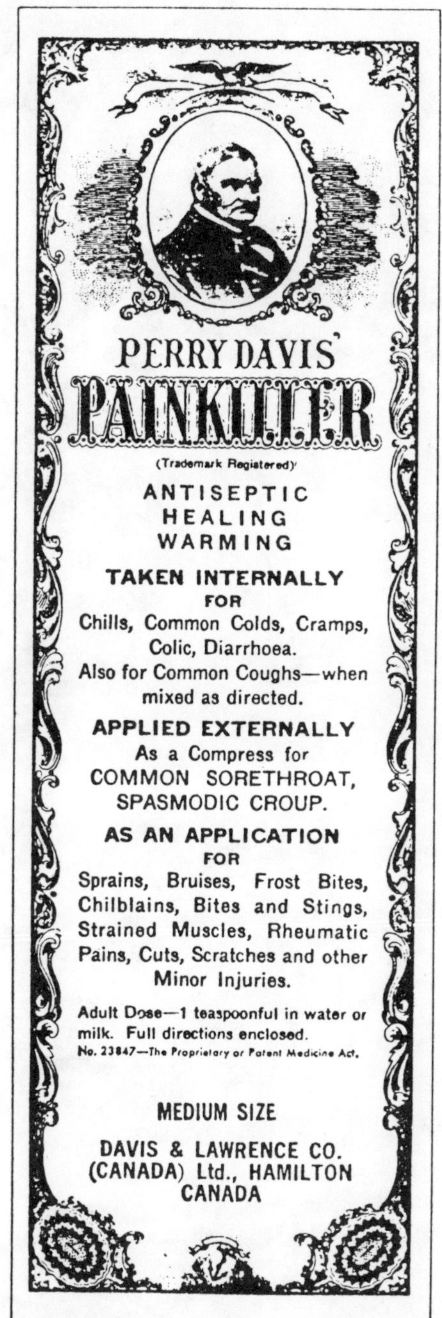

Lieutenant Mitchell in his bed ticking parka cover and with his Winchester in a moosehide case, "ready to mush" at Fort Egbert, 1903.

COURTESY LIBRARY OF CONGRESS,
BRIGADIER GENERAL WILLIAM MITCHELL COLLECTION

UP THE GOODPASTER: ON TO FAIRBANKS

14

Back in the Indian village, I arranged with the Indians to whipsaw some lumber with which we could make boats in the spring. Then we set out upon our return journey. Dutch and the Indian were very sore. Pointer, my leader, and Moose, the wheel dog on Dutch's team, had each frosted one foot pretty badly and had to wear moccasins.

We found that our back trail had frozen hard and had not drifted. The weather was colder than ever, still below minus seventy. That night Joe was very listless in making camp and had nothing to say. I said nothing to him but made a mental note to watch him. Dutch's energy kept up pretty well, although he was very tired. Next morning I had a hard time getting Joe out on the trail. We were running fast with the dogs, without snowshoes, making about five miles an hour. After awhile, Joe got so he could not run at all and I put him on my toboggan. When we came to our camping place that night, Joe would not move and sat on the sleigh. I told Dutch to make a fire quickly while I chopped down a spruce tree and laid the bed boughs in front of the fire. Dutch and I went back, got the Indian, carried him up the bank and put him down in front of the fire, while we went about our camp duties.

Coming back, I sat down by Joe and asked him what was the matter with him. He said "Good Pasture Indians bad men. He look see other people, he makeum sick. Good Pasture Indians, he look see David, he look see me, he look see dogs." He paused. "Dutch foot sick, me foot sick, Pointer foot sick, Moose foot sick. Me no get home. Me no see squaw, me no see papooses, me no see Indians, me die," and he lay back on the spruce boughs.

I told Dutch to put up the tent while I fed the dogs, and to tell Joe we would have dinner as soon as possible. We were now eating the same food as our dogs, of which I still had a good supply, and drinking tea, just plain tea, as our sugar had given out. Joe would not touch a thing, he just lay there. I was convinced that his whole condition was the result of being overtired and thinking that the Good Pasture Indians had cast the evil eye on him. He believed implicitly that they had this power and liked to exercise it, because, as he explained it, if they made people die and they were buried, then all their pots and pans and belongings would be put around their graves, which the Good Pasture Indians could steal and use themselves.

I took Dutch aside and told him we had to do something with Joe or he really would die. I suggested that Dutch go back and tell Joe that he must have noticed that I was not affected by the Good Pasture Indians at all, and that I was not only a soldier chief but a great medicine man, and could make much stronger medicine than the Good Pasture Indians. Moreover, that within twenty minutes I would make medicine to cure him and forthwith he would be all right, and feel better than he ever did.

Into the teapot about half full of water, I put half a bottle of Perry Davis Pain Killer and sat over the fire in front of Joe, muttering and mumbling things, while I put in some pieces of dried salmon, a few pieces of bacon, and finally added some spruce boughs. The concoction was terrible but it was hot and had a lot of Perry Davis Pain Killer in it, and I knew it would have an effect on Joe. If medicine did not have a horrible taste, an Indian thought it did not amount to anything.

Without any warning, I grabbed Joe by the neck and pulled him up to a sitting position. He would not even open his eyes. I forced him to look at me and told him I had learned that the Good Pasture Indians had cast a spell over him, they had looked at him and made him sick, and that I knew they could make him die, but they did not know that I knew all these things, and now I was going to stop it. I talked to him in this strain for about fifteen minutes. At last he replied that I might be a great soldier chief, but he had never seen me make medicine before that time. He knew now I could make medicine, because he could smell what was in the teapot. He said he knew I was good, because I had helped the Indian David and probably saved him.

I told Joe I had made medicine, not for him to smell but to take, and that would dispel the bad spirit. He said he could not take it because he had already begun to die. I told him he had to take it. We had to pry his mouth open and put a stick between his teeth, then began pouring the stuff down his throat until we had given him a pint of it. At first he became very talkative, saying that the spirit was still in him but he felt strong. Then he became very drowsy and I put him to bed between Dutch and myself, this being the place of honor because with a person on either side of you it was warmest.

When morning came I shouted a little stronger than usual for everybody to get up. Joe jumped up with a bound, went out and made the fire, and I never heard another word out of him about his going to die, or about the Good Pasture Indians having put the evil eye on him. He did not mention this to me again until many months later, when we had a long talk about it.

Two days later we came to the Indian David's camp. All of them looked better now and could stir around quite a good deal. The squaw had fixed up the snowshoes and patched up the clothing, made some new moccassins and mended the dog harness. David had made two trips out hunting but had been unable to kill any game. He had broken the trail along his line of traps, and found the remains of several marten, but on account of not having been to them for several weeks, the wolverines had eaten the carcasses of this valuable animal. He had repaired his deadfalls and expected to do very well during the next few weeks.

The traps the Indians make, called deadfalls, consist of a little pen closed at one end and on top, over which a heavy log is placed, supported by a Figure Four trap. The animal goes in at one end, and as it takes the bait, springs the trap and the heavy log falls across his back, breaking it. The Alaska sable is a very easy animal to catch. With steel traps, a piece of salmon is nailed to a tree nearby, which attracts the animal, and as it jumps around so much, it is practically certain to get in the trap. Although there are other furs somewhat more valuable than the Alaska sable, they are harder to get and more difficult to transport. A sable skin weighs about an ounce. Gold was $16.00 to the ounce then, and an A-1 Alaska sable or marten was worth about two ounces, or $32.00, on the Outside.

Joe and David had a good talk about the Good Pasture Indians. Joe advised David to get out of the country just as soon as he could, because he was afraid the Indians would follow up our trail, find David and make a lot of trouble for him.

I was now confident of getting to the head of the Good Pasture River and my caches, without anything serious happening, so I took all the rice, dried salmon, bacon and tea that I could possibly spare and gave it to David, making him promise that he would only use a certain amount each day, which I showed him how to handle, because it must last him until he got game himself. This he said he would do, and as I knew him to be a pretty good Indian, I was satisfied that he would pull through in good shape.

We pushed on up the river, noting as we went the places that would be suitable for the stations for our sled trains. I selected a place for our main post about midway down the river, where we could build our boats and where all our supplies would be brought to finish the whole Alaska system. This place we called Central.[1]

Upon my return to the head of the Good Pasture River, I found that all the men and the sled trains had worked through the intensely cold weather without a casualty, not even any serious cases of frost bite. The government thermometer showed the weather to have been below sixty for six weeks and the coldest temperature recorded was 76 below! This is an unusually long spell of such cold weather, but lower temperatures than 76 below have been recorded. However it was the worst I ever encountered.

My dogs had pretty well recovered from their hard trip on the snowshoe trail, as we had a hard-packed trail on the way back and comparatively light toboggans. Joe was still pretty tired but Dutch was in fine shape again. I changed from toboggans to sleds again and went on to Eagle City over my regular transportation trail which was in perfect condition. Everywhere that it lay along broad stream beds three trails had been broken, one on each side of the main trail, to keep the snow from drifting into the center one. Wherever warm springs existed, the trail gang had built trestles over them and had also trestled over or filled in all the abrupt rises or falls in the trail, so as to make even going everywhere. I made the trip into Eagle City from the head of the Good Pasture, one hundred and fifty miles, in two days.

I was tremendously pleased with the way the whole organization was working. The wire had been completely laid along the right of way to the head of the Good Pasture River, preparatory to being erected the following summer. We often telephoned over this wire during the cold weather, using buzzer instruments, the ground then giving good insulation. If a place on the trail required repairing, or if a blacksmith was needed for an emergency job, these crews could be telephoned for and within a maximum of two days would arrive

---

[1] This was Central Telegraph Station, not to be confused with the village of Central.

Infantry right-of-way construction party on the Fairbanks-Gulkana line. COURTESY U.S. ARMY, 1909

Signal Corps equipment wagon near Gulkana. COURTESY U.S. ARMY

at the appointed place. The outfits were loaded light, moved at a trot and could make fifty miles a day.

Our mules and horses were in excellent condition. I used to think that horses would stand extreme cold better than mules, because mules stood extreme heat better than horses, but I found that mules stood the cold even better. They would not take the lead as well in deep snow but the cold did not worry them to the extent it did the horses. This winter we had had no sore shoulders among the animals from frost bite, because their collars were made to fit them and were never removed at night. Neither did any suffer from frozen feet, because we kept the trail dry, and whenever heavy balls formed on their feet, they were immediately knocked off with the balling hammer which hung on each collar. None of the horses had bits in their mouths, all being handled on halters. This prevented their mouths and lips from freezing.

At the Northern Commercial Company store in Eagle, I learned that an old Swede of 65, who lived up Eagle Creek about fifteen miles, had not been seen or heard from for several weeks. It was feared something had happened to him but people had put off going up there on account of the extreme cold. I had Dutch drive his dog team up to the cabin, to see what the trouble was. He came back with the body of the Swede on his sled, frozen as stiff as an ice cake.

As he approached the cabin, Dutch said, he found not a sign of life around it, no trail, no smoke from the chimney. The wood was all gone from the woodpile, and the only axe he saw had the halve broken. He pushed open the door and looked around the dark interior but saw no one. Going over to the bunk, he put his hand in and felt what he thought was a hard piece of wood, but upon lighting a match, he saw that it was the old man, frozen to death in bed. He had probably been dead two or three weeks. They put his body away until spring, when a hole could be dug in the ground.

I found that my friend, Ben Downing, who had taken me down the Yukon on my first trip in a flat boat, had also passed away.[2] This great brave fellow, who had the mail contracts from Dawson to Circle, always went on the principle that "the mail must move" irrespective of weather, or other conditions. The winter before this he had broken through the ice a couple of times and frozen his hands and feet so badly that some of his fingers and toes had to be amputated. This year, everybody had tried to make him ease up and let the younger men mush the mail through, but Ben insisted on taking the worst and most dangerous trips himself. He prided himself on being able to stand more and go further than any other man. He had again broken through the ice where the warm springs kept it very thin, and had become so badly frozen in all his members, even almost into his heart, that he could not shake off the dread drowsiness. He had been found before he was dead, carried to the nearest cabin, rubbed with snow and Pain Killer, and given stimulants, but all to no avail.

This grand old pioneer of the North lives no more but all of us who knew him will never forget him. Some day a monument should be erected to him for the wonderful hardihood, endurance and bravery he displayed, and the part he played in opening up Alaska.

The news had already spread about my trip down the Good Pasture and I marveled again at the speed with which news traveled in this country. Here in the dead of winter when there was less traffic than at any time in the year, it was known in Dawson, Forty Mile and Eagle City that I had opened up a new trail which gave direct access to the Tanana River and thus to the big gold strike that had been made near Chena.

I heard that men were outfitting at Dawson to go into the Tanana diggings over my trail. The stampede to a new place is a terrible thing, especially in winter. Men go out only half prepared to withstand the cold and rigors of the trip and nearly always run short of food. Some take women and even children with them. I knew that a lot of them figured that by going in over my trail, they would obtain government assistance if they got up against it, but I had just enough food and supplies for my men and animals to last through until the line was finished. If we had to use this up feeding hungry mushers, it might even stop the construction of our line that winter.

Thinking over the situation, I decided to lay in a surplus of supplies to take care of any unusual demand, my plan being to go down the Tanana River until I met Lt. [George S.] Gibbs, who was working up from Fort Gibbon, and arrange with him to ship all the supplies he could to the head of navigation on the Tanana, where there was now a very good winter trail and where steamboats could be used later.

Fortunately none of my men on the trails deserted for the gold camps, but several did from the infantry at Fort Egbert, where they had almost nothing to do.[3] Most of them went to Dawson across the Canadian line, where they could not easily be apprehended. I do not think I ever heard of any of the deserters having done well with mining, as it calls for special knowledge

[2] Downing died some time later. He took a sleigh trip from Fairbanks to Whitehorse in 19 days in January 1905. *Alaska Daily Guide*, 17 Feb. 1905.

[3] Much of the infantrymen's time was spent on field duty helping the Signal Corps men build and maintain the telegraph lines. *The Story of the Alaska Communication System,* op. cit., and monthly Post Returns, National Archives.

which the average soldier does not have. On the other hand, several who remained in the service until they were discharged made considerable money. Some of the men out on the trail made a good deal by trapping valuable fur bearing animals.

There was barely time to finish my trips before the break-up, so after a couple of days stay in Fort Egbert, we turned our faces to the trail again, and after an uneventful trip of five hundred miles, reached the telegraph station at Chena. The few people there were wild with excitement over the strike on Gold Stream [Goldstream Creek] made by Pete the Dago [Felix Pedro].[4] Gibbs met me the day after I arrived. He had come up the river with a team of malemutes, and had with him a man named Love, who had never had much experience in the cold. After talking over plans and disposing of our business, we decided to run up to Gold Stream and look at the area in which the gold lay, travelling light and taking no tent with us.

Gibbs' team, although composed of good dogs, was not well matched. He had picked them up here and there from those already in other teams. They fought each other and had a terrible time. His leader was named "Joe" and carried a sort of dinner bell around his neck. Every time Gibbs called "Joe" to the dog, the rest of the team stopped, thinking he said "Whoa." In the morning the dogs would all run out in the woods, where they would have to be chased on snowshoes, caught and brought back, and sat on while being put in harness.

Arriving at Gold Stream, we saw Pete the Dago, who told us how the pay was running in the gravel. It certainly looked good. I had never staked any claims in my life, because if a person gets the gold fever, it is all off with him, especially if he is engaged in any government work. But my friends, the officers at Fort Egbert, were very anxious for me to stake some claims for them, so I decided to do so now. We worked up the creek a little way, where it looked as though there might be a good lodgment for gold, and staked several claims with their longer side across the creek, so as to cross-cut the whole thing from one bench to another. These claims afterward proved to be rich property. My friends gave "lays" to others, who I think reaped all the benefit. In mining phraseology, to "give a lay" means to rent claims out to others on shares.

By the time we had finished snowshoeing out the boundaries on each side of the claims, it was time to camp. We found a good place in a clump of spruce trees. I noticed that Love looked rather startled when I said we would camp at this place. I don't know what he expected to find, a cabin or a hotel. Dutch began to dig out a place with his snowshoes where we would put the fire, which was to be made of logs about fifteen feet long, banked up so as to reflect the heat toward a bed of balsam boughs that we were preparing in front of it.

Love looked more disturbed than ever and seemed to think we would all freeze to death, as the weather was 42° below zero. The situation appealed to Dutch and he put forth his best efforts at impressing Love. Complaining that he was perspiring so excessively, he kept taking off one garment after another, until finally he had on only a shirt and trousers. He was very funny and I could hardly keep a straight face. Of course when people are working hard, they can take a good deal off, but when they stop, they must put on heavy clothing immediately. Love had never seen anything like this before, and he thought old Dutch was half crazy.

As we were opening our sled mantles to get out our robes and lay them on the balsam boughs, a big owl began hooting in a tree beside us. Dutch grabbed a rifle and said he would shoot it. In spite of the fact that Dutch had been a Boer, he was the worst shot I have ever seen and the owl would have been perfectly safe. But Love grabbed the gun and begged him not to kill the owl, because if he did we would have bad luck and probably freeze to death that night. Gibbs and I were highly amused, Love was so serious about it. After a good deal of pleading, Dutch allowed the gun to be taken from him.

After a good meal of beans, meat and tea, we went to bed and slept well, and next morning returned to Chena. Love enjoyed the experience very much, and told us that although he had been in the country for several years, he never had any idea that men could work and mush entirely in the open in the coldest weather, without tents or cabins. He had always "holed up" in his cabin the minute the cold weather came and stayed there till spring.

With knowledge of the country, good judgment and strong physique, no one need be worried about getting through in good shape, provided there is timber about from which to get wood for a fire. Trees attract animals, so one can usually find game there. Timber is usually near a watercourse, which contains fish.

The tundra country, however, around Bering Sea and along the Arctic Ocean, is terrible to travel in. There are not trees whatever, only small bushes, willows and alders, whose wet roots are the only fuel that can be obtained. The flat, unprotected country makes every gust of wind seem twice as bad as it really is.

[4] The Italian prospector, Felix Pedro, made the first gold discovery in what was to become the rich Fairbanks District, on Pedro Creek, a tributary of Goldstream Creek north of Fairbanks on July 22, 1902.

At Chena, there was great competition over where the post office would be. Two men, Belt and Hendricks, who ran the trading station at Chena, wanted to have the post office established there. Their principal rival was an old boat captain and trader named Barnett [E.T. Barnette], who had come up to establish a store and a bank, sensing that there would be a big stampede into the diggings. Barnett moved up one of the sloughs on the Tanana, ten or twelve miles above Chena. He wired to Mr. [Senator Charles] Fairbanks, then [later] the Vice-President of the United States, saying that if he got the post office at his location, he would call the place "Fairbanks." In a couple of days, a telegram was received that the post office had been given to Barnett's location, under the name of Fairbanks, and these diggings, which attained world-wide fame, were ever afterward known by that name.[5]

U.S. Army Cableship *Burnside*

COURTESY U.S. ARMY

Hauling end of the submarine cable from the *Burnside* to the shore at Valdez in September 1904.

COURTESY COOK INLET HISTORICAL SOCIETY

[5] Judge James Wickersham claimed, in his *Old Yukon Tales - Trails - Trials*, Washington Law Book Co., (Washington, D.C., 1938) that he asked Barnette to name his trading post Fairbanks.

15 HELPING THE FAIRBANKS STAMPEDERS

I started back up the Tanana River to rejoin my outfit. The weather had grown much warmer, the thermometer having gone up almost to zero, which was exceptionally warm for the latter part of February. As we mushed up the sloughs of the Tanana, a snow storm with considerable wind swept down across us, swirling in blinding gusts, and obliterating the trail ahead. I linked my two sleds together, hitching the fourteen dogs as one team and made Pointer looselead ahead. He would feel for the old trail with both his front and hind feet, carefully working his way along it. I followed on snowshoes, also feeling for the trail with a stick, with Dutch behind me handling the leading sled with a gee pole. The dogs wallowed through the snow, pulling strenuously at their traces. It was necessary to find the trail, even though it was covered by a foot or two of snow, as its stamped down surface afforded footing and support. In the deep snow, one simply flounders about, sinking deeper and deeper. We had difficulty making over two miles an hour this way. For two or three days we fought our way through slowly, then the snow let up.

I met a couple of Indians from the Good Pasture tribe, who said they had heard that many white men were going to stampede over my trail to Fairbanks. It was evident now that we were in for it. The stories that had gone out from Fairbanks, added to by traders who were taking goods in there to sell, had spread not only all over Alaska, but also to the United States. With the memory of Dawson and Nome before them, men were making a frantic rush to get to Fairbanks before it was too late.

Passing the Good Pasture Indian village, we turned up the river. That afternoon as we were making camp I heard bells jingling up the trail and soon two stampeders came into view with their dog team, which consisted of four dogs of mixed breed. The sled was heaped high with equipment of all kinds. From their costume alone, we could see that these men had had very little trail experience. They had no snowshoes, no rifle and only a couple of single bitted axes.

When they saw us making camp, they stopped in the trail and one of them came over and asked me how far it was to the diggings, how the trail was, whether I had seen the country, and how the prospects might be. After answering his questions, I asked him where he had come from and where he was going. You could not tell by the looks of a person on the trail who or what he might be. The man said that he and his friend were actors, and had saved considerable money in the last twenty years. They had always been interested in placer mining and had determined to try their luck in the North. Coming into Dawson the year before they had worked as day laborers to learn the game from top to bottom, and had saved their money to outfit themselves when a strike came. This was rare, because most men who came in spent all they had in a comparatively short time, gambling or drinking. If a man could stand a couple of winters in the North without going to pieces in this way, he was a solid fellow.

He said their muscles were very sore, as they had travelled very fast trying to get ahead of everybody and their hands and feet were somewhat frosted. They had had sense enough to rub snow on them, and I gave them a little Perry Davis Pain Killer to help them out. Many outfits were following them, they said, some with women and children.

Soon they began to make camp, going through about three motions where one should have done. Under their sled mantle they had a great quantity of cans and tinned goods. This is the heaviest stuff one can carry on a trail. Almost everything in a can is wet and water is heavy, also canned goods freeze easily. We always carried dried things, such as dried salmon, beans, potatoes, turnips and carrots. We killed game whenever we found it, sliced the meat into steaks and let them freeze separately. They remained like little pieces of board until we cooked them, when they thawed in the frying pan. It is very necessary to vary the diet with vegetables, otherwise scurvy is almost sure to attack one.

I noticed my dogs eyeing the tin cans in the stampeders' sled. They seemed to know what was inside them.

It is amazing to see them open a can in an instant and take out the contents. There were tins of meat and butter on top of the sled, and I could see Pointer looking at the butter cans, which were yellow, with longing eyes.

One of the men came over again in a few minutes and I warned him to be careful about his canned goods, because my dogs had been on the trail a long time and might steal some while I was not looking, or while the sled was not guarded. They had no dog trained for guard duty, but even if they had, our dogs would have overpowered him. The man replied that all his stuff was in strong cans, that he had heard this tale of dogs knowing what was inside the cans and being able to open them, but he knew that was all foolishness, and it did not worry him. So I said nothing more, but merely watched the dogs, while we cooked our dinner.

Soon I saw both men prepare to leave, to carry some wood to their camp and get some ice from the river to make water. Pointer and King, the wheel dog, waited until both men had gotten about twenty yards away, when like a flash Pointer had a can of butter and King a tin of beef. They were out in the snow with them and had them opened in less time than it takes to tell. I yelled at the dogs to drop the cans and called the two men back, and said to them, "I told you to look after your outfit. Now see what has happened." They were overcome with astonishment. I further told them that if they expected to get to Fairbanks alive, with their experience of the trail, they must guard every bit of food they had in the most careful manner and make it go just as far as possible, because we had no stations from this point on to the diggings. There were few Indians and no white men on that part of the trail. They thanked me very much for the advice.

After dinner they came over to our fire and kept us in a perfect uproar of laughter with their jokes and stories about their experiences. They were real comedians.

The next day I ran into several more teams of stampeders. The first ones were two men, Swedes, each pulling his own sled, with no dogs. They were old timers, going fast. They told me they expected to average thirty-five miles a day, with 200 pounds on each sled, and from the way they looked, I believed they would come pretty near doing it.

Other outfits varied in every conceivable way. One man had a team of five collies, which weighed only about sixty pounds each but appeared to be very good. The driver said they had all come from one litter. It was fortunate the weather was warm, because if it had been colder their feet would have frozen. The man also said he had to be very careful about their fighting with other dogs, as a big husky could maim and cripple them easily. These northern husky dogs fight very much the way a wolf does. At the first encounter, they usually bite through the opposing dog's leg, just below the elbow, making it helpless, then bite another leg. Their fangs cut like a razor. With it all, however, they cannot whip a wolf. A wolf, even though he weighs less, is usually able to whip three or four of them if he has plenty of room in the open and is in good condition.

Outfit after outfit passed down the trail, some with scarcely enough food to last for a week but trusting to luck to have somebody help them. People like this should not be allowed to proceed, but as this was a civil matter I had no jurisdiction over them. I determined, however, that if I saw any very aggravated cases, I would take action to stop them.

I sent word down to the Good Pasture Indians that many people were coming with little food, and I thought if they went down the Tanana and killed a lot of moose, they could sell them to excellent advantage to the mushers. I had noticed a good many moose tracks along the river and when snow four feet deep is crusted over, it is no trick at all to kill moose. The Indians sent back the message that three hunting parties were setting out immediately.

That night as I made camp, a sled pulled in with four good dogs, handled by a woman. A man was walking behind the sled, and on it were two children, one eight and the other five. Both the man and woman were great big people. When they stopped, the man sat on the sled and did nothing. The woman unhitched the dogs, got out the axe, chopped wood and did all the camp duties, fixed up a bed and put the children in it, while the man kept sitting there. She was a perfect Amazon of a woman, six feet tall, and strong as any two ordinary people.

Dutch wandered over to see who they were and why the man did no work. He soon came back and told me that two days before the man had spilled a kettle of boiling water over both hands and arms, and that he was perfectly helpless as a result. He had wanted to turn back to Dawson, but his wife insisted that they were going to Fairbanks to make thier fortune, and if he were crippled, she would take care of all of them.

These people were Swedes also. It is remarkable how the Scandinavians stay with it under the hardest conditions. The old timers say that the requisites for success in the North are: "To be low in the forehead and high in the chest, strong in the back and weak in the head." The Indians classed all people in the North under three categories: white men, black white men (meaning Negroes), and Swedes. Everybody who spoke broken English, no matter what his nationality, was a Swede, for whom they had great respect.

Along at this stage, the stampeders had gone about half way and the worst of the trail lay in front of them. Our soldiers at the stations were being offered huge sums of money by these men to sell them food and rations. As our privates only got about $15 a month, the corporals $25, and the sergeants $35, it was a great temptation. I had to watch them carefully but very little of it was attempted.

Our transportation lines and sled trains were now redoubling their efforts as the warmer weather came on and the sleds slipped more easily over the hard packed trails. I now felt confident that we would finish the line that summer which would give communication from one end of Alaska to the other and open up the country for the first time in its history.

We arrived at Eagle City, where I was taken into the Society of Arctic Brothers [Arctic Brotherhood], a secret organization composed of men who have stayed in the country for at least one winter and become "sourdoughs." It really does much good in helping out its members and others deserving of assistance, also in banding together for the common good and for the maintenance of law and order.

Among the things required of an Arctic Brother is that, when he falls out with his partner, he shall not cut a sled in two, nor kill a dog, nor throw away an axe. Things which would be destroyed by dividing them must be drawn for by lot and kept by the lucky person. If two people are together long enough in the North, they are practically sure to fall out and have a fight. Of the things that can be divided, they try to take share and share alike. Usually they hate each other so that when it comes to dividing things like a gun, an axe or a kettle, they throw them away so that neither can have them. Three people get along better, but even they fight sometime. When they do, it will be two against one and they are better able to handle the matter.

In the Society, there is the usual initiation ceremony. While conducting me "down the snowy trails and over the passes" as they called it, which in fact was a snowy trail down which we had to walk barefoot in a temperature of 35 below zero, I was brought before the tribunal of the Arctic Brothers and accused of purposely starving mushers on the trail going to Fairbanks, while I had plenty of supplies available and they had nothing. There was some foundation of fact in this, because I had been very careful to keep our supplies. Naturally we would not let anybody starve to death, but on the other hand we would require them to be pretty short before we would go into our supplies, otherwise we would have run short ourselves. The charge had the exact effect that they desired on me. I got very mad and challenged the fellows that made it to come out and fight me right there. So we went outside and they grabbed me and rolled me around in the snow for about five minutes, then brought me in and gave me a good warm spiced drink and invested me with complete membership in the order.

A couple of days after this, Chief Joseph, with one squaw and a dog team, came to see me. I figured up how much was coming to him and asked him whether he wanted money or other things. He replied that he did not have much confidence in the white men he traded with, that they always cheated him if they could. A few days before, he said, a white man had come through his camp, and one of his squaws having a bad stomach ache, he asked this man if he had any medicine. The white man gave him a bottle of "medicine" and told him to mix a little of it with water and give it to the squaw three times a day. For this Joe gave him two sable skins of A-1 grade, which ordinarily would be worth at least $30. The medicine did not seem to do much good, Joe said, and pulling the bottle out of his pocket, he asked me to look at it and tell him what I thought of it. I found it to be the smallest size bottle of vanilla extract, which apparently had had half the extract poured out and filled up with water.

I told Joe the big trading companies had fixed prices on their things and whether it was white man or Indian who traded with them, they got the same consideration; that the goods were standard and he was perfectly safe. He answered that undoutedly that was so, but if I did not mind, he would rather have me come and buy the things for him. So I went to both the big company stores, the North American Transportation and Trading Company, known as the N.A.T., and the Northern Commercial Company, known as the N.C., the managers of which were good friends of mine. I explained what I wanted and they gave me a special price on everything.

I asked Joe what he wanted and he answered, "Me wantum gunpowder, lead, new gun. Squaw wantum beads, thread, needles." I said to him "Do you want any flour or bacon?" to which he replied, "Oh—yes—me eatum bacon." They needed food, as a matter of fact, worse than anything else, but when they got in a store they were just like children, the gaudy and bright things always caught their eyes.

We went to the N.C. store first and while walking down the counters, saw a good sized mirror, about three feet by four. Joe's eye lighted on it, and he had to have the mirror. I told him it was all right to have the mirror if he got all the other things he needed first, but that he could not have the mirror unless he first got plenty of food to last him until the salmon came, then gunpowder and lead for his firearms, then needles, thread, scissors and things his squaw needed for making clothing.

So he got a good supply of flour and bacon first, also sugar, salt and "Siwash" tobacco, which is composed of the big leaves of tobacco, about the worst grade possible, encrusted with licorice and molasses. It is very popular with all the Indians. He then bought matches and ammunition, a good 30/30 rifle and some new steel traps. The squaw wanted beads of all kinds, which she had been looking at intently. So I presented her with beads on my own account and later she made a lot of my buckskin clothing. When beads are applied to the buckskin with sinew, they last almost forever. Some of the Indians were beginning to use thread, cotton or silk, to put the beads on with, but this soon wears out and the beads fall off.

Then we bought needles, buckskin needles very much like saddler's or surgeon's needles, some of them curved. We got scissors and knives of several kinds, spoons, a lot of good cooking utensils, a stove for the tent with two elbows so that it could be run out the side of the tent, where the cinders would not burn holes in it when they fell. There were two dampers to go in the stove pipe, also. We got a fine lot of heavy bed ticking material with which to make three tents; axes, hatchets and a lot of little knick knacks of various sorts, blankets, bright colored cotton materials to make dresses with, and two pairs of store shoes, which I knew Joe would never wear but which he insisted on having. We got fish hooks and lines, fish spears and some nets.

I checked over the whole outfit and found there was still a little money left, but not as much as the mirror cost. However, the manager of the N.C. Company told me that if I was very anxious for him to have the mirror, he would let me have it for what remained of Joe's money. Joe was perfectly delighted and so was his squaw. They had never dreamed of getting such things in all their lives.

All his purchases were packed up and made into bales so he could take them out on the trail in his dog sleds. The mirror was put into its original case and wrapped around with straw so as to prevent its breaking. It was quite heavy and hard to handle. Joe never asked me for any cash at all but I gave him and his squaw a little on my own account.

A couple of days after this, Joe and his squaw came to my cabin to bid me goodbye before starting for their home, a hundred and fifty miles away. I gave them some tea and some good tobacco, then went out to see them off. Hitched to the sled were five dogs, and on the sled, to my astonishment, was the mirror, which weighed about a hundred and fifty pounds, wrapped, the ammunition for his gun, some beads, and one small piece of bacon.

I asked him why he he did not take out an entire load of food and leave these baubles until the end. He answered that if he came back from his trip without something very unusual, just ordinary food, they would not think he was a very big man. His first consideration, I told him, was to keep his people in food; the other stuff could go later. I made him load up with flour and bacon, tea, sugar and a few other things, and promised to send him the mirror and other goods on one of our sled trains, which I did a few days later.

Skagway's meeting hall of the Arctic Brotherhood, a fraternal order no longer active. (1967)

COURTESY LYMAN L. WOODMAN, 1967

16 PREPARING FOR THE LAST SUMMER'S WORK

March [1903] was wearing on. There would be only two months more before the break-up, and the time when we should finish all our work in the North. I could make one more trip to the Tanana and in to Fairbanks before the melting of the snow, for a final inspection.

My dogs had made upward of two thousand miles, with our constant mushing, and were in splendid condition, with the excellent food and care we had given them. In our own teams, not one with which we had started out that winter had to be killed, or was permanently injured. Dutch's leader, Whiskey, had been hit in the eye with the point of a whip, which destroyed about half the sight, but otherwise did not injure him.

The days were getting long and there was a great deal of warmer weather, from ten to thirty-five below. The sledding was wonderful. At these temperatures, when we worked up the great divides and mountains, we became so hot that we would remove everything above the waist except our undershirts and sometimes even take those off. Our faces were tanned to the color of deep mahogany; in fact, I was darker than the Indians. One sunburns more on the snow than any other place.

On account of the crust on the snow, a great many moose were being killed, and I heard they were being taken into Fairbanks by the ton, which was very lucky, as the mushers got in there almost without food. Had it not been for this providential circumstance, a great many would have starved to death.

On this trip, I made the final locations as to where the lines should run down the valley of the Tanana to the river. In the area between the Good Pasture and Fairbanks, this mighty river spreads over a width of twenty to thirty miles in places and overflows its banks, so we had to be careful about the routing of our lines.

The men at Central [Telegraph Station] on the Good Pasture had cut the biggest logs they could find from which to whipsaw the lumber for the boats and were snaking them in over the snow with mules and dogs. Pits for the sawing were made and the specifications as to size, depth and width of each boat to be built were drawn up. I was fortunate in having an old fellow named McQuade who was a master boat builder.

Whipsawing lumber out of logs is a heartbreaking and backbreaking job. One man stands above the log and the other stands beneath it, each alternately pulling the great whipsaw as it follows the line indicated on the log. This line is marked by taking a string which has been rubbed in grease and charcoal, and stretching it tightly along the place that is to be sawed. When tight, it is lifted up in the middle a little way and allowed to snap back on the log, thereby marking a straight line.

We built these boats without metal fastenings of any kind. The planks were held to the timbers by wooden plugs, driven in with raw moosehide around them, then the moosehide was wet, which caused it to swell and hold them. They were then caulked with pitch from the gum of spruce trees mixed with dried moss.

During the last trips with the sleighs, we sent out the pack saddles and aparejos to be used by the mules as soon as the snow left and the sledding was over. Everything was now ready along the trail for the coming summer.

I came back to the head of the Good Pasture River and determined to try and make a record trip into Eagle City, one hundred and fifty miles away. The trail was in absolutely perfect order, the snow was melting and a little scum of water lay over the snow and ice in some places, which made it very slippery. It was no effort at all for the dogs to pull the sleighs. Dutch and I lightened them up and left the head of the river at 3 o'clock in the morning. We travelled continuously until we reached the Middle Fork of the Forty Mile River, a distance of seventy-eight miles, and over one divide. Stopping there for twenty minutes, we fed the dogs a little dried salmon, drank some tea and ate a few beans, then started on again.

Crossing the high divide at the head of American Creek, we reached Fort Egbert a little after two o'clock in the morning of the following day, having made the whole trip of one hundred and fifty miles in less than twenty-four hours. I believe to this day it stands as a record of the longest one-day trip ever made up there. Both the dogs and ourselves rested for a couple of days afterward.[1]

I now got together my summer outfit, leather shoes, rubber boots for working on the rivers, hats, mosquito netting, gloves and everything required for our trips. We said goodbye to Eagle City and the Yukon for that snow and pulled out over a rapidly melting trail for our camp at Central. There I found that the men were well on the way to finishing the boats.

We had to stay there for two or three weeks, because travel during the break-up is almost impossible, and I took the opportunity for some intensive study. I was due for promotion to the grade of Captain and would have to stand the examination in the North. I had had little chance to study, but from time to time I had taken books out with me and worked on them, making Dutch question me according to queries I had written out. Among other things, as I was in the Signal Corps, I had to stand an examination on aeronautics as understood at that time, all about balloons, their construction, the manufacture of hydrogen gas, how it would be applied, how the balloons would be handled, both free and captive, how to make kites that would lift men. It is strange that away off in the northland there in 1903 I was getting a grounding in aeronautics which I was to apply in the Great War fourteen years later.[2]

As the ice gradually left the river, I made a reconnaissance trip to see if the pack animals could take to the trail. I was near Chief Joseph's camp, so I went over to see him. He had moved out of his winter quarters and his tribe were in tents, beside a beautiful stream in a grove of birches. A few fish had already come up the river and Joe's people had killed a good deal of game and were very happy and contented. When he saw who it was coming in, he ran out and greeted me, saying "Come, come, I want to show you something."

Going to his part of the camp, I found three tents that had been made of the bed ticking we had bought, in two of which his family lived. The third, he told me, he had saved for me and himself, nobody being allowed to go into it or even look in it. We would go in there and sit in it now, he said. Opening the door, I looked in and saw that the floor was covered with bear skins, and at the other end stood the mirror. There was nothing else in the tent. We walked in, sat down and looked in the mirror. I was on the right and Joe on the left. We had a smoke.

After awhile, he said, "You see me and me see you. Me see me and you see you." Then looking around at the back of the mirror, he asked, "What for no see here?" I was unable to explain to him why that was the case, so I took him down to the water and had him look in the stream, where he could see his face. The image in the stream, he said, was due to the Great Spirit, which looked into your face and all through you when you went to take water, which gives life, but the mirror was an entirely different thing. I told him the Great Spirit was in the mirror to the same extent that He was in the water, and that if he broke or damaged the mirror, it was a tradition among the white men that he would have bad luck, Joe answered that that was the reason he kept it in a tent and would not let any squaw look at it, but reserved it for his friends and himself.

While we were talking, we heard a loon call on the wide stretches of the river. I asked Joe if he knew what it was. He said, "Yes, him loon. Him no can walk on ground, only push." When I asked him why this was, he said that when the Great Spirit was making all the birds, he had heads, necks, bodies, wings and legs all around him. He would take a head and put it on the neck, then put this on a body, then adjust the proper pair of legs, and not put the wings on until the last, because if he did the bird would fly away. While he was engaged in making a beautiful big bird, black and white with speckles on it, with a large beak and fine head, the Evil Spirit came up and began to taunt him.

[1] A retired big game guide with 50 years experience in hunting and dog-sledding, and another long-time Alaskan who still traps Goodpaster Valley, feel it is unlikely that Mitchell could have made his trip as fast as he claimed, and in the manner described. ("Slim" Moore, Anchorage, and Charles Boyd, Delta Junction.) On the other hand, a long-time sled team racing driver, Joe Redington, Sr., says it is entirely possible. He and Susan Butcher made 148 miles from McGrath to Iditarod in less than 24 hours in 1979. He believes several mushers in the 1,049-mile Iditarod Trail Race have duplicated Mitchell's feat on the north end of the race route, approaching Nome. In 1967, General Mitchell was elected to the special section of the Mushers' Hall of Fame at the museum in Knik, Alaska, in recognition of his exploits on dog team trails when the telegraph line was built. (Letter to editor from Dorothy Page, Iditarod Race Committee, October 10, 1981.)

[2] Mitchell experimented with kites in the Tanana Valley. Author Emile Gauvreau, a close friend of his, wrote: "His [Mitchell's] favorite story . . . had to do with a contrivance of his own invention which had actually lifted him from the ground when he was stringing telegraph wire in Alaska for the Army. 'With a few materials we had at hand,' he said, 'we made kites, and I found that by putting two large kites in tandem I could evolve a structure that lifted me off the ground. This was long before I learned to fly, but it was the most exhilerating experience I ever had. Those kites, by the way, were able to carry wire into the air for over a mile and saved me a lot of work.'" Emile Gauvreau, *Billy Mitchell, Founder of our Air Force and Prophet Without Honor,* Dutton & Co., (New York, 1942.)
The Alaska Communication System's 49th Anniversary Bulletin, 1949, mentioned Mitchell's work in Alaska in 1903. "Even in those days, Billy Mitchell was a flying enthusiast. He used a box kite to take himself into the air a sufficient height (altitude approximately 100 feet) to survey the surrounding locale so as to choose a route for his pole line."

Without thinking, he put the wings on the bird which immediately began to fly away. Picking up the first pair of legs he could find, which were little ones, he threw them at the bird and they stuck right under his tail. That is why this big fine bird, the loon, has only a small pair of legs and cannot walk on the ground.

We went back to the tent with the mirror, and Joe said to me, "Now me have your medicine. Good Pasture Indians no have mirror. Me see myself, me see everything behind me." By this he meant that as he could see both in front and behind him, no evil influence could approach him without being observed. Indians think that the evil one approaches them stealthily from behind, the same way they themselves stalk game.

The Indian David had returned to his tribe from the Good Pasture territory. We had undoubtedly saved his life by giving him our dried salmon and rice, fixing up his wickiup and getting wood for him. I had also given him some 30/30 cartridges. After we left his camp the second time, he began to have good luck hunting. Of course he was a good deal stronger by that time, having had food. He killed a couple of moose, which put him on easy street for the rest of the spring.

If an Indian has an abundance of food, even though he sees a long winter coming with no prospects of getting more, he may eat it up all at once. He gives "potlatches," that is, feasts where everyone comes, and has a good time generally, and he gives away his possessions, blankets, cooking utensils, firearms, food, and even clothing. It is a system that obtains among the northern Indians which tends to equalize everybody's possessions, in case one gets very much more than the others. When they get down to a starvation diet, however, and only a very little food can be obtained, they are wonderful at husbanding every ounce they have.

It is a tradition with all northern Indians that after they have eaten all the meat off bones and they are picked clean, they must be thrown into the fire. Often the big marrow bones are plucked out, split and the marrow eaten. They must never give these bones to the dogs to chew, even though their dogs are starving. I have seen Indians sit around a fire, four or five of them, chewing meat off moose bones, surrounded by starving dogs, and throwing these bones into the fire to be incinerated.

The big snowshoe rabbit is a great item in their food supply. They hesitate to shoot these with firearms, using bows and arrows instead. Of course, looking at it one way, a rabbit is hardly worth the expenditure of a cartridge, which are expensive and hard to obtain in the North. But the Indians give a different explanation. They say that when rabbits are killed with firearms, the bullets go right through them and kill their souls. The soul, under these conditions, cannot come back to other rabbits. Thus the whole group of rabbits in a vicinity might die and become extinct. They point out that every seven years rabbits almost disappear and it takes a couple of years for them to come back in considerable numbers. This, they say, is because the white men shoot rabbits with firearms, thus killing their souls, and the family of rabbits must increase from those that are left with souls.

As a matter of fact, rabbits are known to get various diseases when any great number is in one place. In about seven years, the epidemic seizes them and they almost disappear. It is also the case with grouse and some of the other animals.

David was very grateful for what we had done, more grateful than any Indian I ever had anything to do with. Ordinarily, Indians do not show their gratitude openly, but almost always manage to repay their benefactors in some way. David came to me with a moosehide bag which he wanted me to accept as a gift from him. It felt as though it contained some light articles, so I looked into it and saw it was filled with sable skins. There were fourteen A-1 skins, perfectly matched for color and size. David told me they had come from two litters of sables caught in the thick timber on one of the tributaries of the Good Pasture River. They were the darkest skins I had ever seen. Of course, the darker the skin, the more valuable it is. I tried to dissuade him from giving me such a costly gift but he insisted, and I kept them, knowing he would have felt keenly hurt had I made him take them back.

Chief Joseph gave me several remembrances of our friendship and the work we had done together. These consisted of buckskin shirts, coats and moccasins with bead work made by one of his squaws. One ceremonial belt he gave me had rabbit's feet connected to the main belt by moose sinews passed through the polished thigh bones of rabbits. This belt made quite a jingling sound when one danced in it. Another belt was made of the lower teeth of about two hundred caribou. The caribou only has lower teeth, like a sheep. These had been carefully saved from each animal killed during the winter and then had been sewn to a thick piece of caribou hide. It made a very interesting ornament and a rare souvenir.

Joe's tribe had made quite a little money out of the stampeders who had gone up to the Fairbanks strike and were unusually prosperous for Indians at that time of the year. The Indians were very improvident, particularly so if they are in contact with white men, whose customs they try to imitate and whose "fire water" has a terrible effect on them.

Clean-up on ''Discovery'' claim, Anvil Creek (Nome), circa 1900. COURTESY U.S. ARMY, NATIONAL ARCHIVES, 111-SC-83802

BOAT TRIP ON THE GOODPASTER

17

After saying goodbye to Joe and his tribe, I went back to [the camp at] Central, to find the boats practically finished. There were five quite large ones, about eighteen feet long, which would hold one ton of cargo, four rowers and a steersman, and for my own use, a double-ender, twelve feet long. Despite their crude tools and equipment, the men had built excellent boats.

The pack saddles and equipment for the mules were there and the packers had been busy getting willow sticks of suitable length and thickness with which to rig their aparejos. Our food supplies were sufficient to last until we reached Lieutenant Gibbs and his party coming up from the lower Tanana, but nothing could be wasted. If by any chance some of our supplies were lost, we would probably be delayed for another year.

I organized the crews for the boats and practiced them in rowing and steering. I put our best men with the two boats containing our reserve food supplies, so as to insure their getting through in good shape. They were to stop at the mouth of the Good Pasture on the Tanana, opposite the Indian village and organize a camp from which supplies could be distributed up and down the river.

I started the pack trains through the water while the ice was still floating on it. They carried the working parties along the line where they were to erect the poles, put on the insulators and tie the telegraph wire on. Our wire had now been laid all along the right of way from the head of the Good Pasture to the Tanana and it remained for me to determine the course of the line from that point on down to where we met the other party.

We had practically continuous light at this time. I started out in the lead with my boat, with orders to the others to come at two hour intervals so that if anything happened to us in front, we would have sufficient time to run upstream and signal to them what to do. Old Dutch was at the oars in my boat. We had a little dog named "Jakey" with us, a halfbred Malemute and shepherd dog that had been stunted in his youth and had never grown very much. He was a very nice dog, and Dutch claimed he was a wonderful bear dog. I thought at any rate he could guard our camp.

Dutch proved to be a pretty fair oarsman. I had two steering sweeps in the stern so that I could use the right or left one to avoid drifts, rapids, or "sweepers," that is, trees which had fallen into the water but whose roots had not been detached, which would be carried downstream to their total length, then spring up and repeat the operation. It was a very dangerous thing to get caught under one of them.

I sat in the stern, with Dutch in front of me at the rowing bench. Beyond him was our camp outfit and grub, while on my right hand was a 30/40 rifle loaded, and on my left a 30/30. At my feet sat Jakey, the little dog, who peered over the gunwales at the shore as we went downstream. The river was beautiful, the trees were beginning to take on their summer aspect, and the bushes were completely clothed with bright green leaves. Wild flowers covered the ground. We were so confident now that we would finish the telegraph line that summer that we had ceased to talk about it.

As we went along, Dutch told me he wanted very much to kill some game, that he had never killed a moose, a bear or a caribou in Alaska. The salmon were then beginning to run and I told him that undoubtedly we would see many bears. In the midst of this conversation, I looked over the long stretch of mossy flat and could see herds of caribou. Dutch went on talking about how he had learned to shoot with the Boers, but I told him I thought their instruction was very poor, and I didn't think he could hit a balloon.

Glancing at the river bank on the left, a little ahead of us, I saw first one, then two, three, four and five caribou leave the bank, jump in the water and start to swim across. From the way we were drifting down the current, we were sure to run into them. I told Dutch to ship his oars with as little noise as possible. The caribou paid no attention to us but swam straight on. Little Jakey stood up and would have barked had I not hit him over the head. I took the 30/30 rifle with eight rounds in the magazine and one in the barrel, gave it to Dutch and told him to wait until the caribou got within ten feet, then to shoot them. When the leader was within ten feet, Dutch began shooting. He shot over and under them, before and behind them, and emptied the whole gun without touching a single one. The caribou apparently knew him, because they kept right on going. I saw that they were making for a bar where they would go up from the water, so I beached the boat, and taking my 30/40, killed four of them as they emerged.

Dutch was overwhelmed and said it was the greatest chance he had ever had to kill game, and he did not know what was the matter. In my opinion, I told him, it was the worst fit of buck ague I had ever seen and unless he could calm down, he would never hit anything.

"Here they were," he said, "so close it was not even necessary to look at them. All you had to do was shoot."

That was where he made his mistake, I told him, because no matter how close they were, you had to single out your individual animal and shoot at a certain place on it, otherwise you would not kill him.

We dressed the caribou, which were very large and fat, and put one on our boat. This carcass sunk it so low it was not possible to take any more along. We hung the rest up on a tree, then chopped another tree off about six feet above the ground, letting it project into the water, then took some willows and cut them off so our axe marks could be plainly seen. Above these we hung the caribou. We knew the other men would be sure to see them and could carry them along in the big boats easily. The boat following us noticed the sign, and as they had had no meat for some time, they were overjoyed to see the caribou, which they promptly loaded on the boats.

Bears were beginning to come to the river to fish and I knew we would see some before long. As I watched the bank, I saw a mother marten or sable, carrying a little one in her mouth, running up to deposit it in a little den in some rocks on the side of the hill. Quickly beaching the boat, I ran ashore and tried to catch her but she got away. Presently I saw her again, with another small sable in her mouth. Dutch pulled his coat off and put it over her, catching her and the kitten. There were three more kittens out, which we had no difficulty in getting. They seemed not at all scared.

The only box we had to confine them in was a little grub box that had contained baking powder, about 12 × 14 inches across and ten inches deep. With pieces from another box we improvised a cage and put the old lady marten in it, with her four kittens. She tried in every way to get out and would not eat any bacon or meat that we offered her. The little ones, however, ate meat without hesitancy and were very friendly and playful. When we rubbed the backs of their necks, they purred. We had to be careful in sticking our fingers through the bars that the old lady did not grab us.

From this point on we began seeing bears more and more, their coats in bad shape, blotchy and looking as though they had the mange. There were many kinds, silver tips, brown bears, cinnamon bears, glacier bears with almost white coats, that live way up in the hills, and the ever present black bear. They were all sitting along the bank waiting for salmon to come. All followed the same procedure in catching fish. Salmon of course run up against the current. The bears sat on the bank, facing upstream, and watched until a fish came within reach, then with one crack of the paw, they would send it shimmering fifteen or twenty feet from the water. Turning quickly, they were upon it in a moment. Sometimes a bear would chase and grab a fish with his mouth. At one place we saw fourteen different bears "fishing." As we had killed the caribou, we did not need any meat, and as bears at that particular time, when eating fish, are not very good to eat, we let them alone.

That night we made camp at the mouth of the Good Pasture River. I decide to wait there until the other boats arrived, and reorganize the expedition. Mosquitoes were beginning to get bad. It is impossible to convey to one who has not been in the North how terrible these insects really are.[1] At night we built long smudges, or slow burning fires, around which the mules and horses stood to escape the mosquitoes. After a while the animals got so they would not even leave the smudge to feed or graze, so great was the pain inflicted by the bites. Two of my mules were literally killed by mosquitoes on this expedition. They were bitten so severely that in the first place they would not leave the smudges to feed and grew constantly weaker. Later, trying to avoid the mosquitoes, they got into the swift water of the Tanana and were swept away and drowned.

Of my family of sables, all but one, a little female, escaped during the night. We called it "Petite." It took to us just like a tame cat, but was even more playful

[1] The ferocity of these insects was described in 1897 by Jack London who came to Alaska gathering material for his *The Call of the Wild.* Said London: "One night badly bitten, under netting. Couldn't vouch for it, but Jim watched them and said they rushed the netting in a body, one gang holding up the edge while a second gang crawled under. Charley swore that he has seen several of the largest ones pull the mesh apart and let a small one through. I have seen them with their proboscis bent and twisted after an assault on a sheet-iron stove." Richard Mathews, *The Yukon,* Holt, Rinehart and Winston, (New York, 1968.)

and affectionate. It was so agile even at three months of age, that it could jump right up on my shoulder from the ground. It would jump four or five feet almost from a standstill and land on the place it desired. While perched on my shoulder, it would rub its head against my face, and when I stroked it, it would purr much like a cat. I never saw a wild animal that could be so easily tamed.

A few days later, some of my men coming down the river reported having seen the same sable mother at her den where we had caught her. She must have found her way back along those many miles, carrying or coaxing her kittens along with her.

Our pet sable now became a member of the family and as is often the case with "members of the family," it grew to be a nuisance when it became too familiar.

Dutch and I worked down the Tanana River ahead of the working parties. When I found a suitable place to land, I would get out on the bank, strike the line where the telegraph should go, then with my prismatic compass lay a straight line from one point to another, and blaze the trail through myself, alone. I laid out from five to ten miles a day in this way. It was difficult work through the underbrush, bogs and wet moss, with the mosquitoes and insects to contend with, but much easier and quicker than to carry a big outfit and several men along with me.

Rounding the promontory which is at the mouth of the Delta River, we entered Bates' Rapids of the Tanana. The water here was much swifter than I had supposed. The river was twenty miles wide, with an interminable number of sloughs. The current ran at a prodigious rate, carrying with it whatever trees or other floating material got into it. These things lodged on the bends, bars or on projections along the banks, and made a great heap like a log jam, under which the current raced and roared. If a boat got under them, it would be all off with it. We only had about a hundred miles more to go to finish the line, so I determined to take one of the large grub boats and handle it myself, to be sure that nothing happened to it on the way down. I had one of my other men take my own boat while I took Dutch and three others, all of them at the oars, two on each side. One was an ex-constable of the Canadian Mounted Police, a very good man on the water. I stood up in the stern and had a twenty foot sweep with which to steer the boat. The channels were crooked and in many places sweepers fifty feet long hung over them, going down with the water, then raising with a swish and falling again.

We made very good time and I was able to avoid both sweepers and the great piles of drift on the bars. I had never before seen such swift water, nor have I since. Suddenly the channel narrowed and the speed of the water increased. I could see there was a sharp turn ahead, on the other side of which there would be an eddy, due to the water hitting the point and then swirling on the other side. Directly opposite this point was a long sweeper, a green spruce tree. Green trees are much more limber than dead ones, and whip in and out of the water with an incredible swing. If this sweeper hit us, we would certainly be swamped and lose our grub, and thus be delayed another year on the work. It was the supreme moment of test, on which hung the success of our expedition.

Shouting to the men to put on all the speed they could so as to get steerage, away we shot for the point. I planned to swing the boat with the sweep as we got there, pointing it to the right and trusting it would hit the eddy on the other side and carry us to safety. As we neared it, I thought I would make it. Standing in the stern, I pulled my steering sweep with all my might, but just as I did so the spruce sweeper caught me squarely across the waist and lifted me from the boat.

Below us was a great pile of drift on a projection of the bank under which the water swirled. I knew if I let go the sweeper, I would be carried under the drift and never heard from again. All I could do was to hold on to the tree. It carried me under the icy water, then flopped up about fifteen feet in the air, then fell again and went under the current. I could hear Dutch telling me to hold on, and the ex-constable shouting to the men to pull for the shore. A quarter of a mile below me the boat landed. By that time I had wrapped both my arms and legs around the trunk and found that I could hold my breath while the sweeper went under the water. I thought I could hold for fifteen or twenty minutes at least, but if I was swept off at the end of that time, I would have so little strength left I could not avoid going under the drift pile.

I saw three men leave the boat the instant it touched the shore while a fourth made it fast with its painter to the trunk of a tree. One of them had a big coil of rope, another an axe. Never have I seen men work faster or to better effect. Going to the bend about thirty feet upstream from me, they tied the rope around Dutch over his right shoulder and under his left arm, then took a turn around his body. They snubbed the rope around a tree and Dutch jumped into the raging current, being let down gradually by the other three until he got to the point where the sweeper carried me upstream and down into the water. As I came up, he grabbed me around both shoulders and I grabbed him. Holding one to each other like vises, we were pulled in by the other three men.

As we landed, Dutch said to me, "I don't know if

we are even, but you saved me from freezing last winter and I have pulled you out of a bad place in this river."

If it had not been for men like these, I doubt if I would have been rescued from the place.

Making contact on the Skagway-Juneau submarine cable, August 1901.
COURTESY ALASKA HISTORICAL LIBRARY, WINTER AND POND COLLECTION

First WAMCATS building in Valdez, early 1900's.
COURTESY WALTER PHILLIPS, PALMER, ALASKA

18

HUNTING ON THE TANANA

We completed the trip twenty miles down the river that day without further mishap. Here we stayed several days, while I ran the course of the line up and down. Then Dutch and I took our small boat and dropped down to the mouth of the Saljacket [Salcha] River, a few miles below. Again I ran the course of the line, meeting my men about 20 miles up the river as they worked chopping out the right of way. Never have I seen greater physical strength or endurance displayed by a group of men. There were twenty in each working party, great bearded fellows in blue denim clothing, high horsehide boots and slouch hats, with remnants of mosquito netting around the edges. Their faces were running sores from the terrible assaults of the mosquitoes and black flies. As they attacked the spruce trees, the forest seemed to fall in front of them. Without such men, the lines in the North could never have been completed.

One evening in camp on the Saljacket, I told Dutch that as we had had no meat for a long time, I was going out hunting soon. Dutch said that he had seen many moose tracks that day and he thought he could kill some. With Jakey, his wonderful "bear dog," he would be prepared if they ran into bears. Jakey, he said, would immediately attack them, and if a bear turned to defend himself, Jakey would avoid him and keep running around behind, biting at his quarters, which would eventually force the bear to back up against a steep bank to hold Jakey off. Then Jakey would bark and make a great noise to attract our attention, when we could come and shoot the bear. I asked Dutch how he knew this, without having had any experience. He replied that although he had never killed a bear with Jakey, one of his friends who had owned him as a pup told him he thought he would do it.

Later that evening, Dutch took me to the place he had seen all the moose tracks. We walked up the Tanana River three or four miles, threading our way over the moss and through the bunches of spruce timber and alders, and came to the dry bed of a slough. Sure enough, there were a great many moose tracks, cows, bulls and calves, and they were quite fresh, some having been made only a few hours before. Dutch thought the moose were feeding on the tender willows and alders there, and that if he worked up under the cut bank of the slough, his dog Jakey could smell them and indicate where they were, and he could kill them. This rather amused me as I could not think much of Dutch's ability as a hunter, or Jakey's as either a bear dog or a moose dog.

On the way back, we went to the mouth of the dry slough where the main river swept majestically by. Quite a long, bare sand bar led out to the river. Glancing across it, I saw a large wolf looking into the water for salmon, which were running strong. At the same instance, he saw us and ran across our front toward some heavy timber to the right. I had my 30/40 repeating Winchester, and kneeling down, I fired at point blank range. My bullet fell short. I set my sights at three hundred. Again the bullet fell short and I set them at three hundred and fifty. I fired just as the wolf was approaching a dense undergrowth, and saw his hindquarters collapse. I had hit him somewhere behind the middle. He dragged himself into the heavy timber before I could get another shot.

Running down there, I picked up his blood trail and followed him into the woods. I could hear him snapping and snarling and at last caught site of him. His hindquarters had been smashed by the bullet and he had dragged himself by his forelegs alone. I gave him another bullet which killed him instantly. Walking up to him, I saw that he was a large beast with pretty good fur for that time of the year, but glancing closer, I saw he had a collar on. He was no wolf at all, but a dog that had escaped from one of the mushers the winter before. These huskies look exactly like wolves and are impossible to distinguish a short way off.

Next day while I worked on the right of way, Dutch went out to kill a moose. His hopes ran high. At last, he thought, he would get some game while in Alaska. I returned late, to find Dutch rather crestfallen. He told me he had seen several moose but they were so wild, he had not been able to kill any. I asked how close he had been to them and he said he couldn't tell. Were they one or two hundred yards away? No, he answered much closer than that. When I asked if he could see their eyes, he said yes, he not only saw their eyes, but their hair; and to end up with, he told me one had nearly run over him. I counted his ammunition and found he had shot six times. I noticed also that Jakey acted very much cowed, as if he were scared. I could get hardly anything out of Dutch about what had happened, so I said, "Tomorrow morning I want you to take me out and show me where this happened."

Next morning, we went almost to the same place where I had shot the dog, thinking it was a wolf. We ran into the tracks of eight or ten moose, all mixed up with Dutch's track and the track of little Jakey. Jakey had apparently left at once; it was easy to see how he had bounded off in the soft mud of the slough. In one place I noticed one of Dutch's footprints on a moose's track and one of the moose's tracks on Dutch's footprint.

"What does this mean?" I asked, and he answered, "I was under the big bull."

"What big bull?"

"The big bull whose herd it was."

It developed that he had seen the bull leading several others down the slough, and he had concealed himself behind a little pile of dry bushes. When they got almost to him, he jumped out and began shooting. The moose ran straight for him, he said, and scared him half to death. In fact, they almost ran over him. He fired two shots before they got to him, and four when they were leaving, without touching one. They went down to the river and swam across it, where there was extremely swift water. I saw their trail, leading to the water's edge.

This country was full of game, especially moose, but it was very difficult to get near them at that time of year, as they stuck to the thick brush to escape the flies.

Next day I took my rifle and went down to the river, to try my luck. Soon I found moose tracks and many signs of bear on the trees. In the spring of the year, bears stand erect and grab hold of the spruce trees with their front feet, stretching themselves. The Indians say they do it so as to measure how much they have grown during the winter. I could not see a moose, although I got within a few yards of some of them. So thick was the undergrowth and so alert were the moose that they either heard, saw or scented me. In those days I could hunt as noiselessly as any man. In my wet moccasins I made not a sound as I crept along on the moss and under the trees.

It was continuously daylight now, only a little twilight around midnight. I had been hunting about eight hours and was returning to camp, along the banks of the Tanana, which were quite precipitous and covered with spruce timber. The spruce needles had fallen to the ground and made quite a heavy carpet. I noticed an otter slide but could see none of the animals. Young otters are very playful. The will make a slide in the mud of some steep bank, and one after another will jump up and slide down it, turning somersaults, chasing one another and having a great time, just like puppies or children. I have sat by the hour watching them. The old otters sit around and watch their young in these frolics, much the same as human parents do.

As I walked up the bank toward camp, rather disgusted by my day's work, I looked down in the water and saw a small object I took to be the head of an otter. Looking closer, I saw that instead of an otter, it was the head of a bear, which was ducking in and out of the water, apparently bathing. He could not have been fishing, because he would have done this with his paws. The wind was away from him and he had not seen me, I felt certain, because bears do not see very well anyway. I sat down to watch him. He continued ducking in and out, then came out on the bank within ten or fifteen yards of me. I rose to get a better look at him, and he must have heard me move, because he stood erect on his hind legs and looked around. Instantly I shot him through the heart. He was a big brown fellow. With a groan just like a man's, he turned to the right and loped away. I fired again and missed him, then I heard him fall just out of sight. Proceeding cautiously, I found him lying across a log with his head on the other side, breathing his last and groaning almost like a human being. I came up and hit him with a stick and he did not move, so I took out my hunting knife and cut his throat. He appeared to be about seven years old, was in good shape and I estimated he weighed around five hundred pounds. He did not look or smell as though he had been eating fish. I thought we could use a good deal of his meat and certainly his fat, which is almost as good as bacon for cooking.

Within a couple of miles I was back at camp, a beautiful place on the banks of the clear flowing Saljacket River. As I stood on the little bluff above it, I could see some beavers working on their dams two or three hundred yards upstream. Some were pulling trees around, others were cutting on the trees around the banks, and still others working on two beaver houses. In our camp, I could see Dutch cooking supper. He had his bread baking in front of the fire. Jakey lay near him, while our pet marten, Petite, jumped hither and thither, trying to worry Jakey or make him pay attention to her. Every once in a while, Petite would make a dive for the bacon Dutch was cutting up, but he had a little stick with which he would keep her away. While

I sat there, idly watching, I saw a man, thin and haggard, approaching on the other bank of the Saljacket, which was only twenty or thirty yards wide here. Coming down the bank, he called out to Dutch in a weak voice that he was very sick, and wanted some soda.

"Are you very sick?" asked Dutch, playfully, and the man answered, "Yes, I've got such a stomach ache I think I'll die." "How soon?", Dutch went on. "Most any time if you don't help me," said the man. Picking up his gun, Dutch said, "Maybe I'd better shoot you right now and have it over with." At this, they both laughed. Dutch put a little baking soda in the end of a salt sack, tied a stone in it and tossed it across to him, then got the boat and went across for the man.

By that time I had come down the bluff and into camp. The man told me he had had nothing to eat for four days. He and two companions, who were a little way up the river now, had been rafting down the Tanana. They had been packed [packing] up from Valdez to the Tanana crossing, some three hundred miles above where we were. Hearing of the strike at Fairbanks, they thought they could float down the river with a raft to the diggings. The other two men were bankers and he was a broker; all of them, he said, had plenty of money.

Their raft had been merely tied together with ropes. They had bored holes through the logs and made pegs to fasten them together, then bound the raft with willows and strips of bark to make it strong. They had tried to chop out some sweeps with their axes but being so unfamiliar with the work in the wilderness, their sweeps when finished were little better than poles. They had had a fine outfit of food, but it had been poorly packed, and when the water got on it, it was wet through and spoiled. (I had my flour and other foodstuffs that could be harmed by water packed in triple sacks of canvas, with the outer one paraffined.)

As they went down the river, they saw many young Canada geese, which were plentiful along this part, but on getting out their shotgun, the only weapon they had, they found that it was a sixteen gauge and they had only twelve gauge ammunition.

One day they caught two young black bears, but never saw the mother at all. I told him they were very brave men to do that, because they had no gun, and if the old she-bear had ever found them, it would have been all off. "It might just as well have been," the man answered, "Because the day after that we ran into some drift on the edge of a bar, and when we unpacked the raft, we piled up our food just at the edge of the water, where the current kept undercutting the bank. While we were still working to get the raft out, the bears got to fighing on top of the grub, overturned it and spilled everything in the water. We recovered very little of it. Still, one of the boys wanted to keep the cubs, so we did."

Two days afterward they hit a projecting log which tore their raft in two, throwing this man into the water, while the other two clung to the remains of the raft. He had gone down three times, he told me, when two Indians who happened to be near came up and rescued him. After this experience, his companions called him "the hell-diver." The Indians helped them fix up a new raft, which was much better than the old one.

He certainly was talkative after he got a little food and tea in him. I told him to go up and get his friends and have them drop down in the raft to where we were. In about an hour, I heard them coming down the river. Two were at the sweeps and one was attempting to steer. They had almost nothing left on the raft except the two cubs. They moved like wooden men, with no power at all, and barely made the mouth of our little river. We cooked a good meal for them, and as I had a little bit of extra tea, rice and bacon, I fixed up a supply for them to take.

I told them I had just killed a bear and they could have some meat if they would come down and help me skin it. All of them were anxious to see the bear, particularly Dutch, who wanted to show how well Jakey would act in the presence of bears, so we set out.

Within fifty yards of where the carcass lay, there was a slough with water in it, about forty feet wide and three feet deep. Across this a spruce tree had fallen, which afforded a means of crossing. The wind was from us to the bear, so Jakey did not smell him until he got within ten feet of him. When Bruin burst upon his gaze, he put his tail between his legs and with a yelp, ran away as quickly as he could, not even taking time to cross on the fallen tree, but taking to the slough. On our return to camp, we found him still under our sleeping robes, where he had crawled in his fright.

Dutch was much taken aback. Everything he had thought about his wonderful bear dog had been disproved, and all his own prowess as a hunter shown up badly, both by the episode of the caribou when they swam in front of us, and by the moose that had almost walked over him.

The men did not know anything about skinning a bear, but helped me a good deal. A bear is a tough animal and even with the best of knives, it is necessary to sharpen them several times before the operation is completed. They were very glad to get the meat, and the bear was really in better shape than I had thought. We kept the loins, a little fat and the heart, and gave them all the rest.

They were determined to push on and keep their little cubs, which they had tied up with twisted willow thongs. We told them about the very bad water that lay below, and showed them how to tie the things to the raft instead of merely laying them on it, so that if the raft was submerged, they would have a chance of retaining their outfit.

The following day they pushed off. Two hours after their departure, two Indians of the Good Pasture tribe beached their canoes in front of our camp. We were just eating supper. They came up, said "How" and sat down on their haunches. I gave them a little tobacco and tea, and asked them where they were going. They said to Fairbanks, to sell fur, pointing to their loaded canoes. Pretty soon one of them said to me, "You see white men?" I answered, "Yes, three white men," to which he responded, "Guess him die in water." On my asking why, he answered, "Him no savvy Tanana, too much fast water." These Indians proved to be the men who had rescued our visitors two days before and they told us about it. One man, they said, had fallen out and they had rescued him in their canoes, which he had almost overturned in his frantic efforts to get out of the water. They were the most helpless white men the Indians had ever met.

I told the Indians they had better push right along and see if they could catch up with the white men, because undoubtedly they would get into trouble again. As soon as they had their meal of bear meat, tea, beans and open fire bread, all of which they ate to their heart's content, they pushed out into the stream.

The telegraph line was strung on tripods across muskeg and in permafrost areas where repeated thawing and freezing would raise and tip over a single pole. (Pictured near Thompson Pass, 1968.)

COURTESY LYMAN L. WOODMAN, 1968

THE MAIN LINES ARE CONNECTED

19

For a couple of weeks we worked with great speed. Already our parties had gotten in touch with those of Lieutenant Gibbs working up the river. July [1903] was approaching, and now I had no doubts that we would finish the telegraph system that summer. Our wire was working well behind us to Eagle City on the Yukon, to Valdez on the Pacific and by way of Valdez to the United States, over our cable. We had to go through no foreign country now for communication to the United States.[1]

About this time the two Indians who had followed the white men came back. Apparently they had been very successful in their trading, as they had a lot of stuff in their canoes, new hats, bandanna handkerchiefs and tobacco, unmistakable signs of prosperity. After some talk about their trading, I asked them where the white men were.

The next day after leaving us, they said, they had come across the white men on a small island in the Tanana River, still with their bears, but with nothing else. The raft had been caught under some drift and entirely lost, and the men had extricated themselves by climbing up on this. They tried to take one white man to the shore in a canoe, but he nearly capsized it and could not ride in it at all. So they tied the two canoes together and made a sort of catamaran, taking each white man ashore separately. They were going to kill the bears, but the white men begged so hard for them that they took them ashore, too. The white men had absolutely nothing to eat and did not want to eat the bears, so the Indians went out to kill some game for them. Fortunately, they killed a yearling moose, whose liver and heart they brought in that night, and got the rest of the meat the next day. The white men walked down the banks of the river, while the Indians kept in touch with them in canoes and got them safely to Fairbanks. Here the white men gave each Indian $500 for what they had done, which certainly was very liberal. These men afterward were quite successful and all of them located good claims.

Petite, our marten, had now grown to full size. Although it was a never ending source of interest and enjoyment to us most of the time, its tricks and thievishness were beginning to make it a nuisance. I debated with myself what to do with the little animal. It would be cruel to take it Outside with me to the United States. The surroundings, climate and other conditions would probably be injurious and unhealthy for it. I could turn it over to some of my friends, but they might not take proper care of it. If I turned it loose, it might become the prey of some other animal or some trapper. However, the latter seemed the best solution, as it was in better physical condition, from our care and feeding, than any of its fellows. It could catch fish, although I never saw it do so, but it would look longingly at the water sometimes, when the salmon were running.

While still undecided as to what I should do with it, I returned to camp one evening after having been running the right of way through a difficult stretch of timber and found Dutch in a fury over Petite's latest trick. He had been having an increasingly difficult time with it, anyway, as it was continually getting into the grub box and taking whatever it could find. On this occasion, Petite had been playing with the dog and jumping all over the place while Dutch was making bread. He had the bread pan full of batter, when without warning the marten, with one leap, was in the middle of it and covered with dough in an instant. With another jump, it landed right on our wolf robe, in which we were to sleep that night, turning over and over on it to rub the dough off, before Dutch could catch it. Dutch had been working for over two hours to get the dough out of the robe, to say nothing of having the bread spoiled. That decided the matter. We planned to leave our little friend when we moved the next day.

[1] The Army's submarine cable connecting Valdez with Seattle, via Sitka, was not completed until October 1904. Mitchell left Alaska in 1903. Before the cable was installed, communications to the States went eastward from Eagle (Fort Egbert) across the boundary to an extension of the Canadian telegraph system, thence south.

The marten always sat in the stern of the boat with me, while Jakey sat at my feet, and Dutch was at the oars. When we pushed off into the swift water of the Tanana, I tossed the little creature ashore. It apparently knew what that meant instantly, and began a terrible chirping, scolding and spitting, and swam right into the water after us. We pulled out into the center of the stream and the current swept it down. It must have lost sight of us, because in a little while it turned back to the shore and I could see it mount the bank, a perfectly free animal, but now thrown on its own resources in competition with the wild animals of the forest, the climate and snows for its existence. I hope some day in our future life that I shall find out what became of Petite.

At last my wire crossed the Saljacket River. Due to lack of transportation, Gibbs had fallen a little behind in his work and I had to extend on beyond, but at length we reached the end of his wire. I made the last connection of the [land lines of the] Alaska system myself [on June 27, 1903].[2]

Then from St. Michael and Nome on the Bering Sea, clear through to New York and Washington, the electric current transmitted our messages with the speed of light. Alaska was open to civilization. No longer was it the land of the unknown, sealed tight by the God of Everlasting Snow and Frost. We had broken the portal with which he shut out the white man from the North. We had worked straight through his coldest winters, over his highest ridges, down his broadest rivers, both in winter and summer. His mosquito scourge had failed to stop us, and we not only had surmounted all the difficulties, but had grown intensely fond of this wonderful country. America's last frontier had been roped and hog-tied.

Step by step, we retraced our route to Fort Egbert. Telegraph cabins were set up every 25 miles, each provided with a personnel of three men and a dog team. The cabins were well made and well supplied with food, rifles, and ammunition, and the men were encouraged to hunt and trap. Prospecting or gold mining was prohibited, as it was apt to cause the men to neglect their work. I found all these things completed, as had been planned during the previous winter. We checked up our property papers, and accounts, and so efficiently had Sergeant Pollner handled these that the expenditure of not one cent was questioned nor was any property unaccounted for. My job was done.

I gathered up my furs and trophies of bear, moose, sheep, goats, and caribou, packed up and took a steamer down the Yukon to St. Michael [in July 1903], where I boarded another steamer, the *Portland,* an old wooden ship built for use in the Arctic, with many feet of solid oak in her nose with which to pound the ice. Her commander, a fine old sea dog, was lost with his ship some years afterward.

From St. Michael we went to Nome, took on a few passengers and then proceeded south through Bering Sea, passing St. Matthew Island, which is sparsely inhabited by native hunters of seal, whale, and walrus; then by the Pribilofs, St. Paul and St. George, our great seal rookery; then to Unalaska, or Dutch Harbor as it is called, at the beginning of the Aleutian Islands which stretch out almost to Asia. We anchored near the old revenue cutter *Bear,* which had rescued the Greely Expedition in 1883, opposite the northern end of Greenland. She was under the command of Captain Tuttle, famous in our old Revenue Cutter Service. The ship's surgeon was Dr. Hawley, from Milwaukee, whom I had known for many years. The *Bear* had just completed a trip up into the Arctic Ocean as far as Wrangell Island, where she had landed a party. They had many polar bear skins on board. The *Bear* was on her way to the Hawaiian Islands where she went every winter after her Arctic cruise. There all her hatches were kept open and she was thoroughly dried out after her drenching in the fog, rain, and snow of the northern seas. Her officers spoke frequently of the Japanese boats just beginning to come in increasing numbers into Bering Sea. These men killed the fur seals on their migrations, and the sea otters, which then were almost extinct and whose killing was prohibited by law. With it all they were supposed to be making maps and charts of the whole area so that in case Japan ever had to carry out warlike expeditions in the North, all the necessary data would be on hand.

Several whaling vessels were also lying at anchor, which we visited. They were well-rigged and well manned, but very oily and smelly. One of the whalers had three sea otter skins, two from full grown animals and one from a pup. This was the rarest and highest priced fur in the world. The sea otters at one time ranged clear from the Japanese Islands to the California coast, but they are now to be found only on the rocky promontories of some of the Aleutian Islands, in constantly diminishing numbers. When Pribilof first went to the islands that bear his name, it was not seal skins he was after, but sea otter skins. These were taken

[2] This refers to the tie-in near Salcha of the north-south and east-west lines connecting Fort Liscum on the south at Valdez with Nome and Fort St. Michael and the posts along the Yukon. Skagway could be reached over the Canadian link. Other connections came later as shortcuts were developed and communities in southeastern Alaska were added. The Chief Signal Officer's annual report for FY 1902 credits Lieutenent Mitchell with supervision of construction of 125 miles of the Valdez-Eagle line. Assuming he also directed the work on the connecting line 65 miles from the mouth of the Goodpaster to the Salcha River, he had been responsible for a total of 190 miles of WAMCATS telegraph line.

to China by the hundreds of thousands and sold to the Mandarins. When the Allied troops went to Peking in 1900, whole robes of sea otter were captured, the value of which were not known to the soldiers then.

Unless something can be done to stop the indiscriminate killing of sea otters, they will probably become extinct before many years. Japanese fishermen and hunters are especially guilty in this regard.

Some of the men on these whalers had been in the Arctic thirty years before, when a whole whaling fleet was caught in the ice and destroyed. At that time, 32 whaling ships were abandoned by their crews in the Arctic Ocean. In 1871 the ice was unusually heavy. The whalers arrived off Bering Straits within a few days of each other, working their way through the narrow passages in the ice, where there was constant danger of being stove in or colliding with other vessels.

About the last of July, they succeeded in getting into the Arctic Ocean, where they raced to get through. From the Straits they worked north and east to Cape Lisburne. The navigation along this coast is difficult on account of the great number of sandbars stretching out from the shore. As the charts were poor, soundings had to be made almost constantly. The tides through here do not amount to much but a change of wind brings on a decided difference in the depth of the water. As the ships were so near the Magnetic Pole, their compasses acted in a strange manner. The needle dips down so low that it is hard for it to turn on its axis.

By August the ice had worked further offshore and the whalers proceeded to the northeast. They passed Icy Cape and were approaching Point Barrow, but toward the last of August, the wind changed to the southwest and the ice began shutting in on them, accompanied by heavy snow storms. The whalers tried to escape the way they had come but the ice closed in more and more. When a ship is really "beset" in this pack ice, which presses on it from all sides, its timbers are crushed in and its decks bent. When it sinks, it leaves no trace nor does any wreckage ever come up. During the first part of September some of the ships were crushed and by the middle of the month the crews of all the ships found they could not escape. They sent down the coast to see if any ships were outside the pack ice, and found that there were seven, about 70 miles away. Hope was abandoned for saving the ships, and preparations made to join those outside. Some of the captains had their wives and children with them, and treasures they had gathered up all over the world. Everything not absolutely necessary had to be left behind. They set out in small boats along the shore. When the ships were abandoned, the colors were left flying. All the liquor was destroyed so the Eskimos would not get intoxicated and burn the ships in their orgies, but the whalers forgot to take out the medicine chests. When the natives found them, they ate and drank liberally of their contents, with the result that some were killed and others made very sick. In revenge, they burned several ships.

After a couple of days in the open whaling boats, the refugees reached the ships outside the pack ice. As soon as they had taken on all the crews, they made sail through Bering Straits and down to Honolulu.

During the winter after the ships were abandoned, some sank where they were from the pressure of the ice, some were burned by the natives, but some went through the whole winter without being injured. Only one was saved by whalers who went up the next year and brought it out.

The destruction of this whaling fleet, that hailed from New Bedford, Mass., was one of the severest setbacks that the whalers had after the Civil War. In 1876, thirteen whaling ships were lost near Point Barrow. It is a ticklish thing to get caught in the Arctic Ocean between the pack ice and the shore, as the chances are very much against the whalers ever getting out.

We left Unalaska in a dense fog and proceeded out of the harbor and through the pass between the islands, guided by the echo of the whistle. A ship's officer stood on the bridge, watch in hand, and blew the whistle. He noted the number of seconds between the time the whistle was blown and when the echo was received, and computed from that how far offshore the ship was. This method of navigation is often resorted to through this part of the world.

We had an uneventful although rough passage to Seattle. From there I was ordered to Washington, D.C. to report on what had transpired during the building of the telegraph lines, and what we should do in the future about maintaining or extending them.

Although many generations will elapse before Alaska carries a heavy population, which will come only when the rest of North America is so overpopulated that people have to go into the frozen north to find a livelihood, still it is capable of supporting hundreds of thousands. Its soil is extremely fertile, its rivers abound in fish and its hills and forests shelter great herds of the finest of game animals.

Officers' quarters, Fort Davis, four miles east of Nome, September 1901. Post named in memory of Col. Jefferson C. Davis, 23rd Infantry. He had, as a major general during 1867-1870, commanded the Military District of Alaska, the designation for the entire new territory.

COURTESY ARCHIVES, UNIVERSITY OF ALASKA, FAIRBANKS, GEORGE WILKENSEN COLLECTION

Telegraph station, Copper Center, built according to the plan shown on the opposite page.

COURTESY U.S. ARMY

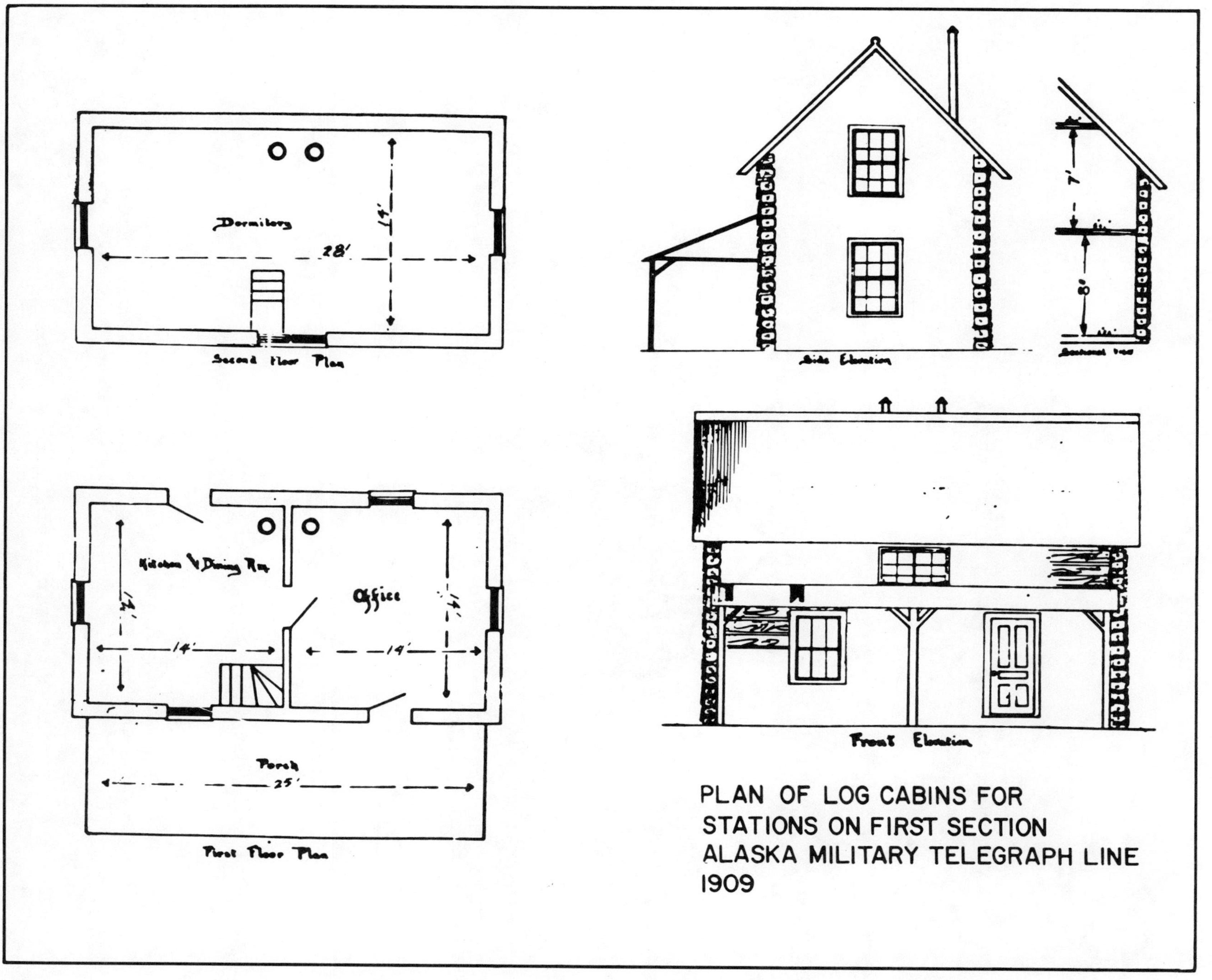
Dormitory
28'
14'
Second Floor Plan
Side Elevation
7'
8'
Sectional View
Kitchen & Dining Rm
Office
14'
14'
14'
14'
Porch
25'
First Floor Plan
Front Elevation
PLAN OF LOG CABINS FOR
STATIONS ON FIRST SECTION
ALASKA MILITARY TELEGRAPH LINE
1909

Appendix A

COMMUNICATIONS CONSTRUCTION 1900-1904*

Funds were appropriated May 26, 1900; construction materials arrived in Valdez in July, and on the Yukon in August. By the end of October 1900 the following progress had been made:

Officer in Charge	Construction	Miles
1st Lt. G.W. Stuart, 7th Inf.	Nome to Fort Davis and Port Safety	24
2nd Lt. W.O. Smith, 7th Inf.	St. Michael and Golsovia	35
1st Cl.Sgt. C. Wahl, Sig. Corp.	Golsovia to Unalakleet	30
1st Lt. R.S. Offley, 7th Inf.	Unalakleet to 22-Mile Cabin	22
1st Lt. O.B. Grimm, Sig. Officer, Volunteers	22-Mile Cabin to Kaltag Portage to Nulato	108
2nd Lt. W.O. Smith, 7th Inf.	Nulato, eastward	13
Two detachments, one led by 2nd Lt. P.M. Cochran, 7th Inf., another by 2nd Lt. J.M. Loud, 7th Inf.	Fort Gibbon to old station, west;	13
	scattered short lengths between old station and Kokrines with poles and wire;	19
	and a part with poles only.	11
2nd Lt. W.M. Craigie, 7th Inf.	Fort Egbert to International boundary	11
1st Lt. C.C. Burnell, Sig. Officer, Volunteers	Port Valdez to Station 3,	37
	and poles set to Ernestine Creek	13
	Total	336

* From Appendix 9, *The Story of the Alaska Communication System, 1900-1943,* op.cit.

Appendix A (continued)

By the time the all-American route was completed in October 1904 these stations were operating on the land lines and cables:

NOME - VALDEZ

	Miles Part	Miles Total
Nome	0	0
Fort Davis	4	4
(1) Safety	20	24
St. Michael (cable)	133	157
Golsovia	35	192
Unalakleet	30	222
Old Woman	50	272
Kaltag	45	317
Nulato	40	357
Koyukuk	30	387
Grimkop	20	407
Louden	30	437
Melozi	35	472
Kokrines	38	510
Birches	40	550
Fort Gibbon (Tanana)	55	605
Cosna	45	650
Baker	25	675
Tolovana	37	712
Nenana	55	767
Chena	48	815
Fairbanks	10	825
Salcha	37	862
Goodpastor	60	922
Central	32	954
Summit	58	1012
Ketchumstuk	54	1066
Dennison Creek	30	1096
Tanana Crossing	25	1121
Big Tokio (Tok)	31	1152
Mentasta Pass	20	1172
Cheslotta	20	1192
Chistochina	26	1218
(2) Talsona	20	1238
Gulkana	20	1258
Copper Center	26	1284
Tonsina	25	1309
(3) Teikhell	24	1333
(4) Saina	24	1357
Keystone	19	1376
Valdez	12	1388
Lowe River	3	1391
Fort Liscum (Valdez)	5	1396

FORT EGBERT BRANCH

	Miles Part	Miles Total
(5) Ketchumstuk	0	0
Gold Creek	11	11
North Fork	19	30
Champion Creek	39	69
Fort Egbert (Eagle)	29	98
Boundary	11	109

RAMPART BRANCH

	Part	Total
Fort Gibbon (Tanana)	0	0
Rapids	35	35
Rampart	40	75
Glen	35	110
Baker	15	125

WIRELESS SECTION

	Part	Total
Safety	0	0
St. Michael	107	107

SEATTLE-VALDEZ (cable)

	Part	Total
Fort Lawton	0	0
Seattle (land line)	9	9
Sitka (cable)	1070	1079
Valdez	640	1719
Fort Liscum	4	1723

SITKA-SKAGWAY (cable)

	Part	Total
Sitka	0	0
Juneau	291	291
Fort Seward	102	393
Skagway	21	414

SUMMARY

Land lines	1396
Submarine cable	2128
Wireless	107
TOTAL MILES	3631

(1) Port Safety
(2) Tulsona
(3) Tiekel
(4) Tsina
(5) Kechumstuk

Appendix B
BIBLIOGRAPHY

Alaska Communication System. 49th Annual Bulletin, 1949; also *The Story of the Alaska Communication System, 1900-1943,* an undated manuscript from the 1931st Com. Sq., Elemendorf AFB, AK, 1967.

Berton, Pierre. *The Klondike Fever: The Life and Death of the Last Great Gold Rush.* New York: Knopf, 1958.

Brooks, Alfred H. *Blazing Alaska's Trails.* Fairbanks: Univ. of Alaska Press, 1973.

Burlingame, Roger. *General Billy Mitchell, Champion of Air Defense.* New York: McGraw-Hill, 1952.

Cantwell, J.C., 1st Lt., RCS. *Operations of the U.S. Revenue Steamer* Cantwell *on the Yukon River Station, 1899-1901.* Washington, D.C.: Government Printing Office, 1902.

Dall, William H. *Alaska and its Resources.* London: Sampson, Low, Son and Marston, 1870.

Davis, Burke. *The Billy Mitchell Affair.* New York: Random House, 1967.

Elliott, Henry W. *Our Arctic Province.* New York: Charles Scribner's Sons, 1906.

Gauvreau, Emille and Lester Cohen. *Billy Mitchell, Founder of Our Air Force and Prophet Without Honor.* New York: E.P. Dutton & Co., 1942.

Hurley, A.F. *Billy Mitchell, Crusader for Air Power.* Bloomington: Indiana Univ. Press, 1975.

Mitchell, Ruth. *My Brother Bill: The Life of General "Billy" Mitchell.* New York: Harcourt, Brace, 1953.

Mitchell, Gen. William. *Papers.* Manuscript Div., Library of Congress, Washington, D.C.

Orth, Donald J. *Dictionary of Alaska Place Names.* U.S. Geological Survey, Professional Paper 567. Washington, D.C.: Government Printing Office, 1967.

Ricks, Melvin B. *The Earliest History of Alaska.* Anchorage, AK: Cook Inlet Historical Society, 1970.

Room, Adrian. *Place Names of the World.* Totawa, N.J.: Rowman & Littlefield, 1974.

Whitehouse, Arch (Arthur G.J.). *Billy Mitchell: America's Eagle of Air Power.* New York: G.P. Putnam's Sons, 1962.

Wickersham, James. *Old Yukon Tales—Trails—Trials.* Washington, D.C.: Washington Law Book Co., 1938.

ABBREVIATIONS USED IN NOTES

AFB	Air Force Base
An Rpt	Annual report
Bull	Bulletin
Com	Communication
Cong	Congress
Dept	Department
GPO	Government Printing Office
H Doc	House Document
Hist Soc	Historical Society
NOAA	National Oceanic & Atmospheric Administration
RCS	Revenue Cutter Service
Sec	Secretary
Sess	Session
S Misc Doc	Senate Miscellaneous Document
USGS	U.S. Geological Survice

INDEX

INDEX (continued)

Cook Inlet Historical Society Publications

The Earliest History of Alaska, Melvin B. Ricks, Editor, 1970. (out of print)

Exploration in Alaska, Antoinette Shalkop, Editor, 1980.

The Opening of Alaska, Brig. Gen. William L. Mitchell, Army Air Corps; Lt. Col. Lyman L. Woodman, USAF-Ret., Editor, 1982.

Lieutenant Castner's Alaskan Exploration, 1890. A Journey of Hardship and Suffering, Lieut. Jospeph C. Castner, 4th Infantry; Lt. Col. Lyman L. Woodman, USAF-Ret., Editor, 1984.

The Alaska Diary of Adelbert Von Chamisso, Naturalist on the Kotzebue Voyage, 1815-1818, Robert Fortuine, Editor and Translator, 1986.

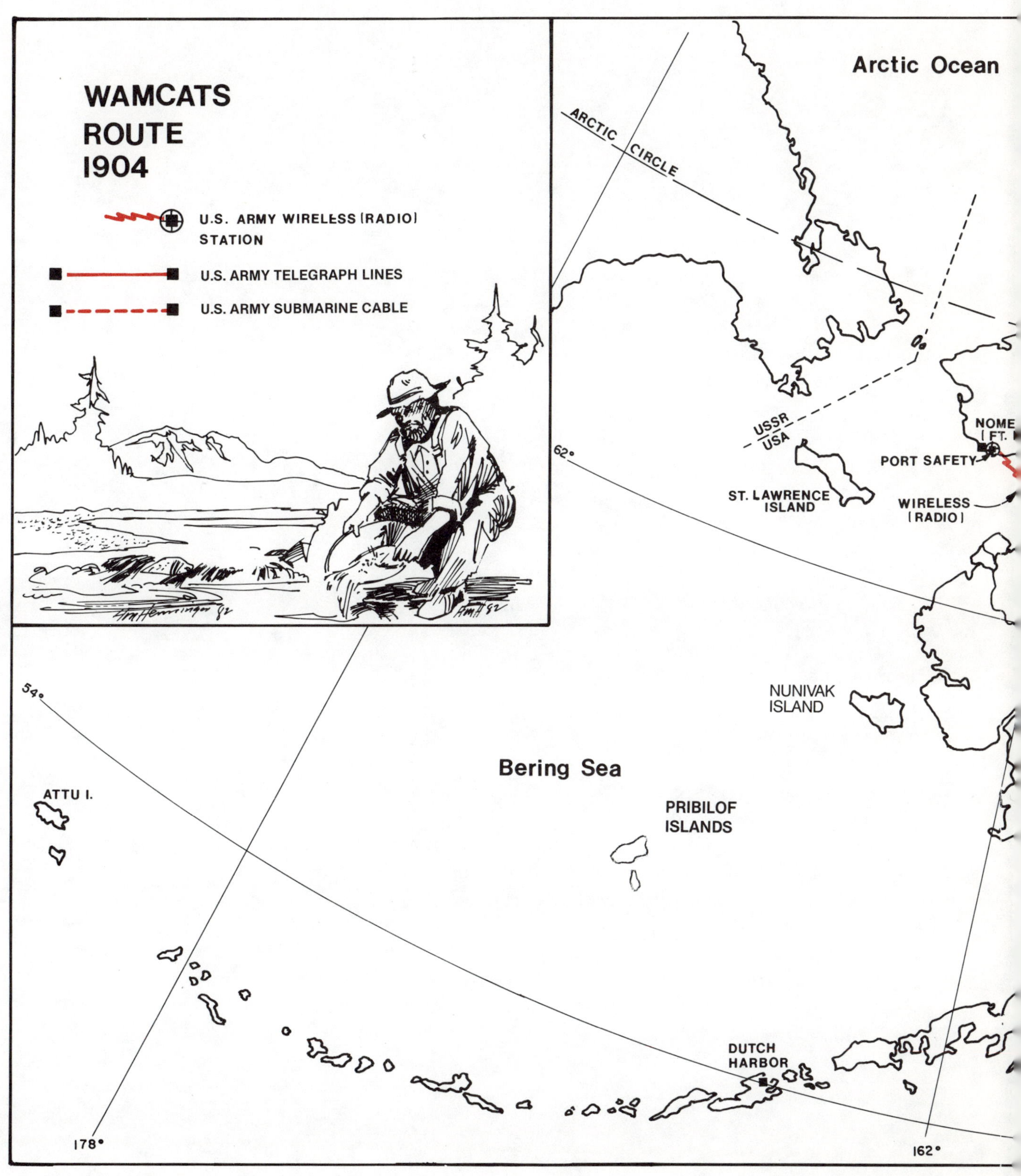

WAMCATS
ROUTE
1904
U.S. ARMY WIRELESS (RADIO) STATION
U.S. ARMY TELEGRAPH LINES
U.S. ARMY SUBMARINE CABLE
Arctic Ocean
ARCTIC CIRCLE
USSR
USA
NOME
PORT SAFETY
ST. LAWRENCE ISLAND
WIRELESS (RADIO)
62°
NUNIVAK ISLAND
Bering Sea
PRIBILOF ISLANDS
ATTU I.
54°
DUTCH HARBOR
178°
162°

Beaufort Sea
PT. BARROW
BROOKS RANGE
ARCTIC CIRCLE
KOYUKUK RIVER
FT. YUKON
YUKON R.
YUKON
AVIS]
TANANA
[FT. GIBBON]
RAMPART
CIRCLE
TANANA
FAIRBANKS
EAGLE [FT. EGBERT]
40 Mile
Goodpaste
DAWSON
RIVER
RIVER
ST. MICHAEL
RIVER
YUKON
RIVER
Denali
62°
KUSKOKWIM
ALASKA RANGE
COPPER RIVER
VALDEZ
[FT. LISCUM]
WHITEHORSE
SKAGWAY
JUNEAU
SUBMARINE CABLE
SITKA
WRANGELL
KETCHIKAN
KODIAK
ISLAND
SEATTLE
Gulf of Alaska
54°
146°